THE
BEATLES
AT THE
BBC

KEVIN HOWLETT

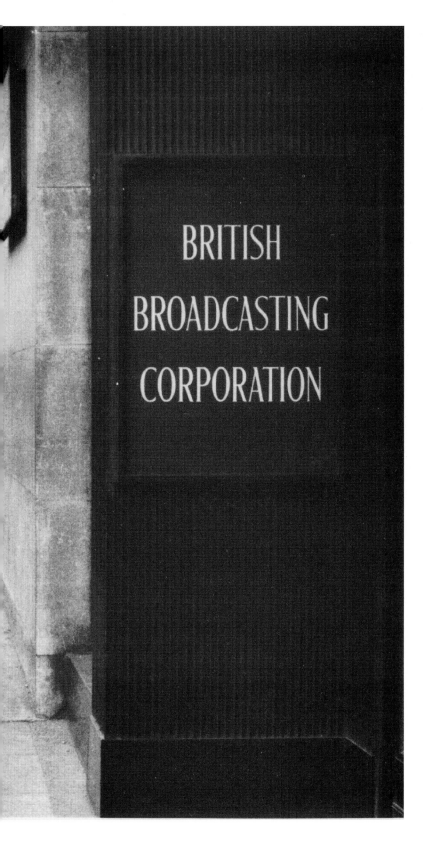

THE
BEATLES
AT THE
BBC

KEVIN HOWLETT

BBC BOOKS

The Beatles outside the Paris Theatre, London.

To Prue, Hugh and Oliver

It is almost fifteen years since I started to trace the history of the
Beatles' BBC broadcasts. During that time many helped with the various
programmes and the album project I have been involved in. Sincere thanks to:

Bernie Andrews; John Andrews; Keith Bateson; Johnny Beerling; Rob Chapman;
Pete Dauncey; John Fawcett Wilson; Pete Frame; Alan Freeman; Debra Godrich;
Ian Grant; Jeff Griffin; Stuart Grundy; Tony Hall; Mike Heatley; Terry Henebery;
Phil Lawton; Stuart Leaver; Mark Lewisohn; Chris Marshall; George Martin;
Brian Matthew;Steffan Olander; Andy Peebles; Peter Pilbeam; Allan Rouse;
Roger Scott; Richard Skinner; Derek Taylor, John Walker,
Richard Ward; Tony Wilson.

For contributing to the production of this book, grateful thanks to:
Nicola Copeland; David Cottingham; Jeremy Neech; Emma Tait; Graham Webb.

Finally, thanks to my elder brother Brian for introducing Beatles records to me;
to my parents for encouraging me with bubblegum cards, a plastic Beatles wig
(very sweaty!) and a red plastic Beatles guitar; and my wife Prue and our
children Hugh and Oliver… for singing along.

Kevin Howlett has explored the Beatles' BBC sessions since
the 1982 programme *The Beatles at the Beeb*. He is an award-winning
and Grammy-nominated producer and his many radio documentaries
for the BBC include profiles of Paul Simon, Leonard Cohen, Frank Zappa
and David Bowie. Inspired by the Beatles in the sixties, at the age
of six he formed his own group, the Spiders.

Published by BBC Books,
an imprint of BBC Worldwide Publishing.
BBC Worldwide Limited, Woodlands,
80 Wood Lane, London W12 0TT.

First published 1996
© Kevin Howlett 1996
The moral right of the author has been asserted
This is a Beatles™ product licensed by Apple Corps Limited™

ISBN 0 563 38770 X

Designed by Design/Section, Frome
Set in Gill Sans and Sabon
Printed in Great Britain by Martin the Printers Ltd, Berwick-upon-Tweed
Bound in Great Britain by Hunter and Foulis Ltd, Edinburgh
Cover printed by Clays Ltd, St Ives plc

Contents

....

Introduction

NARRATOR The boys arrive at BBC Broadcasting House.
EFFECTS *Three loud echoey knocks on a door.*
MAN FROM THE BEEB (*Sternly*) What do you want?
THE BEATLES We have been granted permission, Oh Wise One.
MAN FROM THE BEEB Aah! Pass in peace.

Part of a sketch from the Beatles' 1967 fan club Christmas record that, while obviously jokey, conveys the awe-inspiring reputation of the British Broadcasting Corporation in the sixties and how wondrous it was to pass through its hallowed portals!

This book traces the Beatles' BBC radio career, from their audition in February 1962 through to the last Radio 1 interviews before the group's disintegration in April 1970. The legacy of that time is an extensive collection of unique musical performances and speech tapes that reveal how the Beatles really thought and behaved inside the maelstrom.

The group played on 53 different radio shows between March 1962 and June 1965, giving no less than 275 performances of 88 different songs. Remarkably, 36 of those songs were never issued on record while the group was in existence. With the exception of Lennon-McCartney's 'I'll Be On My Way', these unreleased tracks were cover versions, ranging from familiar rock 'n' roll numbers to some fairly obscure oddities.

The 1982 Radio 1 special *The Beatles at the Beeb* and the 1988 series *The Beeb's Lost Beatles Tapes*, which I produced, allowed these extraordinary tapes to be heard again. In 1994 and 1995, 62 of the BBC performances were released on the *Live at the BBC* and *Anthology 1* albums and also the 'Baby It's You' single. The huge demand for these aural snapshots of the Beatles was emphatically demonstrated by the fact that *Live at the BBC* swiftly sold seven million copies worldwide.

But the appeal of the group was never purely musical. Playful in the early days, thoughtful and confessional towards the end, the BBC interviews capture the enormous charm of the four men who entranced the world. In these 124 radio appearances, there are numerous clues as to how the Beatles were really feeling – whether bewildered and excited on that first mad New York day in 1964 or anxiously preoccupied with business matters in 1969.

This examination of their BBC career also gives us an insight into what radio was like in the sixties. The frequency of the Beatles' live radio performances was, after all, a consequence of a bygone age of wireless innocence. Although millions were hungry for pop music, even in the sixties it was severely rationed on the radio. It was only with the advent of Radio 1 in late 1967 that a BBC radio network was specifically devoted to pop.

And what about the survival of the tapes? The BBC used to be rather reckless when it came to archiving its pop music heritage. This even applied to such established performers as Frank Sinatra, whose conversation with Benny Green about his LP *Great Songs From Great Britain* was not saved in 1962. Fortunately, Beatles programmes survived simply by chance, while others were unofficially preserved by prescient individuals – producers, broadcasters and home-tapers. From the start of my production work on *The Beatles at the Beeb* right up to the release of *Live at the BBC*, more and more excellent tapes kept on surfacing. But quality recordings of a good many historic performances remain sadly elusive. We can only hope that they might one day emerge from the ether...

Kevin Howlett

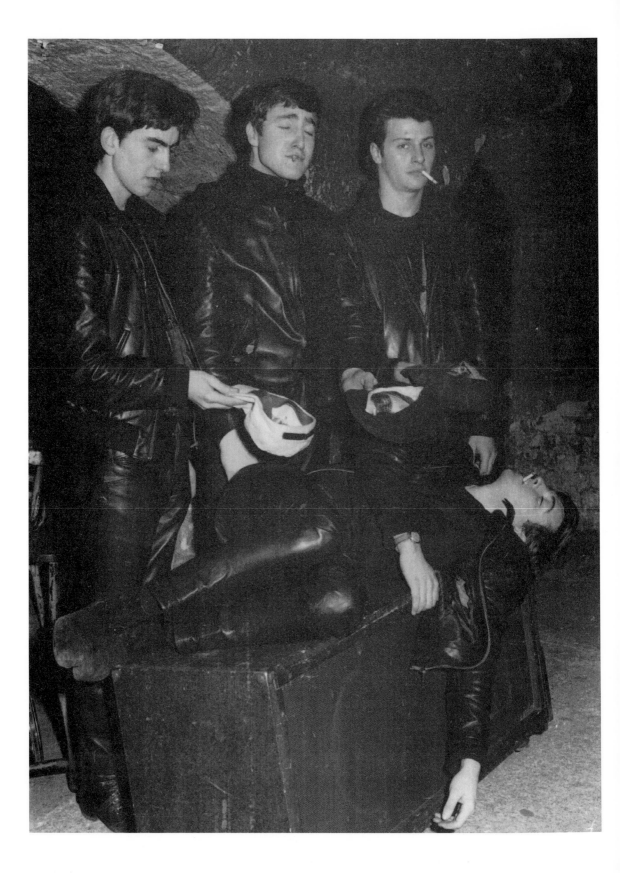

CHAPTER ONE
'A Tendency to Play Music'

....

The Beatles' BBC audition took place in Manchester on 12 February 1962. Ten months before this, the group's line-up had finally stabilized as John Lennon, Paul McCartney, George Harrison and Pete Best. A few weeks prior to the audition they had acquired the services of a solicitous and rather refined local record shop manager, Brian Epstein. Although the Beatles signed the contract making Epstein their manager on 24 January 1962, he had already been at work on their behalf – the application form requesting a BBC audition was dated 10 January.

Epstein's interest in the group had been kindled when a customer inquired at his shop about 'My Bonnie', a record they had made (as the Beat Brothers) with Tony Sheridan in Germany. On 5 January 1962, Polydor issued the single in the UK and Epstein mentioned this release on the BBC application. The same week, Liverpool's music paper *Mersey Beat* published the results of a local group popularity poll which showed the Beatles convincingly on top. So far so good... except that Decca Records, who auditioned the Beatles on New Year's Day, turned them down at the beginning of February. But there was still the chance of some valuable exposure on the BBC – if they passed their audition.

It is important to understand the nature of radio in the UK at this time. Unlike the States, where fast-talking, hip-sounding disc jockeys would spin the latest hit records, British radio was still very sedate. There was only the BBC during the day and, until 1967, of its three national networks, only the Light Programme might occasionally allow Elvis or Buddy

Holly into your home. There was no local radio, no commercial radio. The only alternative was a crackling, phasing Radio Luxembourg beamed across Europe at night. On the rare occasions when the Light Programme did feature pop, the records were often sidelined by emasculated renditions of hits from genial but wrong-footed dance orchestras. The BBC had barely begun to respond to the popularity of rock 'n' roll. Indeed, they seemed to be ignoring it in the hope that it would soon go away.

The Woody Allen movie *Radio Days* brilliantly evokes the character of American radio in the thirties and forties. Kids thrill to the adventures of the Masked Avenger; panic breaks out during Orson Welles' *War Of The Worlds* Martian invasion; perversely, there is a radio ventriloquist; and housewives fantasize about the glamorous lives of on-air personalities.

Even at the beginning of the sixties, the BBC Light Programme was very similar. The mix of comedy shows, daily serials, sport, variety shows, dance band tunes and light classical pieces had originated during the Second World War on the BBC's Forces Programme. The *Music While You Work* slot, for example, featured a live band playing jaunty popular tunes intended to increase the productivity of wartime factory workers. The show survived to the very last day of the Light Programme in 1967. With no daytime competition, the BBC's radio audience figures were colossal and, in fact, equivalent to today's TV ratings.

On weekdays, there was only one daily half-hour show aimed at the many younger listeners who yearned for music with a beat. Timed to coincide with their return from school, *Teenagers Turn* came on to the air at five o'clock. In March 1962, there were five different shows billed under the main title: *The Monday Show,*

'You can't go to the BBC dressed like that!' Clowning at the Cavern: George, John, Pete Best and a horizontal Paul.

The Talent Spot, Get With It, Here We Go and *The Cool Spot.*

Peter Pilbeam was the producer of *Here We Go*, which was recorded in Manchester. 'We used to get some terrific audiences down at the Playhouse for the teenage shows,' he remembers. 'We'd have the Northern Dance Orchestra on stage, trying to look like teenagers with their chunky jumpers on, and a presenter, a singer and a guest group in each programme.'

At a time when Liverpool alone sustained 300 groups, it was hard to spot the genuine, as opposed to the ephemeral, new talent. As Pilbeam recalls, 'In those days, we were spending two or three evenings a week going round the North hearing groups of a similar size and there was masses of rubbish. Then out of the blue this group turned up at one of our audition sessions called the Beatles – a weird name and everybody said "Whoa-yuk!" – but they impressed me at the time.'

The Beatles performed two Lennon-McCartney originals – 'Hello Little Girl' and 'Like Dreamers Do' – while John also sang Chuck Berry's gentle rocker 'Memphis, Tennessee' and Paul turned balladeer for 'Till There Was You'. On his audition report, Peter Pilbeam commented: 'An unusual group, not as "Rocky" as most, more C & W [Country and Western], with a tendency to play music'. He describes this as 'high praise, indeed, because a hell of a lot of noise came out of most three guitars and drums groups'. The Beatles passed the audition.

Despite Peter's note on his report about the singers – 'John Lennon: yes; Paul McCartney: no' – both were featured on their radio debut, recorded in front of an audience on 7 March 1962. For this auspicious event, the group had for the first time consented to wear the suits provided by their manager. After all, this was the BBC! So out went the usual stage gear of jeans and leathers.

The next day, the whole country had its first chance to hear the Beatles. John was heard singing 'Memphis, Tennessee' and the Marvelettes' US hit 'Please Mister Postman', while Paul did Roy Orbison's current hit 'Dream Baby'. Impressed again by their

performance, Peter Pilbeam decided to re-book them for his programme. This significant radio break-through came seven months before 'Love Me Do', their first single on Parlophone, was released.

The next BBC recording took place on a Bank Holiday – Whit Monday – and was once again for Peter Pilbeam's show *Here We Go*. A coach trip was organized to take Liverpool fans across to the Playhouse Theatre in Manchester in order to bolster the audience and ensure an enthusiastic response.

Four days later, on 15 June 1962, 'Ask Me Why' became the first Lennon-McCartney song to be broad-cast on the radio. The group also played their versions of 'Besame Mucho' and 'A Picture of You' – a Top Ten hit at this time for Joe Brown and the Bruvvers.

By their next appearance on *Here We Go*, the Beatles had a record of their own to promote. They played both sides of the single – 'Love Me Do' and 'PS I Love You' – plus the popular standard 'A Taste Of Honey'. There was also a new Beatle behind the drums. Having played his final gig on 15 August, Pete Best was replaced by Ringo Starr from Rory Storm and the Hurricanes. The Beatles' fee increased too. Having previously received £26 18s (£26.90) plus their rail fares to Manchester, for this third booking they were paid £37 18s (£37.90) plus expenses.

With 'Love Me Do' lingering at the lower end of the charts, the Beatles began to venture further away from their stomping ground in the North. In December 1962, they made appearances on local TV shows based in Bristol and Wembley and travelled to Peterborough in the far-off Midlands for a package show with yodelling balladeer Frank Ifield. The same month their first BBC show recorded in London was broadcast at the usual time of five o'clock. *The Talent Spot* featured young jazz vocalist Elkie Brooks (who would wait nearly 15 years for her first hit), plus country singer Frank Kelly, Mark Tracey and compère Gary Marshal, who all sang with the Ted Taylor Four. Having played both sides of their single, the Beatles

Producer Peter Pilbeam's comments on the back page the BBC's form 'Application for An Audition By Variety Department'.

yes. [...]

4

THIS SHEET FOR BBC USE ONLY

Paul McCartne... —— NO
    Dreamers.
    Till There was You.

John Lennon —— Yes.
    Memphis Tenessee.   ok   good etc. Backing

    Hello Little Girl (Quest TK+ Pkn)

      An unusual group, not as Rocky
  as most, more C+W, with a tendency
  to play music.

NO Instrumentals   (Yes)

Booked for T. T's 7th March '62.
                 P.P.

closed the show with 'Twist And Shout'. That unbridled burst of energy must have sounded pretty cataclysmic alongside such gentle musical company!

They recorded *The Talent Spot* the day after their fourth visit to EMI's studios in Abbey Road.

'Please Please Me' and 'Ask Me Why' were completed in that session and released on their next single in January 1963. That month they secured their most important radio engagement so far... an appearance on *Saturday Club*.

CHAPTER TWO
'Bill-Toppers'

....

The four BBC broadcasts in 1962 had helped the steady career progression of the Beatles. But this was all fairly minor compared to their appearance shortly after the release of their second single 'Please Please Me', on radio's premier pop show *Saturday Club*.

From ten o'clock to noon every Saturday, the nation heard their 'old mate' Brian Matthew present everybody from Terry Lightfoot and his New Orleans Jazzmen (for New Orleans read Potters Bar) to Eddie Cochran. The audience figures were enormous, with around ten to twelve million people listening and at least double that number when the General Overseas Service simultaneously transmitted a 30-minute section to the world.

The programme had evolved from a 1958 half-hour show produced by Jimmy Grant called *Saturday Skiffle Club*. Despite the fast-fading appeal of washboards and tea-chest basses, the programme grew ever more popular, was extended to two hours and soon had the word 'skiffle' dropped from its title. Brian Matthew's genial but pacey presentation linked a lively selection of pop, Country and Western, trad jazz and rock 'n' roll taken both from discs and specially recorded BBC sessions. Indeed, much of the programme's success was due to its producers' assiduous search for talented newcomers to showcase in session. By early 1963, it could reasonably claim to have discovered a number of big stars, including Cliff Richard and Adam Faith.

Anyone at all interested in popular music could not help but tune in and the nation's coffee bars remained empty of teenagers until *Saturday Club* was over. It was as much a part of the British Saturday as *Grandstand*, *Juke Box Jury* and *Dixon Of Dock Green* on the telly! Naturally, the Beatles would have listened regularly and, like hundreds of other ambitious musicians, dreamed of one day being invited onto the show.

The contract for their *Saturday Club* booking was dated 31 December, which indicates that the BBC had responded very swiftly and favourably to a preview of their new record. 'Please Please Me' was released on 11 January 1963 and a week later they mimed the song on the popular TV programme *Thank Your Lucky Stars* – also presented by Brian Matthew. During the next seven days they were heard on three BBC radio shows – chatting to Keith Fordyce at lunchtime on *Pop Inn*, playing three songs on *Here We Go* and on 26 January visiting *Saturday Club*.

The BBC's listings magazine, the *Radio Times*, made the Beatles' *Saturday Club* debut one of its highlights of the week and commented, 'Any group with so uncompromising a name as the Beatles has much to overcome to win recognition from those who have little interest in Hit Parade music. Why did they choose the name? John Lennon, their leader, says (and we quote): "It came to us in a flaming pie and spoke these words: *From this day on you are the Beatles with an A*." '

They were well down the bill behind Joe Brown and the Bruvvers, Sheila Southern, Vince Hill, the Vernons Girls and the Ted Taylor Four. No matter, they were on. They played both tracks on the new single and four others: 'Love Me Do', 'Some Other Guy' (a version of a Ritchie Barrett record that was a favourite in Liverpool but absolutely nowhere else), Little Eva's recent minor hit 'Keep Your Hands Off My Baby', and a rocking arrangement of the old chestnut 'Beautiful Dreamer'. Brian Matthew predicted on air that the Beatles' great popularity in Liverpool would soon spread to many other parts of the

Brian Matthew, the presenter of Saturday Club *and* Easy Beat.

John, she had already had five Top Ten hits, including two number ones. Just as she had to miss a couple of engagements because of illness, John's heavy cold prevented his participation in a few concerts on the Beatles' next tour with American stars Tommy Roe and Chris Montez. It also forced them to abandon their pre-recording session for that week's *Saturday Club*.

Bernie Andrews had recently become a BBC producer and was supervising the music sessions for the programme. 'We started it and they couldn't get the vocals together because John had a bad throat and couldn't sing.' With the Beatles playing in York, Wolverhampton and Bristol over the remaining days of the week, the only option was to have them play live during that Saturday's show. As Bernie recalls, 'The studio in Broadcasting House was actually a talks and small drama studio – not really a music studio at all. So we got a few extra mikes in, started rehearsing about eight o'clock and went on the air live at ten o'clock.' This early morning start for the group followed their two shows the night before in Bristol, which in early 1963 was a much longer drive from London than it is now.

It was not their first experience of playing live on air. On 20 February, they had performed in front of a lunchtime audience in the Playhouse Theatre for *Parade of the Pops* introduced by Denny Piercy. But their willingness to take on the challenge was still very impressive.

'I don't think there was another beat group who would have dared to attempt that particular feat,' remembers Brian Matthew. 'The Beatles did it and took it in their stride. This was the first time I saw them perform in one of our studios and I was completely overwhelmed – they were clearly streets ahead of their contemporaries.' The songs selected were 'I Saw Her Standing There', 'Misery' and 'Please Please Me' from the forthcoming album, and three well-worn stage numbers – 'The Hippy Hippy Shake'

country. Three days later, another performance on *The Talent Spot* made that a little more likely.

'Please Please Me' reached number one on most charts – and certainly the BBC's. When it became clear how big this hit was going to be, an EMI session was quickly arranged for 11 February 1963, in which all ten extra tracks required for the *Please Please Me* album were recorded. (In the 1978 spoof documentary about the Rutles, this achievement is celebrated with the words 'Their first album took 20 minutes, their second – even longer.') Their next visit to *Saturday Club* was broadcast on 16 March 1963, a week ahead of the album's release.

Since the last appearance they had travelled the country in severe winter weather on a tour headlined by Helen Shapiro. Although six years younger than

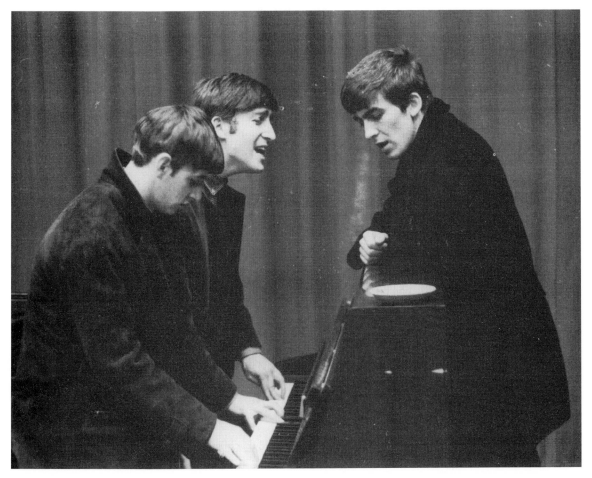

Relaxing at the BBC Paris Theatre during a Side by Side *recording, 4 April 1963. None of their BBC recordings featured any piano playing.*

and two Chuck Berry rockers, 'I'm Talking About You' and 'Too Much Monkey Business'.

Two and a half weeks later, the Beatles met up with Brian Matthew again for a recording of his gentler Sunday morning show *Easy Beat*. Another big audience, of around nine million, listened every week to the resident band led by Johnny Howard and an assortment of singers. Performing in front of an audience at the Playhouse Theatre, the Beatles played 'Please Please Me', 'Misery' and the new single 'From Me To You'. 'How Do You Do It', by their Liverpool mates Gerry and the Pacemakers, was number one at the time and Gerry joined Brian Matthew on stage to introduce the Beatles playing 'From Me To You'. 'This is one that I really think is going to be a hit... hope so anyway. Nothing more I can say except... how do you

do it?!' Within a month, the Beatles' disc had knocked his record off the top of the charts.

John and Paul also took part in *Easy Beat's* record review section 'Going Up?'. Unfortunately, no tape exists to preserve their comments on 'Night Cry' by Bert Weedon, 'It Looks Like They're In Love' by Cleo Laine, 'Do The Bird' by the Vernons Girls or 'The Folk Singer' by Tommy Roe. For their extra trouble, each pocketed a guinea (£1.05).

The next time the Beatles played on the BBC, they were once again in front of an audience – but a much larger one. Their performance of 'Twist And Shout' and 'From Me To You' was broadcast direct from the Royal Albert Hall in *Swinging Sound '63* on 18 April 1963. This was the second of three Light Programme concerts from the prestigious domed venue. The *Radio*

The Beatles' first appearance at the Royal Albert Hall for the Light Programme's star-studded pop music event, Swinging Sound '63.

Times writer Tony Aspler attended the first and witnessed 'the "cats" erupt in a paroxysm of whistles and screams of appreciation. I suppose a good scream does clear the head, but if, like me, you feel like a pigeon among the cats, it's *safer* to hear it all at home, on the radio'.

There was the usual diverse Light Programme mixture. Traditional jazz was represented by Chris Barber's Jazz Band with Ottilie Patterson and also George Melly singing with the BBC Jazz Club All Stars; cheeky pop came from the Vernons Girls and Kenny Lynch; folk from Robin Hall and Jimmie Macgregor; country-folk from the Springfields; novelty numbers from Lance Percival and Rolf Harris.

The two beat groups were Shane Fenton and the Fentones and the Beatles, who were second on the bill to American star Del Shannon. He played his latest release 'Two Kinds Of Teardrops' and one of his six previous British Top Ten hits, 'Swiss Maid'.

After the Beatles' wild performance, Rolf Harris observed, 'Fantastic… people here twisting all over the Albert Hall!'. This reception obviously impressed Del Shannon, who covered 'From Me To You' for his next single. It became the first Lennon-McCartney song to enter the US charts but reached no higher than 77 on the Billboard Top 100. Following the concert, Paul met his future fiancée Jane Asher, who had earlier posed for a *Radio Times* photograph of her screaming with the other 'cats'. She was a well-known teen TV icon, who regularly passed judgement on new records for *Juke Box Jury* and had recently acted in an episode of *Dixon Of Dock Green*.

At the start of April 1963, the Beatles recorded three programmes for a radio series called *Side By Side*. Each week the Karl Denver Trio played host to another group, who, as well as trading numbers, joined them for a quick burst of the show's signature tune, the old standard 'Side By Side'. Karl Denver's yodelling had most famously been heard on the Trio's biggest hit 'Wimoweh (The Lion Sleeps Tonight)'.

The show was presented by BBC staff announcer John Dunn, who at the time of writing (1996) still commands the early evening Radio 2 slot he eased into in 1973. On *Side By Side*, he jollied the proceedings along with such links as 'And here are those four Beatles… up to some no good monkey business' before John kicked in with 'Too Much Monkey Business'.

The humour and personality of the group were evident in the snatches of interviews heard during this series. On the 13 May broadcast, John explained the group's name with the usual zany 'flaming pie' pronouncement of 'Beatles with an A'. Paul introduced 'A Taste Of Honey' as one of his Auntie Gin's great favourites and, before launching into 'Boys', Ringo quipped, 'They did give me a go on the LP and, between you and me, I think that's the track that's selling it!'

Their third appearance on *Side By Side* was heard on 24 June 1963, but had been taped as long ago as 4 April. The programme featured a Lennon-McCartney song that at the time of broadcast, was available on the B-side of 'Do You Want To Know A Secret' by Billy J. Kramer with the Dakotas. But 'I'll Be On My Way' was never recorded by the Beatles, making it one of the most important tracks on the 1994 collection *Live At The BBC*. Incidentally, the front cover photograph for that album was taken outside the BBC Paris Theatre in Lower Regent Street on the day of this session.

During the show, George came to the microphone and croaked a few lines of 'From Me To You' to demonstrate that his voice had all but disappeared. John Dunn reassured listeners that the programme had been recorded a few weeks ago and so if they were seeing the Beatles that night 'there George will be, large as life and twice as beautiful!'. In fact, they were not playing on 24 June but all four did make the gig on 4 April – at Stowe Public School for boys. No girls, no screaming; it must have been the quietest audience they'd ever had!

On 18 May 1963, the Beatles embarked on their third nationwide tour with Roy Orbison. They were great admirers of the Big O's passionate vocal gymnastics on epic ballads like 'In Dreams' and 'Running Scared' and his cool and easy style on 'Only The Lonely' and 'Dream Baby'. Nonetheless, audience clamour for the Beatles meant that they soon had to usurp his position as the tour's headliner. But, unlike other American stars of his era, Orbison's popularity with British record buyers survived well past this tour, with a further eight Top Ten hits, including two number ones.

After three dates, the Beatles used a day off to record two radio shows at the Playhouse Theatre. On the evening of 21 May they topped the bill of a 59-minute concert featuring Mark Wynter, Mike Berry, Maureen Evans, Alan Elsdon's Jazz Band and the Red Price Combo. A special show for Bank Holidays, *Steppin' Out,* was broadcast on Whit Monday – 3 June. Not wasting a moment, they spent the afternoon putting down six songs for their third appearance on *Saturday Club*.

Brian Matthew confirmed their new headlining status when he announced, 'It's time now to hear the first one from our bill-toppers, the Beatles!'. He also indicated that the show was receiving 'as many requests for the Beatles as for everyone else combined'. Some of these were read by the group and included cards from Egypt and Germany for the international listeners who heard the half-hour section of the programme relayed every week by the BBC's General Overseas Service.

Fans were treated to spirited renditions of 'Money' and 'Long Tall Sally', which would not be available on record for some time. Three days later the Beatles were back at the BBC taping some intriguing cover versions for a new series that emphatically confirmed their place at the top.

Just three months after their first number one, the BBC had invited the group to host their own radio show – *Pop Go The Beatles*.

CHAPTER THREE

'We're Ready to Pop!'

BBC executives themselves may not have noticed the rising popularity of the Beatles, but they had been prodded into action by a young studio manager – Vernon Lawrence – who had dashed off a memo on 30 April 1963 suggesting a series called *Beatle Time*. He proposed an evening or weekend slot with guest male and female vocalists – the wholesome Mark Wynter and Susan Maughan – and a rock element to be provided by Brian Poole and the Tremeloes or Russ Sainty and the Nu-Notes.

Donald MacLean, who rejoiced in the title Music Organizer – Light Entertainment (Sound), conceded that 'Young Lawrence certainly has good judgement of contemporary values' and the idea evolved into a series of half-hour programmes featuring the Beatles and a guest group. For 15 weeks in the summer of 1963 the Tuesday evening show became required listening for teenagers all over Britain. 'It's five o'clock, we're ready to pop. It's the *Pop Go The Beatles* spot!' as presenter Rodney Burke put it.

Only three weeks after the first memo, the *New Musical Express* was heralding the new series with the headline 'Group Gets Radio Show'. The article stated that 'four shows have been planned although the series may be extended'. This was an admirably speedy and, in the context of the existing Light Programme, even courageous move on the part of the Corporation. Terry Henebery was appointed producer, with the assistance of a new production trainee Ian Grant. For the initial four-week run, the presenter was Lee Peters (or 'Pee Litres', as the Beatles christened him!). His was a familiar voice on the network, as he played the character of David Owen in the daily soap opera *The Dales*, first broadcast in January 1948 as *Mrs Dale's Diary*.

The title of the Beatles' series was dreamt up by Frances Line, one of the production department's secretaries. As Terry Henebery remembers, 'One of the most difficult decisions is what to call the programme. You can't keep calling it the "Something-Something Show", it's so boring. Frances took a lot of interest in programmes like *Saturday Club* and *Easy Beat*, for which she worked actually, for Brian Matthew. She had a younger sister who was into pop music and she said, "We've been sitting round at home and we thought this wouldn't make a bad title – *Pop Go The Beatles*." I said, "You've got it, that is a super title!"' Frances Line became Controller of Radio 2 (the Light Programme's successor) in 1990.

The BBC loved a corny signature tune and, with this title, they had an opportunity to rock up the nursery rhyme 'Pop Goes The Weasel'. As it happened, the tune was still buzzing around the airwaves in Anthony Newley's jaunty arrangement which had made the Top 20 in June 1961. The Beatles' version of the opening and closing theme was taped in the first session, which they shared with guest group, the Lorne Gibson Trio. Both their leader and Terry Henebery recall the trio lending a hand with the 'Pop Go The Beatles' signature tune.

The Lorne Gibson Trio were the Beatles' guests on the first show, transmitted on 4 June 1963. The other three groups in the initial run were the Countrymen, Carter-Lewis and the Southerners, and the Bachelors. These were all quite safe Light Programme 'combos' and, in the case of the Bachelors, an extremely sugary contrast to the Beatles' repertoire. As Terry Henebery confirms, the choice of guests was solely that of the production team. 'Bearing in mind that the Beatles were new, one wanted to put some solid guest acts in;

The fourth Pop Go The Beatles *presented by Lee Peters was recorded between 10.30am and 1.00pm on 17 June 1963 at the BBC's Maida Vale Studios, London. Following the session, the group adjourned to the canteen and then gave 21st birthday bumps to Paul in Delaware Road.*

a mixture of the attractive units appearing on other programmes. There was no pressure from the Beatles to use mates or anything because they weren't big enough to put "the heavies" on.'

There was also the obligatory reading of listeners' requests. Lee Peters took the role of posh BBC straight man struggling to keep order amid the antics and

send-ups of the cheeky Liverpudlians.

When John interrupted him to explain that he was playing the (blues) harp on 'I Got To Find My Baby', the announcer supposedly stormed off, leaving John to complete the introduction. 'Love these Goon Shows', chuckled John, before the track burst in. He was referring to the radio comedy series, starring Spike

Milligan, Peter Sellers and Harry Secombe, that ran for 200 episodes in the fifties. Like most of their contemporaries, the Beatles were fond of adopting the silly voices of *Goon Show* characters like Eccles, Bluebottle or Moriarty and their sometimes surreal sense of humour was generally reminiscent of the Goons. Incidentally, during *Pop Go The Beatles* and *Side By Side* there are mysterious references to 'Harry and his box'. What *was* that all about?

The Beatles' playful improvisations were dazzlingly fresh for a BBC pop show. Record programmes linked by disc jockeys, for example, had to be scripted in advance and then approved by Anna Instone – the formidable Head of the Gramophone Department. Whereas the Beatles' chat fell under the aegis of another department and sounded highly radical by comparison!

Terry Henebery remembers that the fun was not only confined to the speech content, 'They were very much younger and they'd come to the studio and horse about. You had to crack the whip and get on the loudspeaker talk-back key quite a lot and say "Come on, chaps!". They'd be lying all over the floor, giggling. And I can remember afternoons down at the BBC Paris Cinema Studio, where you were just looking at the clock, throwing your hands up in horror and thinking will they ever settle down? I mean, people would go and get locked in the toilets and fool about. But you were, at the end of the day, getting some nice material out of them.'

An Audience Research report was compiled on the first programme of the new series. It was estimated that 5.3 per cent (nearly three million) of the listening public over 14 years old heard *Pop Go The Beatles*. Members of the Listening Panel were asked for their responses and an Appreciation Index mark out of 100 was calculated. The show received a rather low rating of 52 (which was below the average of 61 for Light Entertainment music programmes at the time). But, after all, this was not *Workers' Playtime* from a factory canteen in Wrexham (a lunchtime show heard earlier in the day); this was one for the teenagers.

That age group gave such favourable responses as 'really with it', 'the finest group in the country' and 'on their way to the very top'. 'Older' listeners, in their twenties and beyond, were positive too – 'a really distinctive sound', 'full of vitality' – but the report concluded that 'those who were not especially fond of this type of music… disliked this sort of 'obnoxious noise'. Oh well, there was always *Stringalong* later on with Bob Clarke, Jack Toogood and the Gordon Franks Orchestra!

Most agreed that Lee Peters had made a 'good compère' and, despite his constant references to

Vernon Lawrence, Studio Manager, L.E.(S)   5070 B.H.

PROGRAMME SUGGESTION: "BEATLE TIME"   *Beatles Progs.*

A.H.L.E.(S)I   Copy to: M.O.L.E.(S)   30th April 1963

I wish to submit the following suggestion for a programme entitled 'Beatle Time'.

This programme would feature The Beatles, the current chart-toppers of the British 'pop' music scene. As proved by recent broadcasts, it could be compered by Paul McCartney and John Lennon, this would also cut down the cost.

To provide a contrast, I would suggest a group directed by Harry Robinson of seven or nine musicians. The object of this group would be to back a guest male and female vocalist each week, i.e. Mark Wynter and Susan Maughan.

As The Beatles produce such a distinctive sound, a group such as Brian Poole and the Tremeloes or Russ Sainty and the Nu-Notes could provide the 'rock' element.

The cost would be approximately £250.

I imagine a programme of this nature would be suitable for a fifty or sixty-minute evening or weekend slot in the Light Programme.

(Vernon Lawrence)

'Ring-oh', the Beatles were tickled by his relentless corny links. John seemed particularly taken with a (very good) James Mason impression during an introduction to 'Baby It's You'. He also bluffed convincingly, when leading a round of 'Happy Birthday' during the show to be broadcast on Paul's twenty-first birthday (18 June 1963) but recorded on 1 June. He even encouraged Paul to talk about his party in a session recorded the day before it! (This actually turned out to be an eventful night, in which John's rowdy altercation with Cavern DJ Bob Wooler was reported in the press.) That session produced the recordings used in the broadcast on 25 June – the final edition of the four-week run.

On its Tuesday highlights page, the *Radio Times* trailed the fourth programme and revealed that 'two days after the first broadcast in the *Pop Go The Beatles* series, the producer Terry Henebery received over one hundred cards from listeners all over the country expressing their delight that this remarkable group now have their own programme'. The previous week's *New Musical Express* also reported that 'following the success of the group's radio series, the show has been given a lengthy extension'. It was actually given a further 11 programmes and returned to the airwaves after a mere three-week break.

For this run, there was a new presenter to be cheeky with. He also had a name guaranteed to cause Beatle amusement. On one show, his opening statement 'I'm

Rodney Burke (where are you now?).

Rodney Burke' was met by John's jibe 'That's your fault!'. (It was too, as the announcer was using a stage name.) Rodney Burke was tirelessly cheerful. 'That was a Little Richard number – "Ooh My Soul" and "Ooh my arms" – we've just flown into Manchester here from London to record the show!' was a typical cringe-inducing link. The production team were swamped with more and more listeners' dedications for the Beatles to read out, which they did with increasing confidence and witty interplay. Although still chosen by the BBC, the guest acts now seemed to be more appropriate. Liverpool groups were represented by the Swinging Blue Jeans and the Searchers, Vernon Lawrence's original suggestions – Russ Sainty and the Nu-Notes and Brian Poole and the Tremeloes – were finally booked... and the Hollies made their sixth BBC recording.

But, of course, *Pop Go The Beatles* was most fascinating because of the songs chosen for the broadcasts...

Just 24 days after this memo from BBC sound man Vernon Lawrence, the first recording took place for the series Pop Go The Beatles.

CHAPTER FOUR

'R-and-B Material Will Be Strongly Featured'

....

For some groups, a series that demanded six new recordings every week might have been daunting; but it allowed the Beatles freedom to try out their newer influences and air some old favourites. Rather than selecting solely from their comparatively small catalogue of songs on record, they began to plunder a long list of cover versions. The hundreds of hours spent entertaining the rowdy clientele at Hamburg night clubs and the friendly regulars at the Cavern in Liverpool had given them a large and varied repertoire to choose from.

Although there were just 18 Beatles tracks available on record in the summer of 1963, they performed 56 different songs during *Pop Go The Beatles*. All six of the cover versions on *Please Please Me* were broadcast, as well as 11 of the 12 Lennon-McCartney compositions released on that album or their singles (the missing song was 'Thank You Girl'). Listeners also heard the six covers featured on *With The Beatles* several months prior to its release in November 1963 – but not the album's original compositons. That left a further 33 songs not on record at the time of the series; 26 of those remained unreleased during the group's existence.

The *New Musical Express* reported that 'R-and-B material will be strongly featured' on *Pop Go The Beatles* and the shows certainly lived up to that promise. For the 1988 documentary series *The Beeb's Lost Beatles Tapes*, George explained that the selection of the songs reflected, 'What we used to do on stage because, whenever you're doing tons of material, you need to sing other people's songs as well. And we started out doing Hamburg where, as the old story goes, we used to play eight hours a night for tuppence a month and [adopting his best *Monty Python* "You

tell that to the kids today" voice] when we got home, Brian Epstein would slash us to death with a carving-knife... if we were lucky! So we used to have to sing all kinds of tunes. We'd play 'Moonglow' and 'The Harry Lime Theme'... and we even played some Shadows songs. We sang all the old Shirelles and the old Tamla Motown tunes, so consequently, as we were doing loads of these BBC shows, a lot of the material was just stuff we'd been singing round the clubs.'

As Ringo has pointed out, the songs taped at the BBC proved 'we were a working band... everyone gets to *Sgt Pepper* and thinks that's what we were... but we were doing every club on the planet!' In his candid interview with *Rolling Stone* writer Jann Wenner, John also emphasized that 'in Liverpool, Hamburg and other dance halls... where we played straight rock... what we generated was fantastic and there was nobody to touch us in Britain.'

During the summer of 1963, the Beatles played theatres at many of the UK's seaside resorts. With their live set shortened to 20 scream-filled minutes and consisting mainly of their hit records, the *Pop Go The Beatles* sessions gave them a welcome chance to romp through some old favourites and pay tribute to some of the musicians who had first inspired them.

Chuck Berry was one of the Beatles' foremost musical influences and they gave nine BBC performances of Berry numbers, six of them included in *Pop Go The Beatles*. Except for 'Roll Over Beethoven', for which George took the lead, Berry's witty rockers were all sung by John.

The following year, 1964, saw fans beginning to divide their loyalties between the 'poppy' Beatles and the 'rocky' Rolling Stones. Jagger and Richard were fervent fans of Chuck Berry, and the Stones frequently covered his tracks. But if the Stones fans had heard the Beatles on the radio, they might have recognized a similar devotion to Berry in the Liverpool group. It's certainly interesting to compare the lighter touch of the Beatles' BBC session take of 'Carol' with their rivals' rougher version on the first album *The Rolling Stones*. And, leaving all the rivalry aside, the *Pop Go The Beatles* dynamic recording of 'Sweet Little Sixteen' is definitely unassailable.

During the series, six Carl Perkins covers by the Beatles were heard for the first time. Three songs – 'Everybody's Trying To Be My Baby', 'Honey Don't' and 'Matchbox' – made it onto record the following year, but 'Glad All Over', 'Lend Me Your Comb' and 'Sure To Fall' remained unique to the BBC. Each Beatle took a lead vocal on at least one of these six tracks and they all seem to have shared a great affection and enthusiasm for this rockabilly material.

Perkins' biggest hit, 'Blue Suede Shoes', was the first record to make the American pop, R & B and country charts. It reached the Top Two on all three listings in 1956 – easily outselling the Elvis Presley cover version – but injuries in a car crash soon afterwards prevented Carl capitalizing on his remarkable breakthrough. His career lost momentum and by 1963 he was a forgotten man in the States.

But the Beatles, like thousands of British rock fans, had longer memories and loyally mentioned him as an important influence – as Carl Perkins gratefully acknowledged in 1994, 'I [later] said to them, "What have I ever done that caused you to say that I had anything to do with the great music you write?" They said, "We noticed on your first records that you wrote your songs, you played your own music and you sang your songs… and that's what we wanted to do."'

Carl was present when the Beatles recorded 'Matchbox' at Abbey Road. 'They struck right into it and I knew then they'd been listening!' During a party the night before this session, John asked Carl to play his version of 'Right String But The Wrong Yo-Yo' in order to settle how the opening was played. 'I kicked it off and John said, "See George, I told you, you were wrong!"' It was no coincidence that when three of the

Beatles adopted temporary stage names in 1960, George became Carl Harrison.

During *Pop Go The Beatles*, the group also performed songs by the three most celebrated figures of the rock 'n' roll era – Elvis Presley, Little Richard and Buddy Holly. They never featured an Elvis number on their records but they covered three in the series: 'I Got A Woman', 'I'm Gonna Sit Right Down And Cry (Over You)' and his debut 'That's All Right (Mama)'. A fourth – 'I Forgot To Remember To Forget' – was taped a year later. Just three days before Paul sang 'That's All Right (Mama)' at the BBC Maida Vale Studios, John gave his opinion of Presley's 'Devil In Disguise' on the 29 June 1963 edition of *Juke Box Jury*. He expressed his disenchantment with the post-army Elvis by saying he sounded like the crooner Bing Crosby! John had loved the Elvis Presley who had swaggered through rhythm and blues tunes and, to prove it, he turned in two inspired performances of 'I Got A Woman' at the BBC.

John was also besotted with the blasts of energy that exploded from Little Richard's records in the late 1950s, but the four covers chosen for *Pop Go The Beatles* were all belted out by Paul. His throat-tearing imitation of Richard's untamed whoops and yells may even have been nurtured a little by the man himself, as he had befriended the group when they were his support act in 1962. All four covers were unavailable at the time of their broadcast and 'Ooh! My Soul' was only unveiled again with the release of *Live At The BBC*. That album also includes a *Saturday Club* take of 'Lucille' but the *Pop Go The Beatles* recording made three days earlier remains under wraps. It is distinguished by Paul shredding his voice even more recklessly and George going wilder with the tremolo arm!

The Beatles all loved the music of Buddy Holly, who wrote many of his own hits and also played dazzling guitar. Back in 1958, the Quarry Men – the early skiffle incarnation of the Beatles – had made a private recording of his number one 'That'll Be The Day'. After his tragic death in 1959, Buddy's music quickly faded from the American charts. Not so in Britain, where posthumous hits continued into the

4   RADIO TIMES September 12, 1963

RADIO TIMES PORTRAIT GALLERY

PAUL McCARTNEY
*Bass guitar, joint composer with John.
Born Liverpool, June 18, 1942*

JOHN LENNON
*Harmonica, rhythm guitar, composer.
Born Liverpool, October 9, 1940*

RINGO STARR
*Drums (newest member of group).
Born Liverpool, July 7, 1940*

GEORGE HARRISON
*Lead guitar.
Born Liverpool, February 25, 1943*

'Very much a do-it-yourself outfit'—the secret of the Beatle Cut

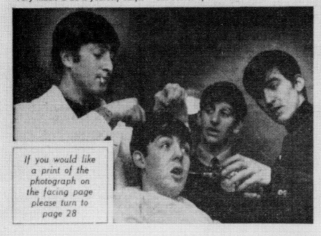

If you would like a print of the photograph on the facing page please turn to page 28

Just how they got their name, even they themselves are not quite sure, although it could have something to do with the fact that they emerged on to the pop scene from a Liverpool cellar club called The Cavern. But there is no dark secret about a success story so big that these days it seems show-business is overrun with Beatles.

Although their average age is only in the lowest twenties, these young musicians are solid professionals. The three founder Beatles—John Lennon, Paul McCartney, and George Harrison—cut their musical eye-teeth on washboards back in the skiffle-happy days of 1956 when they were still at school. For six years they played their way in and around Liverpool, riding the skiffle and rock regimes, collecting en route drummer Ringo Starr and a fiercely loyal following on Merseyside and points north.

Just twelve months ago they cut their first disc, *Love Me Do.* There was no detectable rush on the record shops, but then in January the Beatles burst out all over with *Please, Please Me.* It climbed to the top of the charts, stuck there for four weeks, and earned them a Silver Disc. It was joined by another three months later for *From Me to You.* And only recently they were up among the best-sellers again with *Twist and Shout,* the first EP disc ever to reach the Top Ten.

Very much a do-it-yourself outfit, the Beatles play their own compositions (over a hundred to date), write their own lyrics, score their own arrangements. Equipped with brooding good looks, they inspire devotion of traffic-jam proportions among their fans wherever they appear. If imitation be indeed the sincerest form of flattery, the number of eyebrow-level Beatle haircuts to be seen around the coffee bars is flattery indeed.

Their special plaintive sound is easily recognisable, but less easy to define. Some detect a transatlantic influence, others talk of a unique brand of rhythm-and-blues peculiar to Liverpool. Most, though, are content to call it the Merseyside Beat, switch on the record player, and forget all about definitions. As, indeed, do the Beatles themselves.

The last word is with John Lennon: 'People are always trying to pin labels on us . . . but as far as we're concerned it's just good fun.' It sounds that way—and clearly the sound will be around for a long time to come.

Next week: LOUISE DUNN ('Iris' of 'Compact')

In the week that the penultimate Pop Go The Beatles *programme was broadcast, the BBC's listings magazine* Radio Times *highlighted the group in its weekly 'Portrait Gallery' feature. When readers turned to page 28, they were invited to fill in a coupon with their name and address and send 2 shillings (10p) to the BBC in order to receive a glossy 10 inch by 8 inch print of the group portrait. (This offer is now closed.) This feature was included*

RADIO TIMES *September 12, 1963*

5

The Beatles

in the Radio Times *covering a week of programmes from Saturday 14 September 1963. Following their 15 September appearance at the Royal Albert Hall in the annual 'Great Pop Prom' – with a new group below them on the varied bill, the Rolling Stones – the Beatles flew off for well-earned holidays. Soon after their return in October, the press applied the epithet Beatlemania to describe the hysteria surrounding their every move.*

mid-sixties. Three of his records reached the Top Ten in 1963 and a version of 'Bo Diddley' was there when the Beatles taped two Holly songs on 16 July 1963. John and Paul harmonized on 'Words Of Love' and George took the lead on 'Crying, Waiting, Hoping'.

But, as George has pointed out, the Beatles were not only drawing on the rock 'n' roll era for their repertoire.

They were admirers of the Brill Building songwriters, and the partnerships of Leiber-Stoller and Goffin-King each received three BBC covers (two songs apiece in *Pop Go The Beatles*). 'We want to be the Goffin and King of England!', Lennon-McCartney once proclaimed. In gentler moments, Paul sang the popular standards 'A Taste Of Honey' and 'Till There Was You' but his most unusual ballad was 'The Honeymoon Song' – an exotic item written by the Greek composer Theodorakis and sung by the Italian Marino Marini. John's equally romantic discovery was Ann-Margret's 'I Just Don't Understand' – a real gem. Indeed, the Beatles had long been adept at digging out unusual material – often learning a neglected B-side of a record to trump their many competitors in Liverpool.

Two Arthur Alexander B-sides were recorded for *Pop Go The Beatles* – 'A Shot Of Rhythm And Blues' and 'Soldier Of Love'. Neither of the A-sides – 'You Better Move On' and 'Where Have You Been' – made the British charts in 1962 but they found their way into the set lists of many groups. Like so many indispensable records of the era, they were on the London-American label, an imprint of Decca Records. While Arthur Alexander was unlikely to be featured on the BBC Light Programme, those in the know would spot his latest record in the American chart published in the *New Musical Express* and try to catch a snatch of it on Radio Luxembourg. Travelling hundreds of miles to its British audience, the signal suffered harmful interference from other European stations. But Luxy's distinctive fading in and out almost added to the feeling that you were gaining illicit access to forbidden fruit.

Unashamedly commercial, Radio Luxembourg openly invited companies to pay for the airtime given to their new records. *The Decca Show* presented by Tony Hall, the label's Head of Promotions, was particularly essential because it featured so many of the London-American discs. Once you'd glimpsed the greatness of Arthur Alexander, most towns had a helpful record shop that would order his latest release, if it wasn't already waiting for you there. Meanwhile, the juke box in a local coffee bar might have an esoteric selection picked to click with a cooler crowd and then you could really experience that bass sound on 'A Shot Of Rhythm And Blues'.

In the Beatles' case, perhaps the fact that they lived in a port where ships arrived from America – with the odd bit of rhythm and blues booty in the hold – helped them seek out the right stuff. But Bob Wooler, the man who played the records at the Cavern, thinks the difficulty of getting hold of this material has been exaggerated, 'The R and B records were available on Pye International and London-American; they weren't imported here. It's rather fanciful to say we played very rare records that only we had at the Cavern. We didn't really. We played a lot of pop material of the time, interspersed with lesser known records but which were actually available in this country.'

If you knew who was great – the Coasters, Larry Williams, the Johnny Burnette Trio, the Shirelles, the Miracles – then the race was on to get hold of their records. As Paul confessed in 1990, this might even include a little begging, borrowing or stealing: 'That's what going to parties was about I'm sad to admit. There would be these lovely people who'd bring their whole record collection to a party... bad move! Too tempting leaving that kind of stuff around with the likes of us!'

Pop Go The Beatles also provided a chance to try out some new songs. As Ringo observed, 'It was fine when doing the repertoire we knew but some weeks it'd be real hard. We'd rehearse two or three songs in the lunch break and then go and record them in the afternoon.' One example is George's version of an obscure record by the American girl group the Donays – although 'Devil In His Heart' did creep out on Oriole in the UK, hardly anyone's ever seen a copy!

The *Pop Go The Beatles* tapes are the nearest we can ever get to a good rootle through the Beatles' record collections. We are fortunate to have the unreleased songs caught in a raw state but well-recorded and without the constant jet-engine-whine of screaming fans. For this we are indebted not only to the Beatles' musical talent and resourcefulness but also to the abilities of the BBC studio staff.

CHAPTER FIVE

'Gin Bottles and Old Martians'

....

In many ways the BBC was very similar to the Beatles' record company EMI. Both organizations had a whiff of stuffy Civil Service bureaucracy about them. Unlike their counterparts at EMI, BBC sound balancers did not have to don white coats in the studio but everybody wore jackets and ties.

While Abbey Road did not have the latest recording technology used in the States – for example, Atlantic Records was using an eight-track tape machine as early as 1958, a good ten years before EMI finally acquired one – it was still more up to date than the BBC. Record companies were also not over-generous with the amount of time allotted for a session, but even in 1963 there was usually not quite the same time pressure as at the BBC. An average radio session of three and a half hours would be expected to yield at least five completed recordings.

Multi-track tape machines did not infiltrate the Beeb until the seventies, so if any mistakes were made they could not be isolated from the rest of the music. It had to be 'all right on the night'. The only way of enhancing the group's performances during *Pop Go The Beatles* was occasionally editing together the best sections of different takes.

For *The Beeb's Lost Beatles Tapes* series in 1988, George remembered the speed of these radio recording sessions. 'Everything was done instantly. We probably had a quick set-up of the amplifiers and the drums, plugged in, ran through the songs once while the engineer got a rough balance and then we did them. But before that, we used to drive 200 miles in an old van down the M1, come into London, try and find the BBC

At the BBC Paris Theatre with Liverpudlian comedian Ken Dodd for a recording of his radio show on 9 October 1963 (John's birthday).

and then set up and do the programme. Then we'd probably drive back to Newcastle for a gig in the evening!'

On hand to capture their songs on tape were the BBC's studio managers. (Although they performed an equivalent role to commercial sound men, they were *never* referred to as engineers.) The group soon gained a regular sound balancer for *Pop Go The Beatles*, who was around their age and had similar interests.

As Keith Bateson recalls, he was quite a contrast to their first studio manager. 'The original chap who did the balance on *Pop Go The Beatles* was a lovely guy called Charles Clark Maxwell, who was an old Etonian – he might just as well have been an old Martian as far as the Beatles were concerned because they hadn't really come across anyone quite like Charles before... and there was, I think, a slight communication problem... So I was put in his place because I could become very Mersey when it suited me!'

Although he actually came from Bolton in Lancashire, Keith Bateson proved popular with the Beatles – and not just because of his modified Scouse accent. Brian Epstein often made his group's bookings conditional upon Keith being at the controls. He was also in demand as a sound effects expert and the clash of a Beatles session with a recording of Spike Milligan's *Omar Khayyam Show* once led to a hasty rescheduling of the comedy show. Like several of his pioneering colleagues, he wanted to bring the sound of BBC pop recordings up to date. 'The BBC was still recovering from the wartime scenario of "keep the drums down, don't get the workers jiving in the aisles, keep production up, damp the drums" and we were trying to establish a new sort of pattern to rhythm. We were trying to copy the commercial people and we had a few problems with our microphones [on the drums] at the time because they were rather old. They were "ribbon microphones" and as soon as you expended any energy at them, above the normal, the ribbon used to break – which was quite handy!'

Keith's assistant studio manager on *Pop Go The Beatles* was John Andrews, who remembers, 'we were the first people to start taking the front skin off the bass drum and putting blankets inside along with the old 4033 – the gin bottle we used to call it – a very robust microphone designed for television use'.

The BBC's studios were often old theatres with a cavernous echo unsuitable for the close sound of a beat group. When attempting any acoustic screening the studio managers were forced to improvise. As John Andrews recalls, 'There were quite heavy curtains on either side of the stage to cover sound effects for audience shows and Keith decided he would put Ringo behind these curtains. The group had never seen this before and they thought it was hilarious.'

With his drums encircled by curtains, when it was Ringo's turn to sing, a Heath Robinson-like array of BBC metalwork was constructed to poke a microphone through to him. This was an odd sight, as John Andrews explains, 'The only microphone that was good for drum vocals was the old C12 – a great silver cylinder about 12 inches long and 2 inches in diameter – and the windshield was a great mesh job about 4 inches in diameter. We didn't have your modern steel booms with the little adjustments… we had a huge great hanging device with elastic strings on it and for it to reach Ringo

During Pop Go The Beatles, *Ringo sang just two songs – 'Boys' and 'Matchbox'.*

we had two very large booms with three wheels, a tripod and a great big handle.'

Producer Ian Grant remembers a similar makeshift arrangement for picking up the sound of guitar amplifiers, where microphones were tied to the handles and hung down in front of the speakers.

With its large rotary faders to adjust the levels of sound, a BBC control board in those days resembled the flight deck of an old Lancaster bomber. There was no 'equalization' on the desk to alter the treble or bass, so microphones were chosen for their particular tones. The 'ribbon' microphones gave a warm bass sound and the 'condenser' mikes had a brightness suitable for vocals and guitars. Studio managers employed tricks to change these characteristics – one devised by Freddy

Harris involved a cigarette packet stuffed behind the back-clip of a 4038 microphone, which produced a 'bass-cut'.

Adding any contolled reverberation to the sound was not an easy push-button process either. At the studios in Aeolian Hall, an echo chamber was set up, with a loudspeaker at one end of the room and a microphone at the other. The sound of the music from the speaker bounced around the room and was then added to the recording. Ian Grant was fond of experimenting. 'The only way to change the delay time was to move the speaker towards the microphone or further away... I'd get keys to the room and mess around!'

Despite the technical limitations, the *Pop Go The Beatles* sessions were usually good-natured affairs. The Beatles were apt to joke about in the studio and Terry Henebery's assistant producer for the series, Ian Grant, has not forgotten his boss's exhortations to 'sort this unruly lot out... sit on them a bit more!'.

'They approached it as fun,' Ian remembers. 'But Paul was more the co-ordinator for getting things together. You could liken him to the fixer... he was the guy you could talk to if it was getting a bit out of hand.'

Terry Henebery was perceptive enough to realize that the atmosphere of send-ups and japes should be allowed to permeate the programmes. But the music of the Beatles and their guests was not where his heart lay. He produced the radio show *Jazz Club* and, a little later, BBC TV's *Jazz 625*, which captured historic performances by many legendary performers – Duke Ellington and Dizzy Gillespie among them. The Beatles were not unaware of Terry's musical preferences, as George has explained. 'Yeah, Mr Henebery was a jazz fan and he hated the Beatles! At that time, Paul's girl-friend was Jane Asher and when she'd finish whatever her job was, she'd come round and sit in the control room. And then she'd tell us later what he used to say, because he'd be behind the window and forget that she was there. And he'd be saying, "These bloody Beatles... they haven't got a clue! I hate this music." And all that kind of stuff.'

When the *Pop Go The Beatles* series was extended, the BBC decided to limit the group's appearances on other programmes, and three *Side By Side* recordings scheduled for July, August and September 1963 were cancelled. But summer bookings still took place for the two big audience shows presented by Brian Matthew – *Easy Beat* and *Saturday Club*.

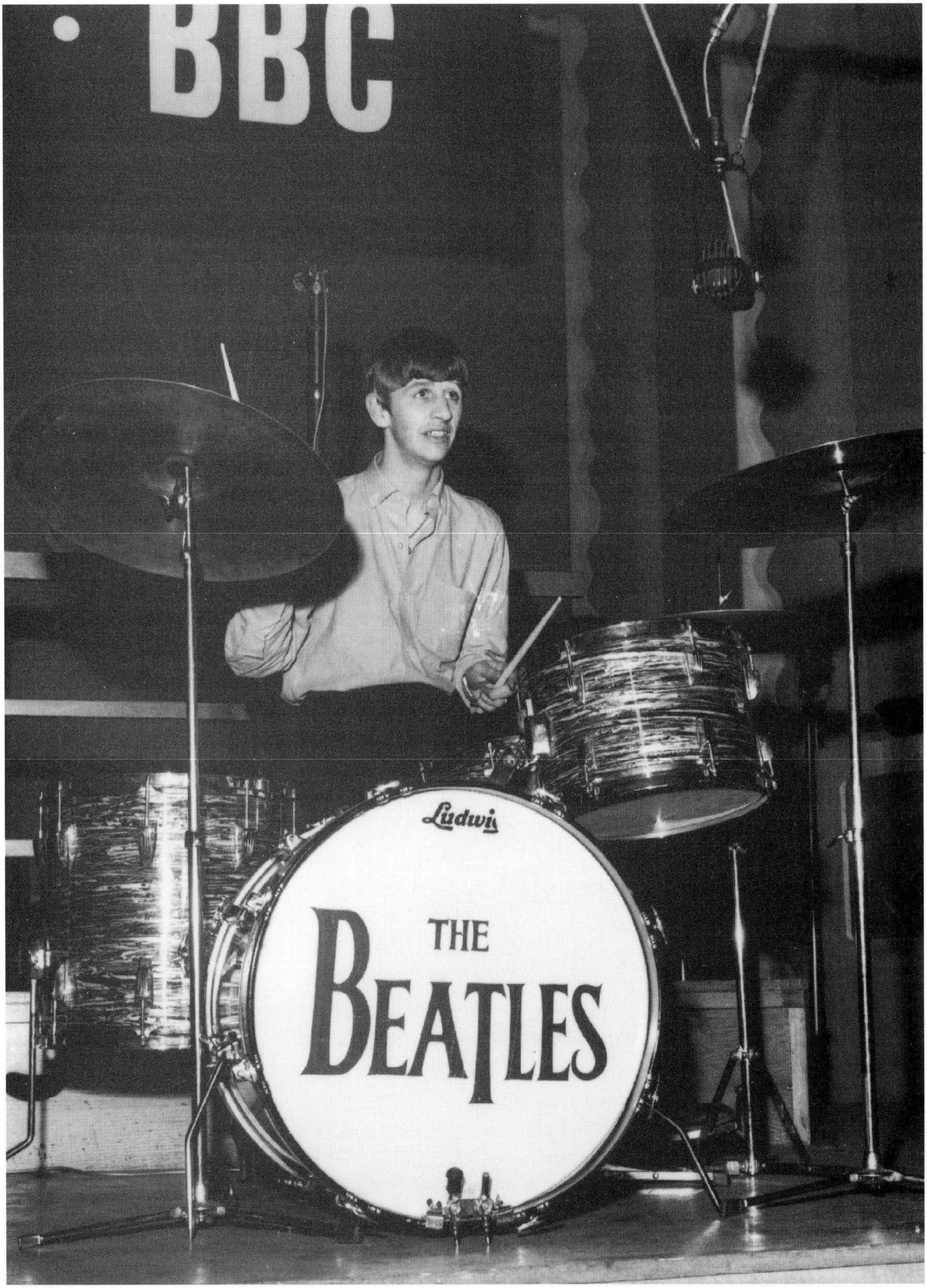
BBC
Ludwig
THE BEATLES

CHAPTER SIX

'The Showbusiness Jackpot'

....

Their *Pop Go The Beatles* series and visits to *Saturday Club* and *Easy Beat* reflected the group's escalating popularity during the summer and early autumn of 1963. In *Easy Beat*, broadcast on 23 June, over the screams of the audience, Brian Matthew said, 'I've been overwhelmed by a shoal of letters all saying, "Will you please ask the Beatles to sing especially for me"… well, now if I were to read out all the names I'd be here right into the middle of Jean Metcalfe's Bumper Bundle!' (Jean Metcalfe presented *Two-Way Family Favourites* – the popular Forces request show broadcast on Sunday lunchtime.)

The following weekend, the Beatles were at the top of the bill for *Saturday Club*. Five of the six songs were covers not available on record, including three Chuck Berry numbers. 'Roll Over Beethoven' with backing vocals on the last chorus sounded quite different to the later released version and 'Memphis, Tennessee' featured a powerful upfront bass part from Paul. The whereabouts of the enigmatic 'Harry and his box' were discussed, leading to John's clarification that 'the truth about Harry and his box is that verypardonoftenthe-parkywalkthrough! Tell me, you know what I mean?' Obviously.

The next time they were on the show was 24 August 1963, the day after the release of 'She Loves You', which they performed along with its B-side 'I'll Get You'. Their growing confidence as radio performers is evident on an amusing recording of John reading a cute request while guitar and piano are played behind him. The writer from Nottingham mentions their enjoyment of *Pop Go The Beatles* and asks for 'You

'We just play how we can and the sound we make is just us and it seems to be selling at the moment.' Ringo at the BBC Playhouse Theatre.

Really Got A Hold On Me' – heard twice in the series by the time of this 30 July recording.

The *Saturday Club* afternoon session was sandwiched between morning and evening Abbey Road studio time used to make tracks for the next album. As if all this wasn't enough, they were interviewed the same day by bandleader Phil Tate for his regular 'Pop Chat' feature in the programme *Non Stop Pop*.

PHIL John, over to you for a minute. You do a lot of songwriting, I believe. Do you always work as a team?

JOHN Mainly. The better songs that we have written – the ones that anybody wants to hear – both of us have written.

PHIL And do you write the words and music together or does one of you write the words?

JOHN Sometimes half the words are written by me and he'll finish them off or we go along a word each, practically!

PHIL And did you write your new record release?

JOHN 'She Loves You', you mean? Yeah, we wrote that two days before we recorded it.

PAUL Actually, we wrote it in a hotel room in Newcastle.

PHIL Well, this brings me to a question from one of your fans – Vicky Owen of Chadwell Heath – how did this distinctive hairstyle come about?

GEORGE Well, I don't think any of us have been bothered with having haircuts and it was always long. Paul and John went to Paris [in October 1961] and came back with it something like this and I went to the [swimming] baths and came out with it [just] like this!

PHIL Are you keeping your homes in Liverpool or do

John, Paul, George and... Bernie – during a Saturday Club recording session, 17 December 1963. The Beatles often visited Bernie Andrews in the flat he shared with Terry Doran in Mayfair: 'Sounds posh, but it was only eleven quid a week for four bedrooms... and I wish I still had it!'

you plan on moving to London or anything like that?

RINGO I don't think any of us are moving... We must have a base in London because we're there more than we are in Liverpool at the moment. But we're not moving our houses.

In fact, all the Beatles were living in London during the last quarter of 1963. Paul was staying with the family of his girlfriend Jane Asher in Welbeck Street, while the others took flats in nearby Mayfair. There they were able to socialize a little with some media folk, including *Saturday Club* producer Bernie Andrews. He was sharing a flat in Shepherd Street with a business associate of Brian Epstein, Terry Doran and his vociferous mynah bird!

As Bernie remembers, 'Paul only came round to the flat once, actually, and just inside the front door of the flat there was this mynah bird in a cage and the mynah bird said "Hello, Ringo!", which I was very embarrassed about as it was the first time Paul had been round. I apologized and said he normally didn't do things like that!'

Bernie even made and preserved a home-recording of the cheeky bird exclaiming 'Hello, Ringo!', which in 1988 was broadcast next to that anecdote in *The Beeb's Lost Beatles Tapes*. The BBC producer was also the regular provider of a favourite Beatle meal. 'The main thing that George used to come round for was egg and chips. He loved egg and chips! When they were at the height of their popularity, he couldn't just go round to some restaurant in Mayfair and order egg and chips.

And he couldn't go to a place where you *could* order egg and chips because he'd get mobbed like mad. He didn't want to know about cooking it himself, so he used to come round to Bern's for egg and chips!'

For some reason a guitar belonging to Ringo remained at Bernie's flat for about three years but he doesn't remember the drummer ever playing it – 'not with his fingers anyway!'.

In the seventies, the Beatles' former press officer Derek Taylor came across the notes he'd made for Brian Epstein's autobiography *A Cellar Full Of Noise*, for which he was the ghost writer. The Beatles' manager had indicated to Derek that Bernie was 'someone who I and the boys have a great deal of affection for, because he is probably one of the best producers in the Corporation'.

The Beatles were produced by Bernie for the fifth birthday edition of *Saturday Club* broadcast on 5 October 1963. It was to feature what the *Radio Times* described as 'the most spectacular bill of stars ever invited to the *Club*'. It was quite a line-up. In addition to the Beatles, there were sessions from the Everly Brothers, Frank Ifield, Kenny Ball's Jazzmen, Joe Brown and the Bruvvers, Tommy Roe, Clinton Ford and Kathy Kirby. Taped birthday messages were played from Roy Orbison, Del Shannon, Rick Nelson, Brenda Lee, and Cliff Richard on the phone from Tel Aviv. Mimicking the arrangement of the current Heinz hit 'Just Like Eddie', the Beatles played 'Happy Birthday Dear *Saturday Club*' and another five tracks, including Chuck Berry's 'Memphis, Tennessee' and Little Richard's 'Lucille'.

Recorded on 7 September, this *Saturday Club* session was their thirty-fifth music session for the BBC in 1963 – all done within the space of 32 weeks. Meanwhile, they had also written and recorded songs for EMI, appeared on many TV shows and criss-crossed the country on tour. The group took a well-deserved fortnight's holiday at the end of September. They returned the next month and found the whole country in thrall to Beatlemania. Undoubtedly, the exposure on the Light Programme's pop shows had helped the nation

fall in love with the Beatles' music and personalities. But the BBC would now find it much harder to tempt them into their studios. And their days of playing for studio audiences were definitely numbered.

Easy Beat was recorded in front of a mainly female audience on a Wednesday evening at the BBC Playhouse Theatre. In 1963 it was produced by Ron Belchier and recorded by his regular studio managers – balancer Bev Phillips and his assistant John Andrews. Wednesday was a very busy day, as John recalls, 'We did *Parade Of The Pops* live at lunchtime with an audience, 12.30-1.30, and then we'd clear down the stage completely and set up again for *Easy Beat*. There was a rehearsal throughout the afternoon, then the audience came in about seven and we did another complete one-hour show "as live".'

One of John Andrews' jobs was to signal from the auditorium to his colleague in the sound booth, who then adjusted the level of the PA system once the recording had started. This fairly primitive system of hand waving usually worked, except for the Beatles performance recorded on 16 October 1963. 'The noise was totally unbelievable… even now I can remember thinking, "God, this hurts!" As soon as the lads came on, it was just solid screams – you could hear a little guitar. Bev was looking anxiously at me and I just turned around, shrugged my shoulders and put my hands in the air! There was just nothing you could do with our 75 watts of PA.'

The performance sounded great on the air, though, as the Beatles performed 'I Saw Her Standing There' and their four hit singles. 'Now, hush, hush!' Brian Matthew implored the fans, commenting that 'Alfred Hitchcock's *Birds* have got nothing on you lot!'.

In this small theatre, the stage was only about 6 feet from the front row of the very excited audience. The authority of Brian Matthew and a few burly BBC commissionaires kept the situation under control but Brian Epstein had already become anxious about the Beatles' safety. An *Easy Beat* recording scheduled for 4 December and contracted on 10 September had been cancelled three days later. After October, there would be no more audience shows with the Beatles in BBC radio studios.

During their last *Easy Beat*, Brian Matthew observed that it was now 'almost a year since the Beatles first hit the showbusiness jackpot'. The announcement of their inclusion in the *Royal Variety Performance*, playing for the Queen Mother and Princess Margaret, now gave their success a regal seal of approval. The media were all agog at this news. BBC reporter (later TV newsreader) Peter Woods couldn't hide his rather patronizing attitude when he talked to the Beatles at their rehearsal for *Easy Beat*:

WOODS Well, lads, almost unknown in January and now going into the Royal Command Performance in November. This is quite a rise – even for your business – isn't it, Paul?

PAUL Yes, it's been very quick and we have been very lucky.

WOODS How much of this is due, do you think, to pure musical talent?

PAUL Er, dunno. No idea. You just can't tell, y'know. Maybe a lot of it, maybe none of it.

WOODS How much would you say?

JOHN I agree with Paul… it varies…

WOODS How much of this is getting popularity by acting the fool a bit and playing around?

JOHN Well, I mean, that's just natural. We don't do it for effect… we do it anyway, whether we're on stage or…

WOODS But your funny haircuts aren't natural.

JOHN Well, we don't think they're funny, you see, cobber!

WOODS As far as playing your type of music is concerned, is this a new thing, do you think, Ringo?

RINGO No, not really.

WOODS The word in the music world is that 'We've heard this type of thing before.'

RINGO We just play how we can and the sound we make is just us and it seems to be selling at the moment so…

JOHN It's rock! Rock 'n' roll.

RINGO It is rock, yeah, as John said, butting in.

WOODS George, can I turn to you now? How long do you think you're going to be successful? You've had this monumental rise. Obviously this sort of thing can't go on but do you think you can settle down to a life in showbusiness?

GEORGE Well, we're hoping to. Not necessarily a life in showbusiness but at least a couple more years… I mean, if we do as well as Cliff and the Shadows have done up till now… well, we won't be moaning… I mean, naturally, it can't go on as it has been going the last few months – it'd just be ridiculous.

WOODS How do you find all this business of having screaming girls following you all over the place?

GEORGE Well, we feel flattered.

ALL Flattened!

GEORGE Yeah, and flattened. But if the screaming fans weren't there, then we wouldn't be here would we?

ALL *(Exaggerated northern accents)* Aye, by gum, that's right!

WOODS Paul, coming quickly back to you again … Mr Edward Heath, the Lord Privy Seal, has said that the other night he found it difficult to distinguish what you were saying as Queen's English. Now, are you going to try to lose some of your Liverpool dialect for the royal show?

PAUL No, you're kidding.

GEORGE We just won't vote for him!

PAUL No, we wouldn't bother doing that. *(Adopting strong northern accent)* We don't all speak like them BBC posh fellas, y'know.

JOHN and PAUL *(Northern accents)* Nay, we don't. By gum, no, we don't. Right up north.

WOODS *(Assuming a northern accent)* Aye, well with that I'd better wish you good luck in the show… What song will you be singing most there, do you think?

PAUL *(In perfect English public school drawl)* Well, I don't know, but I should imagine we'll do 'She Loves You'.

ALL *(Similar voice to Paul)* Haw, haw, haw! Jolly good, jolly good!

Rehearsing Easy Beat *at the BBC Playhouse Theatre, London on 16 October 1963. The previous day's announcement of their invitation to appear in the* Royal Variety Performance *was headline news. For the Light Programme's evening* Radio Newsreel, *Peter Woods asked about their 'monumental rise' and their career plans: 'Not necessarily a life in show business,' said George, 'If we do as well as Cliff and the Shadows... we won't be moaning.'*

The irony of this final exchange was that very soon middle-class youngsters would be endeavouring to give their voices a regional twist in imitation of their musical heroes. For example, DJ John Peel, an ex-public schoolboy, invented a new voice for himself that became gruffer and more northern as his career progressed. And the BBC, in general, would soon start to reflect on air the variety of accents heard around the country.

By the end of 1963, the success of the Beatles and other Mersey artists – Gerry and the Pacemakers had three number ones and Billy J. Kramer three Top Five singles – put the spotlight on Liverpool. BBC TV's *The Mersey Sound* and ITV's *Beat City* were screened in October and November 1963. On the BBC Light Programme, a feature on the Beatles' formative years in the city was broadcast during the 3 November edition of the fortnightly entertainment magazine programme

The Public Ear. There were interviews with *Mersey Beat* editor Bill Harry, Stuart Sutcliffe's mother, beat poet Royston Ellis, some anonymous Cavern fans and former drummer Pete Best – 'I was called into the office by Brian Epstein and for no rhyme or reason I was told that I was gonna be replaced'.

The narrator Tony Hall's enthusiasm could not have been further from the cynicism of Peter Woods – 'For everyone under 20, the Beatles still represent everything worth shouting about… and if you're older and you can't understand the teenagers, then you should *study* this music'. On the same programme, George set the record straight about their financial situation at the time. 'People say we make £7000 a week… I mean, we probably do make quite a bit but we don't actually see it because record royalties, things like that, take months

before they come in. And anyway…'

'Your mother costs a fortune!' interrupts John.

'…Yeah, my mother costs a fortune! But we've also got an accountant and a company called Beatles Limited… They see the money!… Don't forget we played for about three or four years, or maybe longer, earning hardly anything. If we were doing it for the money, we wouldn't have lasted out all those years. We like it sufficiently to do it not for the money too… but the money does help, let's face it!'

In a discussion about their abilities as musicians, Paul singled out George as the most interested in his instrument – 'the other three of us are more interested in the sound of the group'.

Meanwhile George concluded that 'individually, I suppose we're all crummy musicians really!'.

CHAPTER SEVEN

'Happy and Melodious with Plenty of Zip'

....

The Public Ear's profile of the Beatles was broadcast the day before their triumph at the *Royal Variety Performance* on 4 November 1963. This was shown on television the following Sunday night – 10 November – with a cast that included Marlene Dietrich, Buddy Greco, Max Bygraves, Tommy Steele, Flanders and Swann, Wilfred Brambell and Harry H. Corbett (playing *Steptoe and Son*), and Jan and Vlasta Dalibor (*Pinky and Perky* to you and me). There was also a Light Programme highlights presentation the same evening, which broadcast 'From Me To You', 'Till There Was You' and 'Twist And Shout' (omitting their opener 'She Loves You').

In November and December 1963, the Beatles were making their fourth tour of the country within nine months. Audiences now screamed incessantly and the claustrophobic life portrayed a little later in *A Hard Day's Night* was a reality. Indeed, the film's screenwriter Alun Owen observed the siege conditions of this tour for three days. Michael Braun, the writer of the excellent *Love Me Do! The Beatles' Progress*, was also in the entourage for the last two weeks of concerts.

A BBC interview recorded on 10 December in the dressing room of the Gaumont Cinema, Doncaster, gives a vivid picture of life with the Beatles at this crazy time. Australian Dibbs Mather talked to each of them in turn for a feature distributed by the BBC's Transcription Service and not heard in the UK. Throughout the recording, the sound of teenage girls screaming and chanting – 'We want Paul! We want Paul! – is in the background… as well as John munching an apple very loudly! Once more, some of the questions reflected the interviewer's assumption that their incandescent popularity would very quickly fizzle out:

DIBBS George Harrison… you're one of the reputed deep thinkers in this group. Do you see it as a peak in your life? What happens to you after this is over?

GEORGE Well, I suppose we'll stay doing this sort of stuff for a couple of years. Naturally, we won't be able to stay at this level but we should have another two years at least, I think.

DIBBS And what happens to George Harrison then?

GEORGE I dunno. I'll know by the time that comes along. Probably have a little business or something like that.

DIBBS You don't want to go on in the profession?

GEORGE Probably, yeah. I'd like to make records with other artists. I don't mean perform, I mean as a producer.

When Dibbs Mather talked to Ringo, he received an honest account of his earlier life in Liverpool:

DIBBS Ringo Starr, it's been suggested that boys coming from the particular area that you came from – if you hadn't found an interest in music – might have found it much more difficult to get out and make a go of life. Would you comment on this?

RINGO I think it's true. I mean, when I was 16 and that, I used to walk on the road with the rest of the lads and we'd have all our drape coats on. We never got to the stage of beating up old women though. Just we'd have a few 'narks' and that with other rival gangs, sort of thing. And then I got the drums and the bloke next door played a guitar and I got a job…

PAUL *(Shouts)* Teddy boy!

RINGO *(Laughs)*… and we started playing together and another bloke in work made a bass out of an

Dibbs Mather interviews the Beatles for the transcription programmes Dateline London *and* Calling Australia, *distributed to overseas stations on disc.*

old tea-chest… y'know, them days – this was about '58, mind you – and we played together and then we started playing on dances and things and we took an interest in it and we stopped going out hanging round street corners every night.

Like so many of their interviews, there was the standard question of what Ringo would do when it was all over.

RINGO You mean when it's finished altogether? I'd like to open a business. I've been saying, this last year anyway, ladies hairdressing, but you never know what'll happen. I may open something else but I wanna try and be successful.

Dibbs had been swatting up on his subjects and noticed that Paul had graduated to the sixth form at his grammar school.

but I was as well. But I don't think that's made me feel I ought to go on and do better things.

DIBBS What do you think you might have done if this particular thing hadn't come up?

PAUL Well, at the time I was thinking of going to a Teacher Training College. I don't know whether I'd have been any good at all but it just seemed sort of a natural thing to do at the time.

Their chat concluded with a discussion about the immediacy of the Beatles' lyrics:

PAUL Lyrics, as far as we're concerned, are just things that we might say. The main point is that they've got to be feasible. We don't like saying, 'Yeah, she's a movie queen, baby' or things like that because they don't happen to come into our lives. But we will say things like, 'Don't go away because I might miss you' because I'm sure that, you know, that everybody's felt that at some time or another. The things that *can* happen, we'll write about but things that happen in other people's great glamorous lives – Cadillacs and movie queens and Hollywood – I'm sure we'll never write into our lyrics because we couldn't believe it. We've got to believe our lyrics.

So far so good for Dibbs. In a quite respectful and informed way, he was asking questions that were pitched at a different level from the usual 'How did you get that funny haircut?' But his patience was tested when he faced John, who was in a cantankerous mood:

DIBBS What's been the greatest influence in your life… up to this date, up to this experience with the Beatles?

JOHN Neil, that's our road manager.

DIBBS What kind of influence did he have on you?

JOHN Er, none really.

DIBBS *(A little desperately)* Is no influence better than some influence?

JOHN Well, apart from that *(a loud munch)* an apple a day, keeps the docker away!

DIBBS Paul McCartney… you alone of the four Beatles seem to have had a greater incentive to go on and do other things because, on the educational side of it, you've gone further than the other lads have.

PAUL No… Yeah, not really though. It just so 'appens I happened to get a few GCEs – I don't think that makes me cleverer than the others… I know John's not soft at all, maybe he was a bit lazy at school

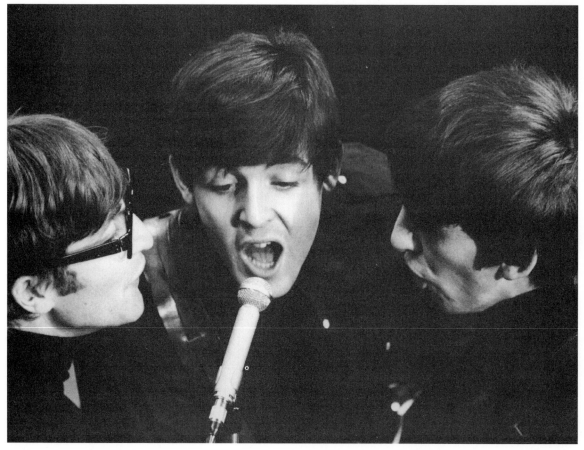

Recording songs on 17 December 1963 for the Christmas Edition of Saturday Club, which also featured Adam Faith and the Roulettes, Mr Acker Bilk and his Paramount Jazz Band, and the boy and girl next door of British pop – Mark Wynter and Susan Maughan.

DIBBS It's said, John Lennon, that you have the most Goon-type humour of the four Beatles.

JOHN *(Quickly)* Who said that?

DIBBS I think I read it in one of the papers *(door slam)*... This is all going wrong, I wanted to get a nice personality bit.

JOHN I haven't got a nice personality.

DIBBS What kind of personality would you say you have?

JOHN *(Cheerfully)* Very nice. *(Laughs)*

DIBBS Um... you were interested in poetry, at school...

JOHN Who said?

DIBBS *(Patience finally disappearing)* It's printed in a book compiled by the Beatles and entitled *The Beatles.*

JOHN I haven't read that book... We don't normally write those things. You can tell they're all written by the same person anyway.

DIBBS *(Despairingly)* Ohh! Well, it's said that you write comic poetry if the mood takes you, about something that takes your fancy.

JOHN Oh yeah, I do that.

John then read a part of 'Neville Club', which was eventually published three months later in a collection of verse, prose and drawings called *In His Own Write*. A week after talking to Dibbs Mather, the Beatles were back at the BBC recording two shows for Christmas week.

The informality of these BBC publicity photographs is demonstrated by John wearing his glasses in the studio, which he never did on stage.

John and Paul catch up on paperwork between takes at the session for Saturday Club *recorded between 3.00pm and 6.30pm on 17 December 1963. A week later, their remarkable year of British success was crowned with the opening of The Beatles' Christmas Show – 100,000 tickets sold for 30 shows.* Record Retailer *magazine came up with the staggering statistic that British consumers had spent £6,250,000 on Beatles records in 1963.*

Their sixth appearance on *Saturday Club* was recorded on 17 December 1963 and broadcast four days later. Following a spin of Kathy Kirby's Top Five hit 'Secret Love', the Beatles' first song was 'All My Loving'. The exchanges between the group and Brian Matthew are typical of the roles they adopted for this and future interviews:

BRIAN 'All My Loving', indeed. I never saw a more belligerent bunch in my life! What's the matter with you lot then?
JOHN What happened to our request, Brian Bathtubes?
PAUL Yeah, we sent it in about two weeks ago and you haven't played it, have you, eh?
JOHN No, he hasn't played it, has he? Oh no, not him!
PAUL Oh no.

GEORGE He won't play our request.
BRIAN Have you done? Well, all right then, now read someone else's request.
JOHN 'Dear John, would you please play "This Boy" by the...'
BRIAN Get on with it!
JOHN... 'fabulous Beatles. Thank you.

After an excellent BBC performance of 'This Boy', the programme continued with Frank Sinatra's record 'Come Fly With Me'. Their next spot in the show followed Susan Maughan singing a version of the current hit by Dora Bryan – 'All I Want For Christmas Is A Beatle'. The group responded with a quick parody – 'All I Want For Christmas Is A Bottle'! In their final set they put a few appropriate Christmas words to the Freddie and the Dreamers' hit 'You Belong To Me', which was then in the Top Three, beneath 'I Want To Hold Your Hand' and 'She Loves You'. The last session track was a 'Chrimble Muddley' based on Duane Eddy's 'Shazam!', in which John sang the titles or snippets of lyrics from the five Beatles singles to date... and 'Rudolph The Red-Nosed Reindeer'!

Their last BBC music session of 1963 was recorded for a two-hour Boxing Day programme introduced by Rolf Harris, who also compèred The Beatles' Christmas Show at the Finsbury Park Astoria. The radio special's working title, *Beatletime*, became *The Beatles Say From Us To You*, allowing 'From Me To You' to be reworked as the all-important signature tune. Their 'guests' – selected by the producer Bryant Marriott – included Joe Brown and the Bruvvers, Jeanie Lambe, the seemingly ever-present Susan Maughan and Kenny Lynch.

One of the most remarkable recordings of the Beatles' radio career happened during *From Us To You*. They were invited by presenter Rolf Harris to provide some backing while he sang a customized 'Tie Me Kangaroo Down, Sport'.

The new lyric ran along the lines of 'Cut your hair once a year, boys', 'Don't ill-treat me pet dingo, Ringo', 'I think George's guitar's on the blink' and 'Keep the hits coming on, John'. Rolf shook his wobble board and called for some 'She Loves You'-ish falsetto 'Woo!'s from the obliging group.

The BBC's Audience Research Department compiled a report which estimated the audience at 22.1 per cent for the first hour and 20 per cent for the second. Around 11 million had heard the broadcast but the 'Appreciation Index' figure was a lowly 49 out of 100. Significantly, of the 323 who completed questionnaires, 31 per cent who 'usually liked listening to this kind of music' gave the show a very respectable 75. There were not many teenagers in this audience sample but some of the 'older' listeners (ancient 23- or 24-year-olds) had enjoyed the show. The report concluded: 'This was definitely family listening. Teenagers, right, left, and centre and across the road had the set on. I found it quite happy and melodious, with plenty of zip. I am quite a fan of the Beatles. To me they are the new "Today", clean and wholesome and gay.'

CHAPTER EIGHT

'The Beatles Arrive'

....

'The Beatles' Christmas Show' ran at the Astoria in London for 16 nights. This meant that the group spent the holiday season working most evenings but at least they were not travelling the length and breadth of Britain. They could, perhaps, relax a little. George may well have popped round to see Bernie Andrews and enjoyed a plate of egg and chips. Certainly, George and Ringo dropped in on a radio presenter who lived opposite their flat in Green Street.

Tony Hall was a Radio Luxembourg DJ, *Record Mirror* columnist and Head of Promotion at Decca Records. He had recently narrated the profile of the Beatles on the magazine programme *The Public Ear*. The group had probably heard some of their favourite records on his Luxembourg *Decca Show* and their respect for him turned to friendship after they met him.

The Public Ear had an 'Air Mail' section, in which letters to the programme were read out. The signature tune, naturally enough, was 'I'm Going To Sit Right Down And Write Myself A Letter'. During the edition broadcast on 12 January 1964, one of the letters was voiced by two of the Beatles. George read most of it:

Dear *Public Ear*,

We heard your programme on December the 29th when Tony Hall said it'd be nice if the people who liked our kind of music would also appreciate the kind of records and music that we play at home – like Mary Wells, [the] Miracles and not to mention Marvin Gaye.

We believe the fans would like these singers if they had the chance to hear them, y'see. Because we don't

Brian Epstein relaxing with the Beatles at the Plaza Hotel, New York and revelling in the group's unprecedented American reception on 7 February 1964.

seem to hear enough of them these days on the radio.

So you'd make us very happy, Tony, and you'd *(Ringo joins in)* absolutely break us up, if you'd play us some.

Yours sincerely,
George Harrison and Ringo Starr

Ringo and George were then heard discussing how Ringo's 'gag' had been missed out. Amid much laughter, Ringo explains, 'You know… Marvin Gaye… and I say "Marvin Gaye" and you say, "I told you not to mention him!" '

Tony Hall thanked George and Ringo for their audio letter and picked up on their request: 'Well, here's one by the Miracles that I know you're always playing at home and the title? "I've Been Good To You".' This was the B-side of the group's second Top 40 US hit for Tamla – 'What's So Good About Goodbye' – released in early 1962. (Have a listen to 'I've Been Good To You' and then compare it to the Beatles' 'Sexy Sadie'…)

Tony Hall remembers, 'I'd never really heard Marvin Gaye, the Miracles and all that until George played me the records up in their flat and they absolutely blew me away and I then went on a sort of a crusade for Motown!'. Unfortunately for Decca, despite Tony's enthusiasm and good personal contacts with Motown boss Berry Gordy, his superiors remained indifferent. ('That label will never mean anything in England,' he was told.) When their licensing agreement expired with Oriole, Motown was picked up by EMI's Stateside label and within months the hits were rolling out.

George and Ringo had been recorded at Tony's flat, which they often visited. Although he lived just opposite them in Green Street, it was not an easy journey to make because their fans held a constant vigil outside. On one occasion, George had to a take a 20-minute detour in a taxi to evade the girls. Tony summarized the manoeuvre as 'two pounds to cross the road!'.

He and his wife threw regular parties for their friends in the business and at one of them Ringo and Cilla Black led the dancing to the Top Ten American single by Shirley Ellis, 'The Nitty Gritty'. Another memorable get-together involved John, George and Ringo meeting Phil Spector and his girl group the Ronettes. After an uncomfortable start, the evening livened up and ended around breakfast time with Spector talking about and playing some of his hits. 'George, who was *the* record man, particularly dug it!' Tony remembers.

The Ronettes were featured in session for *Saturday Club*, broadcast on 11 January 1964. A few days before, the Beatles recorded an appearance that was kept in the can for a month. Before its transmission, the group's success shifted up another gear... much to the surprise of many British cynics. Rather ludicrously, just because the Dave Clark Five's record 'Glad All Over' finally replaced 'I Want To Hold Your Hand' at number one, it had been predicted that the 'Tottenham Sound' would hasten the Beatles' demise.

An Emwood cartoon in the *Daily Mail* pictured a group of girls waiting for autographs outside a Dave Clark Five concert. They are glowering at another girl walking by and one of them comments, 'She *must* be old, she can remember when the Beatles were top-of-the-pops!'. A copy of this cartoon is preserved in a BBC Beatles file attached to a jokey memo from the Chief of the Light Programme, Denis Morris, which simply says, 'Greater love hath no man than not to take money off his friends when he is onto a certainty'. He had sent it to Donald MacLean – by January 1964, the Chief Assistant, Production, Popular Music (Sound) – and to the Head of Popular Music (Sound), Ken Baynes.

But even if Morris was prepared to bet that the Beatles were finished, his colleagues did not think it was all over yet. MacLean wrote to Baynes, 'Do you share my suspicion that somebody's jumping the gun by six months, p'raps maybe?... (And that somebody hasn't yet seen *Billboard* 18 January issue lead story, and pages 3, 8, 16, 38 and 61.)'.

'Indeed I do!' was the response two days later.

The American record business trade paper *Billboard* was trumpeting a new British phenomenon – by 10 January 1964 US sales of 'I Want To Hold Your Hand' had passed the one million mark. Luckily, back in November, Brian Epstein had arranged three TV appearances for the Beatles on the top-rated *Ed Sullivan Show*. By the time they touched down in New York on 7 February, 'I Want To Hold Your Hand' was in its second week at number one and America had rolled over, legs in the air, tongue hanging out, waiting for its belly to be tickled!

Only two British artists had ever reached the top in the States – Mr Acker Bilk with 'Stranger On The Shore' and the Tornados with 'Telstar' – but these had been one-off instrumental 'novelties'. The Beatles were different. They came, saw and conquered. Their exultant visit for the *Ed Sullivan Show* TV recordings was closely monitored by the media at home.

The day after their New York arrival, *Saturday Club* carried two items on their progress. Just before 11 am, listeners heard the Beatles talking from their hotel room over the phone to presenter Brian Matthew. The interview had been recorded the day before at 6 pm – New York time – barely four hours after their feverish reception by hundreds of teenagers:

PAUL It was fantastic... we just didn't believe it...
When we arrived they were all just hanging all over the airport, and thousands of pressmen, and thousands of New York cops. It was just ridiculous... screaming, belting all over the place. It was marvellous, in fact... And we were just driving along, listening to the DJ show on the radio and, as we were going along, it was reporting it... And just as we were getting out of the car, he says, 'Well, we hear they've arrived now!'

Paul said he was hoping to meet the Ronettes, who the

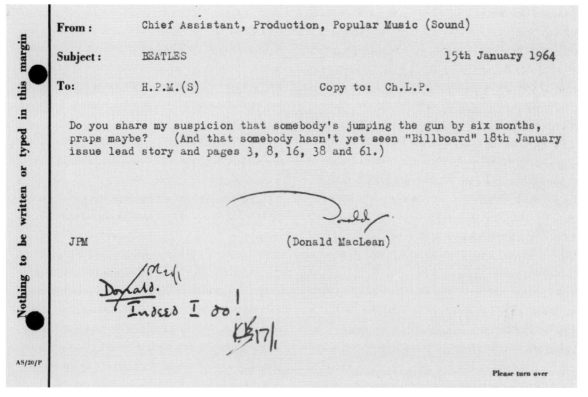

From: Chief Assistant, Production, Popular Music (Sound)

Subject: BEATLES   15th January 1964

To: H.P.M.(S)   Copy to: Ch.L.P.

Do you share my suspicion that somebody's jumping the gun by six months, praps maybe?   (And that somebody hasn't yet seen "Billboard" 18th January issue lead story and pages 3, 8, 16, 38 and 61.)

(Donald MacLean)

JPM

Donald.
Indeed I do!

AS/20/P   Please turn over

The response to a frivolous memo sent by the Chief of the Light Programme: 'Greater love hath no man than not to take money off his friends when he is onto a certainty', pinned to a Daily Mail cartoon with the punchline: 'She must be old, she can remember when the Beatles were top-of-the-pops!'.

others had partied with in London and that a DJ (Murray the K) was hoping to fly in the Miracles to meet them. Then Brian talked to John:

BRIAN Have you seen any TV yet, John?

JOHN Yeah, we've just been watching it for the last hour or two… 'cause they've got so many programmes, so we're on all the news. Yeah, it's ridiculous.

BRIAN What are your first impressions of arrival in America?

JOHN They're wild!… They just seem all out of their minds!

BRIAN John, is there anything you want to say to the fans back here at home?

JOHN Yeah, well, tell 'em not to forget. We're only away for ten days and we'll be back and we're thinking of them. We're coming back to do the film for seven weeks anyway.

BRIAN Oh yes, that film and why haven't I got a part in it, pray?

JOHN Well, we'll try and get you one pushing a barrow or something!

BRIAN Thank you very much. Now let's have a word with Ringo, could we?

RINGO Hello, Bri.

BRIAN Hello. How are you?

RINGO Fine.

BRIAN What was the first thing you did when you got there, Ringo?

RINGO Well, we had this big mass press interview with about 100 people there. And then we got out of that and then we had a Cadillac each! Marvellous cars.

BRIAN Now, what sort of things did they want to know at the press reception?

RINGO Oh, all things. Are we bald? What do we do with our money? All the usual things.

BRIAN You proved that you don't wear wigs, I hope.

RINGO Yeah.

BRIAN What did you do?

RINGO We took 'em off!... Here's George now.

BRIAN How many of your records are in the American Hit Parade at the moment?

GEORGE We've got six in the 100... 'I Want To Hold Your Hand', 'She Loves You', 'Please Please Me', 'From Me To You', 'My Bonnie'... which is a laugh!... and 'I Saw Her Standng There'. You know in New York, three records – 'Please Please Me', 'She Loves You' and 'I Want To Hold Your Hand' – are all (joint) number one.

BRIAN Well, that's marvellous and we're all very proud of you.

GEORGE All our best... see you in two weeks' time... and give our regards to Bernie Andrews.

BRIAN I'll do that.

GEORGE Tell him to get his hair cut!

Extracts from this chat were also included in a report compiled by BBC New York correspondent Malcolm Davis. Broadcast in the last ten minutes of the show, he played tapes of screaming fans at the airport and outside the Plaza Hotel and an interview with Murray the K, who was confident that the Beatles had already made an 'initial impact' bigger than Elvis Presley. *Saturday Club* listeners were left in no doubt that the Beatles had arrived.

The next week, listeners heard the music session recorded in January. There were two unreleased performances. John duck-walked with the best of them on Chuck Berry's 'Johnny B. Goode' and Paul introduced 'The Hippy Hippy Shake' as 'one that we used to do a long time ago at the Cavern and I think it's one that most people know by now'. The song was a current Top Three hit by Liverpool group the Swinging Blue Jeans. The version of 'I Wanna Be Your Man' was interesting, with an excellent Bo Diddley feel that distinguished it from the record.

It was known that on the broadcast date of 15 February, they would be rehearsing for a second live appearance on *The Ed Sullivan Show* in Miami Beach, Florida. 'It's amazing that you can hear us, seeing as we're in America now,' said John. They also discussed their forthcoming film:

PAUL We won't be acting 'cause we'll just be ourselves... we hope... None of us can act, that's the thing.

RINGO John can act the goat! *(Laughs all round)*

JOHN Ringo! If I wasn't in America I'd punch you!

The next week's *Saturday Club* – 22 February – was the day the Beatles landed at Heathrow and the programme featured Brian Matthew talking to the group over the telephone. Paul described the British fans' reception as the 'best ever' and John agreed 'it's the biggest thing I've ever seen in my life, it's marvellous... I'm deaf with all the noise!' Brian joked that Bernie Andrews had wanted him to go to the airport, which prompted John to ask after him. He was told that Bernie – as George instructed! – had had a haircut. 'Oh dear, well, he's out of the club then,' John joked.

Ringo and George described their meeting in Miami with Cassius Clay, who was challenging Sonny Liston for the World Heavyweight Boxing Title on 25 February. 'You didn't fancy sparring a couple of rounds with him then?' Brian asked.

'Well, I didn't want to hurt him!' Ringo replied.

The day of the fight was George's twenty-first birthday and his mother had sent in a request to the show for her son. Not surprisingly, it was a disc by his beloved Miracles, the very appropriate 'Shop Around' ('When I became of age, my mother called me to her side...').

In February 1964, anything could happen. Against the odds, Sonny Liston was floored by Cassius Clay and, just as unlikely a few months back, America had been well and truly knocked out by a British pop act.

CHAPTER NINE

'From Us to You'

....

The day after their return to Britain, the Beatles took part in the TV show *Big Night Out* and throughout the following week they worked in recording studios – EMI's Abbey Road and, on Friday 28 February, the BBC's Piccadilly Studios.

The BBC session was for a second Bank Holiday *From Us To You* special on Easter Monday – 30 March 1964. The Australian DJ Alan Freeman ('Fluff') was chosen to present the show, taking over from Rolf Harris. Fluff had visited the UK in 1957 and ended up staying forever as one of the country's best-loved DJs. From 1962, he had been presenting the BBC's chart show *Pick of the Pops* on which such catch phrases as 'Greetings, pop pickers' and 'All right? Right! Stay bright!' were impeccably delivered over the signature tune 'At The Sign Of The Swinging Cymbal'. For the BBC at this time, it was about the most exciting record show on the air.

Alan Freeman linked together performances from the Beatles and their guests – Mr Acker Bilk, the Swinging Blue Jeans and singers Marion Williams and Vince Hill backed by the Kenny Salmon Seven. Fluff had first worked with the Beatles in September 1963 at the 'Great Pop Prom' concert at the Royal Albert Hall. For the radio, he brought each of them to the microphone for a chat.

As he remembers, 'There wasn't anything terribly intellectual about it. I used to say the most inane things and they were terribly intelligent, so when I uttered inanities, they would match me with them!'. These verbal vignettes were quite different in character from the banter that went on with Brian Matthew:

ALAN George, is it true that you're a connoisseur of the classics?

GEORGE No, it's just a rumour.

ALAN It's just a rumour. Do you enjoy singing Beethoven?

GEORGE No. Been singing it for 28 years now.

ALAN For how long?

GEORGE Twenty-eight years.

ALAN That's incredible. Could you manage one more performance?

GEORGE Um, possibly.

ALAN Oh, go on, say yes.

GEORGE Yes. *(Clap)* Thank you!

'Roll Over Beethoven' then followed, of course. Before Paul sang 'Till There Was You', he was asked about his musical influences – with John in the background, anxious to plug his book *In His Own Write*.

ALAN Do you have any particular idol that you've copied your singing style from?

JOHN What about my book then?

ALAN John, go away.

PAUL Used to be sort of influenced by Elvis in the old days, I think.

ALAN Really?

PAUL Yeah, used to love him.

JOHN *(Shouting in the distance)* What about my book then?

PAUL Chuck Berry, Carl Perkins and Marvin Gaye and things. Can't really sing like 'em but I like 'em though. Love 'em.

That was about as informative as it got in *From Us To You*. But the tongue-in-cheek exchanges amusingly played up the different personalities and Ringo was cast as the lonely drummer away from the main action.

Twenties to the Twist

ALAN FREEMAN is the compère of a new series of programmes of popular music ranging over forty years and interpreted by today's stars (Thurs., Light)

THE BEATLES—From Us to You

LIGHT · 10.0 a.m.

THOSE Liverpool lads look as if they're starting their own personal fan clubs for Joe Brown, Jeanie Lambe, Susan Maughan, and Kenny Lynch. Actually all four are guests with The Beatles in a two-hour pop show this morning that should have the ghosts of Christmas Past, Present, and Future shaking around the Christmas tree—all the more since Alan Elsdon's Jazzband with Mick Emery, The Kenny Salmon Seven, and Rolf Harris are also on the bill.

The Highlights page of the Radio Times *focussing on a new series for the versatile 'Fluff' and the first* From Us To You *presented by Rolf Harris.*

ALAN Ringo.

RINGO Yep.

ALAN Do you ever feel lonely at the back there playing the drums?

RINGO Yep.

ALAN Do you ever feel that you'd like to sing?

RINGO Yep.

ALAN Do you ever say anything else but 'Yep'?

RINGO Nope.

ALAN Would you like to be someone's loving man?

RINGO Yep.

ALAN Now?

RINGO Yep.

ALAN I thought you'd say that.

RINGO Yep.

There was a brief conversation about the film they were about to make and, of course, when John had his *tête-à-tête* with Fluff, they had to discuss the book.

ALAN Alongside all your singing commitments, I'm told that you're budding into a real blooming Somerset Maugham. Is that right?

JOHN No.

ALAN Why not?

JOHN Hah! Well, I'm not blooming.

At this point Paul broke in with a retaliatory 'What about my song, then?' and George and Ringo asked 'What About Us?', which triggered John's singing of the title of the Coasters record of that name.

In just two and a half hours, the group recorded the opening and closing 'From Us To You' themes and eight songs that were all available on record. They turned down a request read by Fluff for the old Cavern favourite 'Young Blood' but it was nice to hear 'This Boy' with an ending rather than a fade.

The programme was produced by Bryant Marriott with studio managers Keith Bateson and John

Andrews. As Andrews remembers, George discovered that the 4038 microphones were magnetic, and so endeavoured to throw his metal cigarette case towards some audience mikes hanging from the ceiling. 'I was torn between thinking, "I must let him do what he wants, this is George Harrison and I'm a lowly gofer", and "My God, if he gets that stuck on there, how the hell are we going to get it down?" Luckily, his aim wasn't very good.'

Although the session had been kept a secret, Alan Freeman recalls the Beatles' presence in Piccadilly being 'sussed' and a mob of girls chasing their car as they left. When it manoeuvred into a side street, 'the door flung open, hit a lamp post and came off its hinges. I thought, "How can they live like this?".'

The show's audience in the first hour was estimated at 24.1 per cent, and for the second hour 22.1 per cent, of the population. Its Appreciation Index figure was once more 49 (71 from 'fans'). Two-thirds of the sampled audience did not describe themselves as 'pop music fans' and had the wireless on 'mainly for the children', preferring the contributions of Acker Bilk and Vince Hill – 'an under-rated artist, who should be heard more often'. A security guard found the Beatles 'vastly over-rated; their performance was decidedly amateur, and their entertainment value nil'.

There was no pleasing some people. But a solicitor, who described himself as 'definitely over-twenty' wondered how anyone could fail to like them: 'Their music is so gay and uninhibited, and they themselves are full of *joie-de-vivre*.' Incidentally, Alan Freeman – and Brian Matthew – were 'definitely over twenty' too. Both were in their mid-thirties in 1964. 'Their music and persona freed me from middle age,' Fluff remembers. 'Because the things that were coming from the Beatles made me feel like a ten-year-old! They made us all feel tremendously happy.'

The week before the Easter Monday *From Us To You*, all the Beatles were featured in the last of the series *The Public Ear* and John's book and their movie-making were the main talking points. Their friendship with one of the programme's contributors, Tony Hall, meant that the show featured some very surprising speech material. George assumed the role of a BBC interviewer and sought Ringo's opinion of *In His Own Write* and then persuaded John to read 'Alec Speaking'. 'Some of you might have found it a bit difficult to understand,' said George. 'Because it's in a sort of funny lingo. Well, we get it, you see… I don't really know how you'd describe it but it's sort of rubbish!' The very word John himself had used to describe his book to Alan Freeman.

George also interviewed Paul during a car journey. They were travelling to the Dorchester Hotel in Park Lane, where they received their Variety Club award for 'Showbusiness Personalities of 1963'. George wanted to know about the film:

GEORGE Are you having any difficulty learning your lines or anything like that?
PAUL Well… I'm a bit lazy about that. I normally learn them about ten minutes before we do the scene, actually. I feel it gives an air of 'impromptuity'!
GEORGE I see. How's the director of the film?
PAUL Dick Lester's directing the film… What's your name?… George?
GEORGE Er, George, yeah… BBC… I'm from the BBC, *Public Ear*.
PAUL Oh yes, it is a bit!
GEORGE You can see it's sticking out!
PAUL Anyway, his name's Dick Lester… and he's one of the nicest fellas I've ever met. He's a great director and I think he's gonna save the film in the cutting rooms.
GEORGE What exactly do you mean by that, Paul?
PAUL Well, you see George, the acting may not be very good but if he can cut it up and slice it around and slot bits in here and slot bits in there, he may make it into a good film, y'see.
GEORGE I see. Well, thank you Paul and you'll receive your three-shilling fee at a later date!

At the end of a day's filming at the Scala Theatre, the group recorded seven songs in a session for the 4 April 1964 edition of *Saturday Club*. 'Can't Buy Me Love' and 'You Can't Do That' were available at the time – on that week's number one single. 'Everybody's Trying To Be My Baby', 'Long Tall Sally' and 'I Call Your Name' were eventually released later in the year. 'Sure To Fall' and 'I Got A Woman' remained unreleased. As usual, the Beatles joked around with Brian Matthew, read out listeners' requests and described the movie.

In the 11 April edition of *Melody Maker*, Ray Coleman described the relaxed atmosphere of that session. 'Only about ten people are in the big theatre, with compère Brian Matthew and producer Bernie Andrews giving the world's most popular artists plenty of freedom. *And the Beatles accept it.* They cavort about the stage, and take their time. They mutter, smoke, eat, drink and smoke.

'Producer Bernie Andrews comes down from the control box to confer with the Beatles about their programme. "Don't forget, next time we're down I'm going to do some of that Bob Dylan stuff," says Lennon. "You know, 'Blowing In The Wind' and that." Andrews nods.

'John plays the introduction to 'Needles And Pins', although it is not in their radio schedule. " 'Ere, it's the gear, that, eh?" he remarks to Paul. "Great song. We ought to do it."

"It's so long since we played a proper date, like this, honest," says George.

"Shurrup," says John. "You're on the radio now." The red light appears. Another couple of songs are recorded.'

'Needles And Pins' by the Searchers, after a three-week run at number one, was still in the Top 30 when John picked out the distinctive guitar intro. George's comment shows how a BBC session – not quite live work or record-making at EMI – could still be a refreshing experience for the group.

Another Bank Holiday was coming soon, so on 1 May the Beatles shoe-horned another BBC session into their frantic schedule. Just the day before, they had played two shows at the Glasgow Odeon and taken part in two Scottish television programmes. During an evening session at the BBC Paris Theatre in central London, they recorded eight tracks, chatted to Alan

Freeman and celebrated the holiday with their 'Happy Birthday' adaptation – 'Whit Monday To You'. The other recorded artists at this session were Manfred Mann, Joe Brown and the Bruvvers, and the singers Mark Wynter and Lulu, with accompaniment from vocal group the Breakaways and the Kenny Salmon Seven.

In contrast to their previous *From Us To You* sessions, only three of the eight tracks had been released. George sang the Elvis Presley track 'I Forgot To Remember To Forget', and there were three Carl Perkins numbers – 'Honey Don't' sung by John, Paul's version of 'Sure To Fall' and Ringo bopping through 'Matchbox'. George was in fine guitar form for Little Richard's 'Kansas City/Hey!-Hey!-Hey!-Hey!' and his solo on the last BBC performance of 'I Saw Her Standing There'.

Only Fluff could make a song title sound so naughty when he announced, 'That's right, it's the Beatles with the caution... Honey?... Don't!' When he encouraged Paul to give a request writer 'a nice juicy kiss', he was told, 'I think you're disgusting... You are, you know!' In his skit with George, in which he feigned confusion over 'I Forgot To Remember To Forget', their exchange ended on what seemed like a sour note!

GEORGE 'I Forgot To Remember To Forget'
ALAN You forgot what?
GEORGE No, 'I Forgot To Remember To Forget'.
ALAN But what do you have to remember?
GEORGE No, 'I Forgot To Remember To Forget', you see.
ALAN What did you forget though that you...
GEORGE No, you see that's the song, that's what it's called.
ALAN What's the song?
GEORGE The song what I'm just gonna sing, any minute now, just watch me.
ALAN What's it called?
GEORGE 'I Forgot To Remember To Forget'.
ALAN This could go on all morning.
GEORGE It could... if you weren't so thick!

'It's so long since we played a proper date like this, honest,' says George. 'Shurrup,' says John, 'You're on the radio now.'

They liked each other really. George – and John – both gave long, friendly interviews to Alan in the mid-seventies and, in 1987, Paul recorded a special version of 'Sgt Pepper's Lonely Hearts Club Band' for Fluff's on-air sixtieth birthday celebrations – 'It was *60 years ago today...*'. The Whit Monday *From Us To You* received a higher than usual Appreciation Index figure of 63, although the audience was estimated as slightly lower – 16.3 per cent and 14.5 per cent for the two hours.

A fourth *From Us To You* was broadcast on August Bank Holiday Monday – 3 August 1964 – and was introduced by Radio Luxembourg DJ Don Wardell. There were five songs from the Beatles' movie *A Hard Day's Night* and three favourite cover versions – 'Boys', 'Long Tall Sally' and the not yet released 'Kansas City/Hey!-Hey!-Hey!-Hey!', which had a more swingy feel on the guitar and another very different solo. The guests included two other Epstein acts – Billy J. Kramer with the Dakotas and Cilla Black – and Lulu and the Animals (one of their tracks was 'My Favourite Things' from *The Sound Of Music*!).

The presentation was more conventional than Fluff's, with the Beatles reading requests in a fairly straightforward manner. John delivered the presenter and producer credits over the closing 'From Us To You' theme and changed his voice from 'BBC-posh' to broad Scouse in the space of seven seconds!

While highlights from the first *From Us To You* of 1964 were pressed on a BBC Sound Archive disc, unfortunately the other two were not preserved. Only the efforts of home-tapers have allowed us to hear

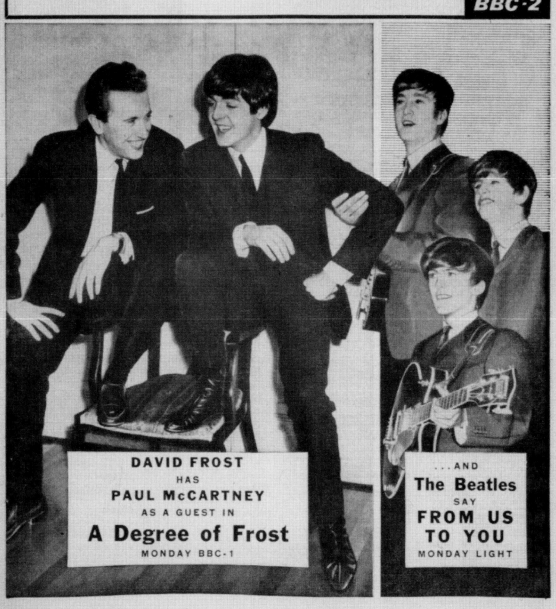

these Beatles' performances. It was often only by chance that taped items survived from the 1960s. For example, in the BBC's Archive there is a mysterious undated reel with the Beatles requesting records to be played. Their introductions give intriguing clues to the music that was inspiring the group around May 1964.

Ringo asked for Cilla Black's 'You're My World', which climbed to number one that month, and, showing his love of Country and Western music, 'Pen and Paper' by Jerry Lee Lewis and the Kitty Wells version of 'I Forgot More Than You'll Ever Know'. Paul picked 'Hitchhike' and 'Pride and Joy', both featured on the 1963 Marvin Gaye album *That Stubborn Kinda Fellow*. George chose two Tamla Motown records – the Miracles' 'I've Been Good To You' and the first UK hit for the label, 'My Guy' by Mary Wells. He also asked for the Impressions' big US hit 'It's All Right' and an early Elvis Presley track 'My Baby Left Me'.

John requested the Tommy Tucker hit 'Hi-heel Sneakers' and anything by Little Richard – 'He was my favourite when I was about 16, after Elvis. I didn't know which one I liked best... but I like Little Richard best now!'. His other selection was an unusual choice – 'Gonna Send You Back To Georgia' by Timmy Shaw. 'I like it because the beat's marvellous, the voice is marvellous and it's a good song. And it's great, so play it!'

Paul also made a record choice on a new show put together by the *Saturday Club* team of Brian Matthew and Bernie Andrews and launched in July 1964...

All smiles for the front cover of the 1964 Whitsun edition of Radio Times *promoting the Beatles bank holiday radio appearance on* From Us To You *and Paul's television interview with David Frost.*

The Beatles

A new film release, an L.P., E.P. and single— it'll be another 'Hard Day's Night' for them

BRIAN MATTHEW

Introduces this two-hour pop programme every Thursday night

TOP GEAR

Carl Perkins

The man in the 'Blue Suede Shoes'—one of the original rockers and at the head of the rock revival

LIGHT **10.0** THURSDAY night—end of the financial week— can be a bit of a drag. Easy-on-the-ear background music is all very well if there's something in the foreground. Top Gear is going to be all foreground. 'It's meant to be the sort of thing to make you want to get up and dance,' says **Bernie Andrews**—and Bernie is a producer who knows what he means.

'Your Chairman' (as the original Edwardian mods would have called him) is the with-it man from *Saturday Club* and *Easy Beat*, **Brian Matthew.** And his first show takes a wide-angle view of the current pop scene. First the Groups: and that does really still mean The Beatles back from being stood on their heads down under, with a recent film release, an L.P., an E.P., and a single— it's going to be another 'Hard Day's Night' for them. Then there's the Challenge of the Girls: **Dusty Springfield** will sing 'I just don't know what to do with myself'—not those Thursday night blues again, but a song to make a long date with the populace. The Rock Revival? Here is **Carl Perkins**, original rocker and leading rock-revivalist. And by way of contrast **Mark Wynter**, who made the Top Twenty with his easy-on-the-ear way when the first wave of rock rolled back.

Bernie also promises each week to keep in touch with standards in the making and an eye open for future trends. Thursday is going to be a night when the youngsters send the oldsters to bed.

Mark Wynter

Easy-on-the-eye, easy-on-the-ear, a Top Pop favourite since 1960

Dusty Springfield

'I just don't know what to do with myself' is a ballad to challenge the Groups and to keep her up with the leaders for a long time

CHAPTER TEN

'Fab Gear, Top Gear'

....

When the Beatles appeared in *From Us To You* on 18 May 1964, they were featured on the front cover of the *Radio Times* and, inside, a page of pop star photos was headlined 'Pop for a Holiday in the Light Programme'. 'Last week we introduced *Saturday Swings*, a new two-and-three-quarter hour programme of non-stop pop in the afternoon to add to the two hours of *Saturday Club* in the morning. On the swings were up-beat, folk-beat, rhythm and blues, ballads, the whole pop lot.'

The proud boast followed that, with the Bank Holiday specials – *From Us To You* and *Pop Luck* (with the Searchers) – and regular shows, 'the whole lot adds up to more than twelve hours in which to sort out the Top Ten, Twenty, Fifty – and to spot a few up-and-comers of your own'. The BBC was finally trying to respond to the beat boom and, no doubt, keeping an anxious ear on some new competition that had arisen a few weeks before.

In March 1964, Radio Caroline began broadcasting from a ship in the North Sea – the first of a flotilla of pirate radio stations that were soon anchored around the coast of Britain. Transmitting from outside British territorial waters, they operated beyond the reach of the law. They grabbed frequencies without licence, took advertising and paid no heed to any Musicians Union regulations in force on the mainland. With no restrictions on 'needletime' – the amount of airtime devoted to records – the pirates could fill their shows with stacks of discs.

In stark contrast to the BBC Light Programme,

pirate radio provided a poppier mix of records, with DJs who were more like the informal and irreverent personalities to be heard on American radio... and also brash exciting jingles! British listeners could now hear, for the first time, syrupy American vocal groups extolling the virtues of Caroline or Big L – Radio London. (There were no vulgar jingles on the BBC.) Despite all this, in its early months, Caroline offered almost as much Ray Conniff, Mantovani and stage musical standards as the Light Programme. Nevertheless, faced with unprecedented opposition, the BBC's executives were now prepared to run with an idea developed by Bernie Andrews for a new late-night pop show called *Top Gear*.

The presenter was to be the tried and trusted Brian Matthew, who recalls: 'It was supposed to be a sharper programme, all round, than *Saturday Club* had been. In other words, it didn't mix skiffle, trad jazz, early rock – it was pretty hard rock right from the word go.' The first programme was broadcast on 16 July 1964 with an amazing *13* records and live sessions from Dusty Springfield, Carl Perkins, Mark Wynter... and the Beatles.

Bernie Andrews remembers, 'I wanted to get the pre-recorded sessions at a higher standard... somewhere near matching the record quality. When I started *Top Gear*, I tried very hard to do that.' Certainly by 1964, *Saturday Club* sessions (and those for other shows too), had been enhanced by using a primitive method of overdubbing. 'We'd record one complete track including the whole band with one vocal and then we'd play the tape again and, as we were recording onto another mono tape machine, we'd add another vocal.'

With four-track tape machines becoming more

Top Gear was launched by the Beatles on 16 July 1964 and given both a Radio Times *front cover and this page featuring the session guest joining 'the with-it man' Brian Matthew.*

Although continuing as the presenter of Saturday Club, *Brian Matthew left the Sunday morning* Easy Beat *to present the new Thursday night show* Top Gear. *'It was supposed to be a sharper programme, all round, than* Saturday Club *had been… it was pretty hard rock right from the word go.'*

common in commercial studios, artists began to expect the convenience of separate tape-tracks for instruments and vocals. The Beeb's old overdub method was time-consuming, where there was no luxury of time, as Bernie explains, 'For purely practical reasons, the mere fact that we had another group coming in at seven o'clock that evening, meant we had to get the previous group out by six-thirty. The balance engineer would have to get round to the old Ship and Shovel, the pub round the corner, and have a bacon and mushroom sandwich and a quick pint and then get back for the evening session.'

Bernie's session time began to expand and his BBC bosses found it difficult to understand why. 'The time I spent on that work did give me an awful lot of problems. At the time I got more support from people like the Beatles and Brian Epstein than I did from those more immediately around me. I was very pleased when they went along with me and helped launch this programme.'

At Bernie's flat, spoken trailers for the new show were recorded, with Paul, George and Ringo reminding listeners of the time, the day and the artists appearing with them on the first *Top Gear*. During the programme, the group were invited to officially open the proceedings but first Brian attempted to discuss Lennon-McCartney's songwriting:

BRIAN Now all these songs in the film you had to write to a deadline. Did you find this a bit more difficult than the way you usually do them on the back of bus-tickets?

JOHN, PAUL and GEORGE Yeah, yeah.

JOHN *(Surprised)* George? George!

PAUL It was hard because we normally do them as hobbies, sort of things.

BRIAN Hello, Ringo's just joined us!

RINGO I thought I'd just come round.

JOHN Did you have a hard time writing them, Ringo?

RINGO Well, the first one was about the worst because I had a lot of trouble with these glasses!

BRIAN The ones he's wearing, he means, folks.

PAUL Yes, it was 'arder.

JOHN We did most of them in Paris and some in New York, didn't you Ringo?

BRIAN Right, the serious bit having got over, let's get round to the funny chat and we would like you chaps to launch the good ship *Top Gear*.

RINGO The good ship what? 'Top Gear'?

BRIAN Bernie's new vessel.

JOHN Ah, is it? When was the accident?

PAUL I hereby name this ship 'Top Gear'.

BRIAN Thank you Duchess. Right, now then, another song from the film…

GEORGE Pity we had to sink it the first week!

BRIAN It is a shame.

JOHN We had a hard time writing them, Brian, anyway.

RINGO Yeah, Brian.

BRIAN You did – all of you. Ringo, what about your songwriting? How's that coming on?

RINGO Oh, yes. I've written a good one but no one seems to want to record it.

PAUL Now…

RINGO Oh, Paul may record it.

PAUL No.

RINGO Yes, Paul. You promised.

PAUL The thing is, I was doing the tune for you to sing it.

RINGO I don't want to sing it, you sing it.

PAUL *(Sings)* Don't pass me by…

RINGO Rhythm and blues, soul.

PAUL Don't pass me by, don't make me cry, don't make me blue, baby, 'cause you know why…

RINGO I got the ice-cream for you.

BRIAN He wrote all those words?

PAUL Yeah, blues and all that.

BRIAN He's the Dylan Thomas of Liverpool, isn't he?

In their interviews with Brian Matthew, Ringo was usually cast as 'the one who doesn't talk' or the one who gets picked on in the playground!

BRIAN Now, look in my young days, when I was a lad, they used to have actors in films.

JOHN Hey, listen.

PAUL It's all changed now. No actors.

BRIAN In those days, the actors used to say their best bits were left on the cutting room floor. Did you find that?

JOHN No. Oh, no. Those were the good bits in the film. You should have seen the rest.

BRIAN Yes?

JOHN Rubbish.

BRIAN Was it really?

JOHN Even worse.

BRIAN Who was worst?

JOHN Oh, Paul.

PAUL I think John was about the worst.

JOHN No, it was you.

PAUL Oh, Ringo was very good; he's a good lad.

JOHN He was miming.

BRIAN They're saying he's a new Charlie Chaplin. Do you think that's right?

JOHN Oh yes… he's an old one! *(Shouts)* OK Ring?

RINGO *(In the distance)* All right, John. Can you hear me?

JOHN Can you hear him?

BRIAN Not really. I hope not.

JOHN *(Whispers)* We've brought you the flowers.

RINGO Oh, good.

JOHN And the grapes.

RINGO Oh, I like grapes!

PAUL He likes grapes, you know.

JOHN Brian's nose is peeling, listeners.

BRIAN Been in the sun.

GEORGE Been to Portugal.

BRIAN Guess who's top of the pops in Portugal, then?

ALL Who?

BRIAN *Os Beatles*.

JOHN *Os Beatles*? Great, great laugh.

BRIAN I don't suppose you know the title of your film in Portuguese?

JOHN *Crinsk Dee Night*?

BRIAN Could be. Let's hear the number shall we?

JOHN *(Obligingly)* Right!

Cliff Richard was also interviewed on *Top Gear* and towards the end gave his reaction to the new show – 'I like it very much indeed, fabulous!' He also chose a favourite new release – 'How Glad I Am' by Nancy

Wilson. Paul was asked to select a single too and came up with 'Mockingbird' by Inez and Charlie Foxx – the first release on the UK version of the Sue label. He told Brian Matthew that the duo had recently shared a couple of drinks with the Beatles in a club. Bernie Andrews had promised in the *Radio Times* that *Top Gear* was 'meant to be the sort of thing to make you want to get up and dance' and Paul's stylish choice was just right for that.

Brian also made a tantalizing reference to having 'a smashing little bit of tape that the lads don't know anything about, that we recorded at rehearsal, with Paul and the other three giving a fabulous impression of the Animals and "The House Of The Rising Sun" but… we daren't play it!'. Whatever happened to that?

Top Gear followed a half-hour magazine programme called *The Teen Scene* and the edition broadcast the previous week – 9 July 1964 – featured *New Musical Express* writer Chris Hutchins interviewing John about acting in the new movie. 'We're satisfied, but we're not self-satisfied. There's a lot which is embarrassing for us, you know. For instance the first bit, which is a drag as far as we're concerned, because that was the first sort of acting we had done and it looks it. It stands out more than the rest of the film… We know that we're dead conscious in every move we make… we watch each other. I know Paul's embarrassed when I'm watching him speak and he knows I am.'

A Hard Day's Night was a wonderful film and enormously influential on the development of pop movies. However, in the cinema, audiences just reacted as if they were at a Beatles concert. Each close-up triggered yet another paroxysm of squealing from the girls, who seemed unconcerned about the realism of the acting.

The Beatles' workload was merciless during the remainder of 1964 – comprising a North American tour, British concerts and the recording of 16 tracks for a Christmas album and single. At the end of November, they loyally returned to BBC studios for two sessions. On *Top Gear*, 26 November 1964, four tracks from the new album and both sides of the latest single were broadcast. Brian Matthew had witnessed the staggering growth in their popularity in two years of programmes with them and wondered if they ever felt tired of being the Beatles. He was met by a chorus of stage yawns but then a surprisingly serious reply to his question:

PAUL I don't think so really. Just occasionally, you get cheesed off with certain things but it doesn't bother you that much, you know. Just occasionally, like people writing rubbish about you, which you get often. Especially in America, to roll a few points into one.

BRIAN Do you agree with that, John?

JOHN I agree with that. I've had 'a divorce and half a dozen kids and attacked young girls' according to…

BRIAN Yeah, we know all that. What have they been saying in the American press?

ALL *(Laughing)*

JOHN Funny, funny! I love this Pete Murray!

BRIAN Isn't this a big sort of drag? Don't you have to go around explaining to your wife that you're not divorced and all that?

JOHN No, she knows I'm not divorced 'cause I keep seeing her every day, you see.

BRIAN Yeah, there's a point. Now what about the simpler things in life like…?

PAUL Like riding on a bus?

BRIAN Yeah, or going to just about any restaurant…

PAUL Oh yeah. You miss those sort of things.

JOHN I don't. I don't miss riding on a bus, Paul.

PAUL Don't you? I do.

JOHN I like the red buses though.

PAUL I like a bus… red buses, green buses.

BRIAN What about restaurants? You've got to eat.

JOHN We go to certain ones.

GEORGE And we go to ones where the people there are so snobby, they're the type who pretend they don't know us. So we have a good time 'cause they're pretending they don't know us.

PAUL Joe's caff! Social comment that, you know.

GEORGE It is.

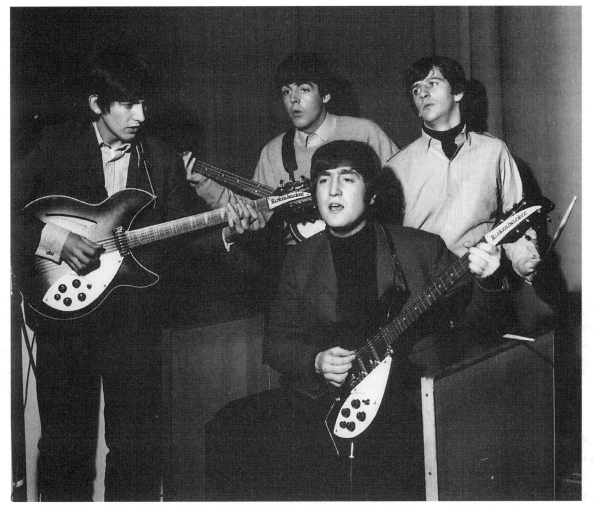

Recording their second and last session for Top Gear *at the BBC Playhouse Theatre in London on 17 November 1964. 'You like this programme, do you?', Brian Matthew inquired. 'Yes,* Top Gear *is our fave-rave-fab programme, as they say in all the comics!' replied John.*

BRIAN This is what we want.

PAUL *(Northern 'brass tacks' accent)* We want real hard facts, son.

The Beatles were sounding a little weary in this interview. Their album for the Christmas market was given the rather cynical title *Beatles For Sale* and the faces on the cover now looked more jaded than cheeky.

BRIAN I've heard it said that a lot of these would make good singles. Do you think there's any likelihood at all of them being released?

PAUL Actually, one of them nearly was.

JOHN But the wrong one, anyway.

PAUL But it wasn't as good as the single, we don't think, but it was nearly at one point…

JOHN You can't release singles off an LP after the LP's been out.

BRIAN A lot of people do.

PAUL Well, in America they do…

JOHN Well, they're different over there, aren't they?

PAUL In America they do that, but it's a bit of a drag. Yes, a bit of drag that!

Brian Matthew asked about 'Another Beatles Christmas Show' – a marathon 38 'houses' over 20 nights at the Hammersmith Odeon – with Freddie and the Dreamers, the Yardbirds, Elkie Brooks and DJ Jimmy Savile. George was quizzed about any marriage plans he might have – 'He wants to stay simple!', John joked – and Ringo described the black opal ring he was given in Australia.

BRIAN Now then, what can we talk about next?

JOHN How about records? That's what we're here for, isn't it?

BRIAN That's what you're here for. Records. All right, talk about records. Tell me about your new one – apart from the fact that it's marvellous.

JOHN and PAUL Oh, Brian you shouldn't... OK, go on!

BRIAN No, seriously. I know we always have a little laugh in our chat about your records... I think this is the best one you've made, this single.

JOHN Oh, thanks a lot, Brian.

PAUL Thank you, Brian.

BRIAN I know nobody cares but I do.

JOHN Oh, we care. We get fed up of people saying, 'What's that rubbish?'

BRIAN No, it's the best one you've ever made and I think the B-side's better than the A-side.

JOHN Oh, well I don't.

PAUL Thank you, Brian.

JOHN Well, as long as they buy the record they get both sides anyway.

BRIAN Well, that's for sure. It doesn't really matter. Did you both write them?

JOHN and PAUL Yes.

JOHN Community effort.

PAUL In fact the B-side was written the morning of the session.

JOHN *(With upper-class voice)* Actually in the studio.

BRIAN You're joking. What – the whole thing?

JOHN *(Same voice)* No, no. Most of it. We had about one verse and we had to finish it off rather quickly and that's why they're such rubbishy lyrics.

PAUL Just a bit of soul in the studio there, you see.

Recorded on 25 November and broadcast on Boxing Day, 26 December 1964, their next chat with Brian for *Saturday Club* was a little more enthusiastic. In the section of the show also transmitted by the General Overseas Service, they were asked which of the countries they'd visited during the year was their favourite:

JOHN America, I think.

RINGO Yes, I'll agree with that.

JOHN Ringo agrees with that.

BRIAN Why, in particular?

JOHN 'Cause we make a lot of money! No! No, 'cause it's good. It's like Britain, only with buttons.

BRIAN I see, yes.

JOHN That's a sort of abstract simile.

PAUL There's more people in America, so you get big audiences and it's all wild and happy.

GEORGE Mind you, there was quite a lot of people in Australia.

PAUL True, true.

BRIAN There were one or two.

PAUL Britain's, however, still the favourite, you see Brian. Favourite place.

BRIAN Never mind, this is the place where we chat up the people overseas!

Some of their future plans were discussed, including work on their next film project which started with a recording session on 15 February 1965. Along with new recordings of 'She's A Woman' and 'Rock And Roll Music', four songs from the earlier *Top Gear* session were repeated in the *Saturday Club* broadcast.

Brian Matthew mentioned that the group's appearances on this programme were now 'few and far between'; as it turned out, the Boxing Day visit was the tenth and last ever for *Saturday Club*. Compared with the 40 sessions for the BBC in the previous year, 1964 had brought a much lower number. But even that year's total of eight sessions was never matched again.

CHAPTER ELEVEN

'They Could Almost Hear Us!'

....

On 7 December 1963, towards the end of the first year of Beatlemania, the group completely dominated Saturday night television. On *Juke Box Jury* at 6.05, the four seats on the panel were occupied by the Beatles. Later, at 8.10, *It's The Beatles!* starred the group on stage at the Empire in Liverpool. Before the concert, *Wells Fargo* was on at 7.20 and *Dixon Of Dock Green* at 6.35, one scene of which even included a burst of 'She Loves You' coming from a transistor radio! Brian Epstein joked at the time, 'a BBC man told me... they were thinking of renaming it "the Beatles Broadcasting Corporation"'.

But from around this date the BBC started to find it increasingly difficult to secure the sevices of the Beatles who had previously been eager to broadcast for them. Delicate and often frustrating negotiations took place in order to lure them back into the studio. At the beginning of December 1963, BBC executive Donald MacLean sent two telegrams to the Beatles' manager – the second rather desperately asking 'Please phone me as soon as you have 45 seconds.' Epstein's NEMS offices, swamped with requests, could not respond swiftly enough to the BBC's inquiries and soon nerves started to fray within the Corporation.

The Light Entertainment Booking Manager Patrick Newman, feeling the duties of his staff were being usurped, expressed his resentment at the personal overtures being made to Epstein by production staff and executives. Hoping to pour oil on troubled waters, Donald MacLean met with Epstein in January 1964. He reported on their meeting in a memo to the Head of Popular Music, Ken Baynes, 'He said that the boys were enthusiastic about *Saturday Club* and would like to do a reasonable amount of appearances during the year; secondly, they would like

to do studio sessions for programmes such as the Boxing Day 10.00am to noon programme (providing they had little talking to do); that he would accept no bookings for audience shows of any sort due to the problems of crowd control.'

Donald MacLean invited Brian Epstein to lunch on 21 April 1964 with some big guns from the Beeb: R. D'A Marriott, DFC (Assistant Director of Sound Broadcasting); M.F.C. Standing, CBE (Controller of Programme Organization); D.E. Morris, OBE (Chief of the Light Programme); and K.S. Baynes (Head of Popular Music). Things were getting serious.

Meanwhile, Patrick Newman conceded in a memo that the arrival of Bernard Lee (from Lew Grade's organization) should get the NEMS office 'more on the rails'. He summarized the recent spate of BBC internal correspondence as 'a case when, with nobody actually wanting it, nuclear war was jolly nearly breaking out'!

He had also visited the NEMS office in London and wrote, 'I, too, have now had the excitement [sic] of meeting Master Epstein face to face, though I doubt whether he was any more impressed with me than I was with his "shouting for his assistant" act'. Clearly, Mr Newman did not relish the Corporation being dependent upon the whims of a young upstart pop group and their manager. It had always been the BBC who had called the tune, but the times they were a-changin'.

Donald MacLean wrote a significant memo to Ken Baynes on 16 March 1965 concerning future Beatles programmes that year. The BBC was looking for the participation of the group on Bank Holidays but approaches 'through normal channels' had resulted in rejection. Following conversations with Brian Epstein, MacLean secured 'firm promises' that programmes for

Whit Monday

The Beatles in holiday pop

LIGHT
10.0
a.m.

TRYING to forecast the future of the Beatles has become something of a national sport. Some critics are hailing them as the new Marx Brothers; others predict their rapid decline. So much adulation and hectoring, advice and criticism have fallen on the heads of the unbarbered four that it's not surprising that their new film is simply called—*Help!*

Today you can hear John, Paul, George, and Ringo speaking up for themselves when they talk to Denny Piercy about what makes them tick and what lies ahead. It will probably be the last chance for some time to hear the Beatles 'live.' Next week they are off on a tour of France, Italy, and Spain, and in August they start another mammoth American tour.

Smuggling four live Beatles across London for a hush-hush recording session in a BBC studio was an 007-sized undercover job. Exhausted but showing no visible wounds, the producer Keith Bateson, a battle veteran of Beatlemania, rallied long enough to report that the group will be singing a half-dozen or so numbers, old and new. Among the other artists to get you into that holiday mood from ten until noon are The Ivy League, The Hollies, and Julie Grant.

Whitsun pop continues in *Happy Holiday Beat* from two to four, when Brian Poole and the Tremeloes, Kenny Lynch, Sheila Buxton, and The Seekers are among the stars lined up. And from four to five the mood stays positively on the bright side in *Yeh! Yeh!* with Billy Fury, Cilla Black, and other artists.

J. B. Priestley's Holiday Play

HOME
3.15

I FIND it hard to believe that this is the fourth time I have produced *When We Are Married* for the BBC: twice for television—Christmas Day on BBC-1 some years ago, and last New Year's Eve on BBC-2—and now twice for radio.

It must be obvious that we consider this comedy of J. B. Priestley's a 'holiday' play—and so it is. But the most endearing thing of all is that however often you hear or see it, act in it or produce it, each time the fun is fresh. You never know which are going to be the most hilarious moments or when you will suddenly feel sorry for the three 'happy couples.'

This time the cast is such a star-packed assembly of comedy players that even Ruby Birtle, the Helliwells' maid, might have been impressed. **Frank Pettingell** again plays Henry Ormonroyd, the drunken photographer, **Thora Hird** and **Deryck Guyler** play the Helliwells, and **Betty Driver** plays Lottie, that very friendly barmaid from Blackpool. But there is no point in trying to list them all—one look at the cast-list and you will see why.
VIVIAN A. DANIELS

LIGHT

5.30 a.m. WEATHER: NEWS
followed by
MORNING MUSIC
GEOFF LOVE AND HIS ORCHESTRA
THE MIKE SAMMES SINGERS
MRS. MILLS
THE DEREK NEW QUARTET
BOB POTTER AND HIS ORCHESTRA
BBC MIDLAND LIGHT ORCHESTRA
Conductor, JACK COLES
including some records
Introduced by BRYAN MARTIN
Bob Potter and his Orchestra are appearing at the Top Rank Hanley Suite

8.0 FAMILY FARE
A record menu for all tastes
Introduced by RODNEY BURKE

8.55 METCAST
A visit to the London Weather Centre for a report on the latest weather position

9.0 FAMILY CHOICE
TED RAY introduces
request records for the family

9.55 FIVE TO TEN
DAVID KOSSOFF tells
the story of Joshua
1: Following a star

10.0 THE BEATLES
invite you to take a
Ticket to Ride
on the Whit Monday
Beat Special
Denny Piercy introduces
a few new records
and
THE HOLLIES
THE IVY LEAGUE
THE ATLANTICS
THE LORNE GIBSON TRIO
JULIE GRANT
DANNY STREET
THE KENNY SALMON SOUND
† Produced by KEITH BATESON

12.15 MIDDAY SPIN
presents
DON MOSS
spinning along on the
Pop Track

1.0 STARTIME
BILL GATES introduces
JOAN TURNER
THE COUNTRYMEN
FELIX BOWNESS
MARTIN LUKINS
THE RAINDROPS
Carnival
Around the World in Song
† THE STARTIME ORCHESTRA
Conducted by MALCOLM LOCKYER
Felix Bowness is in 'Merry-Go-Round' at the Pavilion Theatre, Sandown, Isle of Wight

1.50 CRICKET SCOREBOARD
followed by an interlude

* Approximate time
† BBC recording

GEMINI SPACE SHOT

It is expected that the U.S. two-man 'Gemini' space-craft will have been in orbit over the week-end, and that 'splash-down' will be some time this afternoon.
If the flight takes place as planned, the Light Programme will broadcast first-hand accounts of the final stages of the flight from the BBC Correspondent at the central-centre in Houston, Texas, and from N.B.C. reporters.

2.0 HAPPY HOLIDAY BEAT
so it's time
to tap your feet to
BRIAN POOLE
AND THE TREMELOES
KENNY LYNCH
SHEILA BUXTON
THE SEEKERS
THE KESTRELS
THE LAURIE STEELE NEW SOUND
and a big spinful of discs
THE HOLIDAY BEAT BAND
Conducted by TOMMY WATT
Introduced by DON WARDELL
Produced by DOREEN DAVIES

4.0 YEH! YEH!
TONY HALL
introduces
BILLY FURY
CILLA BLACK
SOUNDS INCORPORATED
THE GAMBLERS
THE BREAKAWAYS
and the pick of the records
from the pop scene
Produced by BERNIE ANDREWS

5.0 ROUNDABOUT '65
Switch on the off-beat circuit
with JOHN ANTHONY
for news, views, comments
and the best on records
plus
THE DENNIS WILSON QUARTET
Script by TONY ASPLER
Produced by PETER DUNCAN
and ROGER ORDISH

6.45 THE ARCHERS
Written by DAVID TURNER
† Produced by TONY SHRYANE
Edited by GODFREY BASELEY
Repeated Tuesday, 12.40 (Home)

7.0 NEWS
RADIO NEWSREEL
and SPORTS REVIEW

7.31 ROUND THE HORNE
Five characters in search
of the authors—
BARRY TOOK and MARTY FELDMAN
starring
Kenneth Horne
with
KENNETH WILLIAMS
HUGH PADDICK
BETTY MARSDEN
BILL PERTWEE
Music by
THE FRASER HAYES FOUR
KENWIN BRADEN
AND THE HORNBLOWERS
Announcer, DOUGLAS SMITH
Produced by JOHN SIMMONDS
† Sunday's broadcast

8.0 DELAYED ACTION

A series of six plays for radio
by Eddie Maguire
with Hugh Manning
1: *Rough Justice*
Jim Starkie, convicted for robbery, is released from gaol after three years but still insists he was framed.
Superintendent George Wallis
..................GEORGE HAGAN
Ex - Detective - Inspector John Burns........HUGH MANNING
Helen Burns...........EVA STUART
Jim Starkie.........JOHN HOLLIS
Detective-Sergeant David Mills
..................MARTIN JARVIS
Ted Becker...NORMAN MITCHELL
Rose Starkie.....MYRTLE REED
† Produced by DAVID H. GODFREY
Hugh Manning is at the Nottingham Playhouse

8.30 THE NEWS
and Sports Results

8.40 MELODY HOUR
MICHAEL COLLINS
AND HIS ORCHESTRA
MARGARET BUXTON
and EDWARD RUBACH
Introduced by PETER LATHAM
† Produced by Eric Arden

9.35 SONGS FROM THE SHOWS
A selection from stage and screen productions on LP's
Introduced by MARTIN LOCKE
Produced by Johnny Beerling
News Summary and
latest Sports Results at 10.30

10.35 THE TEEN SCENE
Holiday Edition
with
MIKE HURST
Special guests,
GORDON WAITS
and GENE PITNEY
Produced by WILFRED DE'ATH

11.15 JAZZ CLUB
Rhythm and Blues Night
with
ALEXIS KORNER's
BLUES INCORPORATED
LONG JOHN BALDRY
AND HIS HOOCHIE KOOCHIE MEN
Introduced by GEORGE MELLY
† Produced by Bryant Marriott

12.31 AFTER MIDNIGHT
some swinging recordings
for the late birds
with
HAROLD ROGERS
and musical assistance from
THE TOMMY WHITTLE QUARTET
and JO SEARLE
† Produced by STEVE ALLEN

2.0 NEWS SUMMARY
and Weather Forecast
Close Down at 2.2 a.m.

At Five to Ten
This morning David Kossoff begins another series of stories from the Bible

---

Your swinging Light Programme line-up for Whit Monday 1965. Start the day with honky-tonking Mrs Mills, savour 'a record menu for all tastes' with Rodney Burke, eavesdrop on Ambridge village life in The Archers and chuckle at the comic brilliance of Round the Home. All this and 'holiday pop'!

Easter, August and Christmas could be made, with the group introducing their choice of records. These were not made in the end but a proposed Whit Monday show with musical performances did take place. MacLean wrote, 'The Beatles would like to do this coincident with one of their recording sessions at EMI studios. (George Martin has agreed this in principle – we may have to offer a studio hire fee.) The Beatles would like a change of title instead of *From Us To You* and will try to think of one.'

The mention of using the Abbey Road studios indicates that the group, used to the more advanced recording techniques at EMI, were feeling reluctant to struggle at the BBC with mono equipment and the pressure of time. Even so, on 26 May 1965 at the Piccadilly Studios, they made their fifty-third and last musical performance for a show broadcast by the BBC.

The Beatles Invite You To Take A Ticket To Ride was broadcast on 7 June 1965 and presented by Denny Piercy – drummer with Bob Miller and his Miller Men – who admitted his script was 'all Monday and no wit'! Three of the guest groups had previously been featured in *Pop Go The Beatles*: the Lorne Gibson Trio, the Hollies and the Ivy League (using their names Carter and Lewis). Bank Holiday regulars the Kenny Salmon Seven backed up vocalists Danny Street and Julie Grant, and the line-up was completed by the Atlantics. Out of 49 musical items in two and a quarter hours, only seven records were played.

There were seven Beatles tracks. 'Honey Don't' was taken at a faster than usual pace with two very good rockabilly solos by George. 'She's A Woman' was given an ending. And there were faithful renditions of 'The Night Before', 'Everybody's Trying To Be My Baby'and 'Ticket To Ride', as well as a storming take of 'Dizzy Miss Lizzy' and a somewhat playful reading of 'I'm A Loser' ('Although I laugh and I act like a clown/Beneath this wig I am wearing a tie,' indeed!). The group chatted briefly but amiably enough to Denny Piercy:

DENNY One big question right now... the film.
PAUL Yes?
JOHN Yeah, that's not a question!

DENNY Is it not a question? It's July 29th isn't it, the premiere?
ALL Yes.
JOHN Unless something goes wrong.
DENNY The title is *Help!* Is that settled on now?
JOHN Oh yes.
DENNY What's the story behind the title?
PAUL Well, it's just they're trying to get Ringo's ring – the baddies, you see, and we're the goodies.
DENNY Are you a sort of Double-oh-seven, Ringo?
RINGO No, no. I'm a sort of *double entendre*!

Nothing very spectacular was revealed but the Beatles seemed genuinely amused by one introduction:

JOHN Why do you have to do this 'imperative'?
DENNY Because the producer asked for it. It's for his wife called Liz. Any suggestions?
JOHN Well, Liz, how about 'Dizzy Miss Lizzy'... Liz?
DENNY What a brilliant idea.
PAUL 'Dizzy Miss Lizzy' – what a great idea!
JOHN I just saw it on that piece of paper you've got there.
DENNY Let's hear it then... 'Ticket To Ride'!'

The producer was Keith Bateson, who had been the sound balancer for many *Pop Go The Beatles* and *From Us To You* programmes. Although this session had its moments of fun, Keith was not optimistic about the group returning to the BBC's recording studios. 'I had a sort of feeling that it may well be the last. I don't think they did but things were getting out of hand in those days, and it did appear to me that... they weren't so much getting fed up... but they'd got lots of other things to do as well. And I know that I had a certain amount of sadness. When I finished it I thought, "Well I'm not sure whether we're going to get one at Christmas."'

An audience research report was compiled for *Ticket To Ride*, which gave a Reaction Index figure of 47 (68 from 'the fans'). An estimated 10.6 per cent of the population tuned in at the beginning of the show, falling to 9.4 per cent by the end (roughly five million listeners). There was disappointment that the Beatles were not present more during the show but they were praised as 'brilliant professional performers', who when chatting to Denny Piercy were 'great fun'. The 'non-fans' were for the first time in the minority (just over a quarter of the sample). They described pop music as 'ghastly', 'insane' and 'jungle music' and the Beatles' tracks as 'monotonous bangings' – 'Oh, the deadly monotony of this kind of music!'.

Tracks from the Beatles' last three sessions had been re-used in a weekly show pressed on LP disc and distributed to radio stations abroad by the BBC's Transcription Service. This division of the Corporation had been established with the aim of disseminating British culture to far-flung corners of the Empire. Recognizing that British pop music was now a very successful export, *Top Of The Pops* was launched in October 1964 and featured BBC recorded sessions showcasing homegrown talent.

The presenter was the ubiquitous Brian Matthew and, around the date of the *Ticket To Ride* recording, he interviewed the Beatles for his global programme. John's second book *A Spaniard in the Works* was about to be published in June 1965:

JOHN You get more for your money this time – there's more pages and drawings.

PAUL Same kind of rubbish.

JOHN Yeah, same kind of rubbish. That's right, Paul.

PAUL Pardon? I liked the first one – hate this one!

BRIAN Heard lots of rumours and reports that you two are thinking of writing a musical. Is there anything in this?

PAUL Thinking of it.

JOHN Paul's thinking of it, I'm doing it.

PAUL John's actually doing it, I just do all the brain work behind this operation.

GEORGE Ringo and I are painting Buckingham Palace!

BRIAN I was coming to you next.

GEORGE That's a point of interest.

BRIAN Marvellous. What colour?

RINGO Green.

GEORGE Green with black shutters.

BRIAN I see. Do you know when you're going back to America, by the way?

GEORGE and RINGO August.

RINGO For two and a half weeks.

BRIAN Thank you, George and Ringo. And this'll be a tour?

RINGO Yes.

JOHN Well, it won't be a one-nighter!

BRIAN I wondered if it was just for television.

JOHN Oh.

PAUL I certainly hope not.

BRIAN If I might ask you one thing on the music side. When you started hitting it big you were very much…

PAUL Smaller than we are now.

BRIAN … suggesting a trend which has since happened all over the world. Do you yourselves foresee any new trend at this stage? What are you listening to right now?

PAUL We like folk kind of music, like Bob Dylan… man! No, we do, y'know. Country and Western music, 'cause we've always liked that anyway. I think all the kinds of things we like now, we always liked but we like a few particularly.

BRIAN You mentioned Bob Dylan – he says you write folk. What do you think about that?

PAUL We don't.

JOHN We don't, y'know.

PAUL We get influenced like everybody else does.

JOHN *(In mock working-class voice)* I mean, as much as it's the music of the people of the day.

PAUL *(Similar voice)* Yeah, the music of the working-class masses.

BRIAN Thank you Spotty Muldoon [a character created by comedian Peter Cook]. Well, we'll take you into some of your folk, Country and Western influenced, Bob Dylan inspired music now, I think. What shall it be? 'Ticket To Ride'?

GEORGE No.

JOHN and PAUL Yeah, that's very folk!

Some of the topics of their conversation would be Beatle talking points throughout the summer of 1965

From: Light Entertainment Booking Manager, 305 H.H.   PABX 2684/4250

Subject: THE BEATLES   19th March 1965

To: C.A.P./P.M.(S).   Copy to: Ch.L.P.; H.P.M.(S).; Mr. J. Grant;
                                      Mr. B. Willey; Mr. B. Marriott;
                                      Mr. B. Andrews; Miss A. Barr.

Your memo of the 16th March caused me some concern.

"Normal channels" means contact between one of the staff of my Section and Bernard Lee of NEMS Enterprises. He is extremely helpful and reliable ..... but suffers from the same ailment as do all Mr. Epstein's employees. That's to say, they are never in a position to say a 'yes' or 'no' to anything without first going to Epstein. As Epstein spends a lot of his time (when he's not in China or Peru that is) behind locked doors in his own office with his own staff not even being able to get him on the telephone this – from my point of view – is not exactly satisfactory. (A point which I made to Epstein when I was vouchsafed the privilege of a personal interview in his office ..... during which time he went through an embarrassing routine of ticking off various members of his staff on the telephone.)

In this case "normal channels" requested performances on Easter Monday and Whit Monday (2. and 3. of your memo). We received a turn-down. For Easter Monday the turn-down is now lightened somewhat with the acceptance of an interview. The Whit Monday has become an acceptance for a proper performance. Naturally enough I'm concerned if only mildly with the changed picture for Easter Monday, and very concerned indeed for the complete reversal for Whit Monday.

Bernard Lee tells me he still had the Whit Monday offer "on the stocks" as it were, but at one stage it looked so impossible that he gave a firm 'no' to Miss Lipscomb. He tells me he was wrong in this instance and accepts full blame for misleading us.

Having given you the facts from my end let us all hope that we get the five items outlined in your memo.

(Patrick Newman)

vm

Patrick Newman, the Light Entertainment Booking Manager, making clear his department's frustration in trying to secure the services of the Beatles.

– John's book, the American tour with the record-breaking concert at Shea Stadium, and even Buckingham Palace. On 12 June 1965, the news broke that the Beatles would become 'Members of the Most Excellent Order of the British Empire' – an honour more usually bestowed on retired colonels and civil servants. The group's rather bemused reaction was recorded in a BBC interview with a Mr Moran. Their casual and mischievous remarks would not have helped pacify former recipients of the award, who protested that its gravity had been violated:

MORAN Did the form come in with the rest of your fan mail or did it come separately in a very sort of impressive envelope?
RINGO Yes, we all thought it was call-up papers!... But when we opened them it was, 'If you'd like to have an MBE, sign here.' So we did.

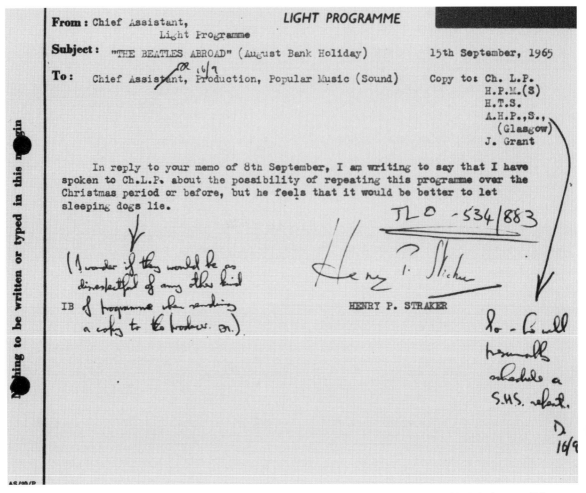

From: Chief Assistant,
    Light Programme

LIGHT PROGRAMME

Subject: "THE BEATLES ABROAD" (August Bank Holiday)   15th September, 1965

To: Chief Assistant, Production, Popular Music (Sound)   Copy to: Ch. L.P.
                                                                    H.P.M.(S)
                                                                    H.T.S.
                                                                    A.H.P.,S.,
                                                                      (Glasgow)
                                                                    J. Grant

In reply to your memo of 8th September, I am writing to say that I have spoken to Ch.L.P. about the possibility of repeating this programme over the Christmas period or before, but he feels that it would be better to let sleeping dogs lie.

HENRY P. STRAKER

An attempt to repeat the documentary The Beatles Abroad *at Christmas is nonchalantly dismissed by the rulers of the Light (see page 74).*

PAUL Send two bottle tops and we got it!

MORAN Paul, do you think you really deserve an award like the MBE?

PAUL I don't know, y'know. What does it matter? We got it.

MORAN What about when you go to the Palace for the investiture... What about the gear, how will you dress?

PAUL Oh, some fella was just saying you have to have top hats... I hope you don't have to have top hats.

MORAN Will you all wear top hats?

RINGO If we have to.

PAUL Have white rabbits coming out of them.

MORAN And what about the hair?

PAUL What about it?

RINGO We'll put that in the top hat as well.

MORAN John, having the MBE, what does it mean to you?

JOHN I don't know until I get it. I'll read about it and see what it is really, 'cause I'm not sure what it is. I only know what I read in the papers. So I'll just check and see what I've really got. I'll find out, then I'll tell you.

MORAN What did your wife say when she knew you had it?

JOHN She said, 'Oh.' *(Laughs)*

MORAN Just like that?

JOHN She didn't have a clue really what it was but she's pleased, you know. I tried to get her one, but I couldn't! *(Laughs)*

MORAN George, now the MBE, what does it mean to you?

GEORGE I don't know. I thought it was the Northern Dance Orchestra at first, but that's NDO! Um, it's great, y'know, but I don't know what we'll have to do when we've got it. I doubt if we'll have to walk up and down Buckingham Palace, will we? Showing people what it's like. I don't know. It'll just be the same, only we've got a medal.

On 16 June 1965, John was interviewed about his writing for the BBC Home Service programme *World Of Books* broadcast on 3 July. He talked to Wilfred De'Ath, a producer who worked on the Light Programme show *The Teen Scene* and an enthusiastic advocate of popular culture. Around the same age as John and aware of pop music, De'Ath endeavoured not to patronize:

DE'ATH Let me ask you first of all, how do you write? Do you write in a disciplined way or do you write when it comes into your head?

JOHN It's more disciplined… The second book was more disciplined because it was starting from scratch. They sort of say, you've got so many months to write a book. In the first book, a lot of it I'd written [already] at odd times during my life.

DE'ATH Do you set aside certain hours in the day to write or do you…

JOHN No, none of that. I haven't written enough. It's not a job, you see.

DE'ATH Would you like to discipline yourself? Do you feel a need to discipline yourself as a writer?

JOHN No, I'm not very keen on being disciplined. It seems odd being a Beatle because we're disciplined but we don't feel as though we're disciplined. I don't mind being disciplined and not realizing it.

DE'ATH You know, these little pieces in the book. They give an appearance of great finish, perfection… Do you revise them?

JOHN Do they?

DE'ATH Yes, they don't look all that spontaneous, they look as though they've been worked over. Do you work them over?

JOHN They're not at all. Nobody's ever said that to me… wonderful! They are spontaneous and I hardly ever alter anything because I'm selfish about what I write or big-headed about it. Once I've written it, I like it and the publisher sometimes says, you know, 'Should we leave this out or change that' and I fight like mad. 'Cause once I've done it, I like to keep it. But I always write it straight off. I might add things when I go over it before it's published but I'd seldom take anything out. So it is spontaneous.

DE'ATH Now the puns and all the other technical things – the puns, the onomatopoeia.

JOHN The what… what?

DE'ATH That's a long word.

JOHN That's three words I've learnt today!

DE'ATH I'll tell you. Onomatopoeia is when I say a word like 'buzz' – 'buzz' is an onomatopoeia because in the word is captured the noise of the bee… and you probably without realizing it,… your book is full of them.

JOHN Is it? Well, I'm glad to know that. Lot of onomatopoeias.

DE'ATH Well, you've rather answered my question because I was going to ask you whether these were contrived…

JOHN No, I just haven't got a clue what you're talking about really. Automatic Pier, sounds like to me. That's probably why I change words, 'cause I haven't a clue what words mean half the time!

On 30 July 1965, the day after the film premiere of *Help!*, the Beatles took time off from a rehearsal for a TV show and talked to Dibbs Mather for the BBC Transcription Service. The Australian broadcaster had first met them in a dressing room at the Doncaster Gaumont in December 1963. Back then, he had wondered what they might do after their 15 minutes of fame had expired. This time he took a different tack:

JOHN We enjoy English records selling in America…

That's the best bit, taking over there instead of them running everything.

DIBBS And, as a result of this and your increasing popularity, how's it affected you? Is it possible you're going to become bored being the Beatles for year after year at the top?

JOHN You don't get bored because there are so many different things happening… like MBEs or premieres… so as soon as you start getting bored with something like a tour, the tour's over and something else starts. And there's always Ringo, isn't there!

ALL *(Laughing)*

DIBBS If you had not got so rich and famous, what do you think you might be doing now?

JOHN We'd probably be bumming round.

RINGO Still working in clubs in England.

DIBBS And Paul would have been teaching?

PAUL I might have been teaching but I would have hated it. I think all of us, if we hadn't stuck with the group… might have ended up doing things we didn't enjoy much.

GEORGE I think we'd probably be playing modern jazz now in some crummy club.

JOHN Do you?

GEORGE Yeah.

JOHN Do we like modern jazz?

GEORGE 'Cause we would have been so fed up playing the same thing, we would have progressed. But now we don't progress because we play the same things every time we play somewhere.

DIBBS Isn't there a progression though, in that the style has altered slightly?

GEORGE Yeah, slightly. But the thing is we used to improve at a much faster rate before we ever made records… because we used to get so fed up playing the same things so we'd always learn new songs all the time.

JOHN You'd have to improvise every time. Even with the old songs you'd do 'em different anytime but when you make records you've got to reproduce, as near as you can, the record – so you don't really get a chance to improvise or improve your style.

George and John's dissatisfaction with having to constantly play just a handful of songs was aired just as the Beatles undertook their third trip to the USA in August 1965. The tour's first concert was another of those Beatle events that, as John saw it, kept boredom at bay. Their appearance in front of 55,600 fans at the Shea Stadium in New York broke the world records at that time for attendance and box-office revenue ($304,000).

The BBC's advance publicity for the next Bank Holiday in August had predicted a Beatles special but the plan for a show with their choice of records had eventually fallen through. At the beginning of the month, however, Brian Epstein agreed that Brian Matthew – who else? – should join the tour. His on-the-spot tape recordings of the group and some of their fans were compiled into *The Beatles Abroad* – a 45-minute documentary for the August holiday.

Produced by Jimmy Grant, the programme was extremely innovative for its time. Pop music – even of the stature of the Beatles – was rarely investigated with the seriousness applied to books or other art forms. (In fact the BBC did not attempt an artist profile series until the 1972 project *The Beatles Story*.) As Scottish public holiday dates differed from those in the rest of the UK, *The Beatles Abroad* (like previous Bank Holiday specials) was not broadcast there. The BBC correspondence that ensued, so that Scotland might hear a repeat broadcast, is indicative of the hierarchy's haughty attitude to pop.

On the side of Scottish Beatles fans was Donald MacLean, who eventually received a brief note from the Chief Assistant, Light Programme, rejecting the idea of a repeat broadcast. 'I have spoken to the Chief of the Light Programme [Denis Morris, so eager for the Beatles' fall in January 1964]… he feels that it would be better to let sleeping dogs lie.' The memo had been sent to Jimmy Grant and a note on the file-copy observed, 'I wonder if they would be as disrespectful of any other kind of programme when sending a copy to the producer.' This lofty attitude was similar to that noticed by Brian Matthew in his first *Top Gear* broadcast, when he asked, 'Why is it these so-called intellectuals go cloth-eared when asked to review anything popular?'

In *The Beatles Abroad*, the Beatles were relaxed and honest with their 'old mate':

PAUL I don't really get nervous when there's that many people because they can't hear you! So we just listen to them… The thing is, even if something really terrible goes wrong…
BRIAN …Nobody's going to know?
PAUL I don't know, maybe they will!

The extraordinary event was filmed and shown on British television in 1966. From the moment the group bounded out of a Wells Fargo armoured truck onto the baseball field, it was clear that John was enjoying himself.

JOHN It was marvellous… It was the biggest live show anybody's ever done, they told us, and it was fantastic. It was just great. They could almost hear us as well, even though they were making a lot of noise, because the amplification was terrific.
BRIAN It was very good actually. I must confess I could only distinguish about three of the numbers which I happened to know.
JOHN Yeah, well the well-known ones you can pick up.
BRIAN Did you do anything that you don't normally do in your concerts.
JOHN We did 'I'm Down', so, 'cause I did the organ on the record, I decided to play it on stage for the first time. I didn't really know what to do, 'cause I felt naked without a guitar so I was doing all Jerry Lee – I was putting my foot on it and George couldn't play for laughing! Y'know, I was doing it for a laugh.

Brian Matthew witnessed the all-too-real mania surrounding their every move in America. 'It was quite bewildering… You can hear about it but until you actually experience it first hand, you've no conception of what it could possibly be like. Kids crawling up the wires and just wanting to get out and touch. Being with them when they ran onto the ball park in Chicago and a cop with a night stick grabbing me and saying, "Where are you going, buddy?" and Paul

turning round saying "It's all right, he's with us!" and dragging me in.

As a 'fellow prisoner' in hotel rooms, cars and planes, he asked George how he coped with the lack of freedom:

GEORGE We don't mind. When we start a tour, we know very well it's going to be wild, with lots of people, and that we're going to be stuck in a hotel. We don't think we're coming over here to see the sights… In fact, over the last few years we've been in hotel rooms, we find a way of keeping ourselves amused!

Having broken the 'shyness barrier', as Brian Matthew put it in the programme, he asked Ringo why the two Beatle wives were not present on the tour:

RINGO It would be unfair to fetch 'em on tour 'cause we travel about so much and they'd have to keep packing their bags the same as us. And if they go out, they get bothered as well when we go abroad.
BRIAN Would you think that it's made any difference at all to the Beatles as a group that two of you are now married? Once upon a time it did make a difference to pop stars.
RINGO I think about 1957–58, it was a big thing that pop stars weren't married.
BRIAN Why do you think this has changed?
RINGO I think all the fans realize that we're just human beings and we drink, smoke and get married like anybody else.

Unusually for a pop music programme, the invaluable insight into the Beatles' life on the road revealed in *The Beatles Abroad* was preserved in the BBC Archive. It remains there on an LP disc but not in the form broadcast on the Light Programme; it is a speech-only version prepared by the BBC Transcription Service with some new interview material added but some omitted. Its survival had been recommended by Donald MacLean. In October 1965, he was once more negotiating with Brian Epstein for a Christmas special.

DAVID AND JONATHAN
Join them for a Happy Holiday Time at 10.0
and again in Swing into Summer at 2.30

BILLY COTTON, KATHIE KAY, AND ALAN BREEZE
Billy calls Wakey-Wakey on another Bandshow at 2.0

HOLIDAY TIME
IN THE LIGHT

JOHN LENNON
and **PAUL McCARTNEY**
talk about their
songs which are sung
the world over by top
stars—at 4.30

JAIRO AMBROSIO AND
EDGARD ZALDUA
in a Cavalcade of Music at 8.40

STEPTOE AND SON
Another chance to hear
about their proposed holiday
—at 10.0

LIGHT

5.30 a.m. WEATHER; NEWS
followed by
BREAKFAST SPECIAL
with David Symonds
and the
Music of the week: see Thursday

8.30 NEWS
and Motcast

8.34 FAMILY CHOICE
Leslie Crowther
introduces request records for
the family

9.55 FIVE TO TEN
' Beside the Seaside '
† Arthur Dean, a Methodist
minister in Morecambe, on the
problems of a seaside town

10.0 HAPPY
HOLIDAY TIME
with
Dave Dee, Dozy, Beaky,
Mick, and Tich
David and Jonathan
The Ray MacVay Show Band
with
Patsy Jones
Jim Fagan
and
Tony Scott
and swinging pop sounds
on record
Introduced by Tony Hall
† Produced by Jimmy Grant
Ray MacVay is appearing at the
Orchid Ballroom, Purley, Surrey

12.0 MIDDAY SPIN
presents
The Sam Costa Show
including records for people
with birthdays today

1.0 GOING PLACES
with
Casey Love conducting
The Scottish Variety Orchestra
Leader, Ian Tyre
Lyn and Graham McCartney
Marion Davies
Introduced by David Symonds
† Produced by Michael Shrimpton

2.0 THE BILLY COTTON
BANDSHOW
Alan Breeze
Kathie Kay
Rita Williams
and The Bandits
and Mr. Wakey Wakey himself
Script by Eddie Curtney
† Produced by Richard Willcox

2.30 SWING INTO SUMMER
Chris Denning introduces some
of the best sounds around
This week's studio artists
Joan Anderson
Johnny Arthey and his Band
Kenny Ball's Jazzmen
The Big Ben Banjo Band
David and Jonathan with
The Michael Hill Trio
Gerry and the Pacemakers
The Lorne Gibson Trio
Brian Green's Jazzmen
Adam Faith and the Imp-acts
Vince Hill
The Ivy League
The Tony Jackson Group
Harry Leader and his Band
Ray MacVay and his Band
The Migil Five
Mrs. Mills at the piano
Ronnie Pleydell
and his Orchestra
The Jung Friction Quartet
Stan Reynolds
and his Orchestra
The Searchers
Shine and Don Leather
Wout Steenhuis
Harry Stoneham
at the electric organ
Danny Street
The Transatlantics
The Danny Wesley Quartet
and a round of records
† Produced by Derek Mills and
Derrek Davies
Ray MacVay is appearing at the
Orchid Ballroom, Purley, Surrey

4.5 ROBINSON CLEAVER
at the Theatre Organ
† From the Granada, Tooting
Robinson Cleaver broadcasts by per-
mission of the Management of the
Richmond Ice Rink

4.30 THE LENNON AND
McCARTNEY SONGBOOK
Introduced by Keith Fordyce
† with John Lennon
† Paul McCartney
and records of their songs
sung by some of the world's
greatest stars, including:
Ella Fitzgerald, Lena Horne
Pat Boone, Andy Williams
Produced by Derek Chinnery

5.31 ROUNDABOUT '66
Fun, fact, and fiction
with John Anthony plus
The Ronnie Aldrich Quartet
Script by Tony Aspel
Produced by Peter Duncan
and John Cassells

6.45 THE ARCHERS
Written by John Keir Cross
Edited by Godfrey Baseley
Produced by Tony Shryane
† Repeated: Tues., 1.30 p.m. (Home)

7.0 THE NEWS
and RADIO NEWSREEL

7.25 SPORT
including
Cricket close of play scores

7.31 DOES THE TEAM
THINK ?
Members of the public and
invited personalities
put questions to
Jimmy Edwards, Ted Ray
Tommy Trinder, Cyril Fletcher
In the chair, McDonald Hobley
Guest, June Whitfield
From an idea by Jimmy Edwards
Produced by Edward Taylor
† Broadcast on February 12, 1966

8.0 ESCAPE
A new series of plays, each of
which tells an exciting or
amusing story on the same
theme
Natalia
by Lester Powell
Cast in order of speaking:
Phillips .... Anthony Jackson
Andrew Chard
.... Michael Kilgarriff
Natalia .... Carol Marsh
Dorer .... Michael McClain
† Produced by Norman Wright

8.30 NEWS
and Weather Forecast

8.40 CAVALCADE
Leslie Mitchell introduces
a programme of music
for everybody
with
Stephanie Voss
Jairo Ambrosio and
Edgard Zaldua
and
The London Studio Orchestra
Leader, Reginald Leopold
Conducted by Kenneth Alwyn
† Produced by Elizabeth Johnson

9.30 REMEMBER
THE WORDS ?
With records of the stars
† Eric Maschwitz
recalls some of the
outstanding lyrics of our time

10.0 STEPTOE AND SON
starring
Wilfrid Brambell as Albert
and
Harry H. Corbett as Harold
in *The Holiday*
with Colin Gordon
Written by Alan Simpson
and Ray Galton
Adapted for radio by
Gale Pedrick
Produced by Bobby Jaye
† Sunday's broadcast

10.30 NEWS SUMMARY
and Sports Results

10.35 MUSIC THROUGH
MIDNIGHT
in the company of
Roger Moffat who introduces
Ken Mackintosh
and his Orchestra
The Nigel Brooks Singers
The Dave Shepherd Quintet
Tonight's record feature,
The Lettermen
your midnight request spot
and Showtime
† Produced by Paul Williams
Ken Mackintosh and his Orchestra
are appearing at the Empire Ball-
room, Leicester Square, London

1.0 IT'S ONE O'CLOCK
Jon Curle
with swinging sounds
from
The Tommy Whittle Quartet
Jo Searle
and some recordings
† Produced by Steve Allen

2.0 NEWS SUMMARY
and Weather Forecast

Close Down at 2.2 a.m.

---

† BBC recording
* Approximate time

CHAPTER TWELVE

'Bashing It to the BBC'

In late October 1965, BBC executive Donald MacLean met Brian Epstein for lunch and reported back to Ken Baynes, the Head of Popular Music. 'I managed at last to get Emperor Epstein to talk business again... I told him frankly that we were disappointed at the now total absence of Beatles on radio except for their discs, and asked how we could do business. We had a long – very honest – talk, and at the end he as good as promised them for Christmas morning *Saturday Club* – perhaps as a self-contained 30-minute feature.'

There had been previous discussions about recording the group for the radio during one of their sessions at EMI in October and November. But, although they did turn up on the Christmas Day *Saturday Club*, it was only for some banter with Brian Matthew. There was no exclusive music performance for the BBC.

Following the August tour of North America and a six-week rest, the Beatles spent a busy month working on their Christmas album and single. Fourteen original songs were recorded for *Rubber Soul*, as well as the double-A-sided single 'Day Tripper'/'We Can Work It Out'. In 1965 pop music had taken some giant steps away from frothy beat music towards something more heady and mature: Dylan's electric albums; the Rolling Stones' 'Satisfaction'; the growth of protest music; exciting debut hits by the Byrds, the Who and the Yardbirds. Always hip to the tip, the Beatles once again set the pace. *Rubber Soul* inspired Brian Wilson, for example, to aim for the heights reached on the Beach Boys' LP *Pet Sounds*.

After the advanced studio techniques used on

The ultra-conservative fare offered by the Light Programme on August Bank Holiday, 1966. Not surprisingly, transistor radios at many of the UK's coastal resorts will have been tuned to the illicit pleasures of pirates.

Rubber Soul, the idea of the Beatles submitting to a BBC music session seemed pretty unlikely. On the other hand, so was the brief British tour that was thrown together in December. Four days before the first concert, 29 November 1965, the group visited the BBC to record some speech inserts for the Christmas Day *Saturday Club*.

The first item recorded was a sung version of the show's instrumental signature tune 'Saturday Jump', prefaced by a quick burst of tomfoolery. 'Ad lib, man, you're famous for it!' John tells Ringo on the unedited tape that has survived. Next they were asked to comment on Brian Matthew's version of the Stanley Holloway monologue 'Brahn Boots' (which they hadn't heard!) in 'Beatle Box Jury'.

This was a parody of *Juke Box Jury*, the Saturday night TV institution presented by David Jacobs. They all sent up the fossilized phrases trotted out by the jurors – 'A nice fat tapper... really get the kids swinging' (Ringo); 'The beat the kids adore these days' (Paul); 'I thought it was nice to dance to but I don't know about the Top Twenty' (John); 'I don't like all these protest songs about boots' (George). The familiar phrase 'Two say will, two say won't' brought 'Beatle Box Jury' to a 'Hit or Miss' end.

Brief Christmas greetings were delivered with some thoughts on how they might spend the festive day – eating and watching television were their unsurprising choices. As the tape rolled between takes, it captured John enthusing to Paul about a new Chuck Berry record (probably *Fresh Berrys*) and receiving an album he had ordered by jazz bassist Charles Mingus. Paul is also heard asking whether the *Saturday Club* audience might wonder 'why we didn't happen to play on this one'.

The next day – 30 November 1965 – Brian

Matthew met up again with John and George to record separate interviews for BBC Transcription's series *Pop Profile*. The programmes were distributed on 7-inch discs running at 33⅓rpm and featured around eight minutes of speech, with a cheesy version of the Booker T and the MGs' track 'Outrage' as a theme tune.

The intention of the series was to sketch in the personal background of 'top personalities from the world of popular music'. John talked about his house in Weybridge, Surrey, his all-black Rolls Royce car, plans for two-year-old Julian's future schooling (the Lycée 'until he's 12 – the most classless school I can think of') and his thoughts about fatherhood. 'I'm trying not to do all the things I disliked but not all of them – because some of the things I disliked, they were right at the time even though I was so annoyed… But it's a joke in the family now, you know. "The guitar's all right for a hobby but it won't earn you any money." I was obviously musical from very early and I just wonder why nobody ever did anything about it. Maybe 'cause they couldn't afford it.'

After a discussion about whether owning a Rolls was 'a passport to anywhere', John was asked whether he had any political leanings. 'Not [to] any party I've ever heard of yet. I don't object to people inheriting money or having a big lot of money. I never did. But I do object to people being stoney broke and starving.'

George's *Pop Profile* was an enlightening and honest feature. Asked why he was regarded as the silent Beatle, he expressed his disdain for the ephemeral nature of most pop interviews. 'I think I'm more quiet than the others because I got fed up, before the others, of all these questions like "What colour teeth have you got?". You know, just stupid questions you've no interest in any longer and I think everybody, well all fans, know what colour eyes we've got and what we drink for breakfast! So I just shut up till somebody asks me something worth answering.'

He said he had a growing interest in folk music, mentioning Dylan, Donovan, Pete Seeger and Ramblin' Jack Elliott, and he described his bungalow in Surrey: 'the man who built it told me [it's] like an Australian ranch house'. He also reflected on his

school days. 'I was a very bad pupil. In fact, I was probably one of the worst pupils they've ever had in the school. I realize that now [but] at the time I was all for having a good "laff". The only thing I liked, really, was art and it was because the teacher was a nice fella. He'd come round and say, "Why don't you do it this way?" With the others, if you'd go up and say, "I'm a bit doubtful about…", they'd shout at you or give you a belt in the gob!

'If this hadn't have worked then I don't really know what I would have been doing. I left school and I was an apprentice electrician for about four months. I remember asking my big brother, "Would you pack in work and have a go at this, if you were me?" And he said, "You might as well… you never know and you're not going to lose anything."'

Paul and Ringo's interviews for *Pop Profile* came five months later, on 2 May 1966, in the midst of recording sessions for *Revolver*. The album merged a variety of unusual elements. Interwoven with exotic Indian instruments, dreamy drones, loops, backwards tapes and a string quartet, clavichord and French horn, its aural texture alone made it a dazzling leap forward from *Rubber Soul*. Paul's *Pop Profile* clearly revealed his willingness to absorb inspiration from new sources. 'There are all kinds of music… that I suddenly realize I like and I always thought I didn't. And it's funny to suddenly realize, "Yes, that's quite good, I wonder why I always turned that off when it came on the radio"… You know, Indian music… George got this big Indian kick and he's dead keen on it and we've been round to his house a couple of times, and he plays it to you… and it's so boring! No, no, it's good, you know. And you hear millions of things that I never realized were in it… and [the same with] some classical music.'

Open to anything innovative – he'd recently attended an *avant garde* concert by electronic composer Luciano Berio – Paul also speculated about a future project in a different medium. 'There are some things I'd love to be able to do. The whole idea of making films is good. I don't mean very big expensive ones. But films you just do because you fancy making a film. The only thing is that, already having the image we've got, if any of us wanted to do anything like that, we would tend to get beaten down. Because people'd say, "Oh look, he's not trying that old trick of making a film" or "He's not going classical". And I thought exactly like that. I used to think, "Oh, there he goes, going the same old path they all go – all-round entertainers." But it's just that you find there are things that are just as interesting as what you've been doing.'

A little over a year later, Paul was the main driving force behind the do-it-yourself film *Magical Mystery Tour*. In the *Pop Profile* featuring Ringo, the drummer recalled the time when he first became seriously interested in music. 'When I was about 14 in hospital, to keep all us kids happy, they had a sort of ward band. A teacher came along and she put up a big board with all yellow dots and red dots. When she pointed to red, yellow or green, the triangles or the drums [would play]. It was great fun and I would never play unless she gave me a drum, you see. So I used to fight for the drums [even] then. Then I used to bang on the locker next to the bed and things.

'I came home and I put little bits of wire on top of biscuit tins and used to bash them with pieces of firewood. And then I got a 30-bob bass drum, which used to drive them all mad. I was about fifteen and a half, sixteen, I think. Just a one-sided bass drum and I used to bang it – bashing it to the BBC!'

When Brian Matthew remarked on the fact that the group no longer toured so much, Ringo replied, 'We used to work every night practically. We were always tired and hungry! [But] I like playing and things like that. I think I would turn into a blob if I was left to do nothing!'

The same day that Paul and Ringo were recorded, all the Beatles talked to Brian Matthew for the four hundredth edition of *Saturday Club*:

BRIAN Don't you think it's cutting it a bit fine with the fans generally, who wish they had a little bit more of you?… You don't perform on radio, television or anything?

GEORGE We spend more time on recording now because we prefer recording.

JOHN We've done half an LP in the time we would take to do a whole LP and a couple of singles. So we can't do it all and we like recording.

BRIAN Can you disclose any secrets about this LP? Have you introduced any unusual instruments this time?… You can't use a sitar 'cause everybody's using them.

JOHN Yes we can!

GEORGE I play sitar on another track but I don't care if everybody's using them. I just play [it] 'cause I like it.

BRIAN When's it going to be finished?

GEORGE It should be finished in about two or three weeks time really, because if it's not, we won't be able to get another holiday before we go away again.

PAUL If we don't get it done soon, guv, we'll lose our jobs!

They never did get that holiday. Just two days after completing work on *Revolver*, they were on tour in West Germany, then Japan and the Philippines, where they were alleged to have snubbed the First Lady, Imelda Marcos. Their Asian expedition came to an undignified and dangerous end amid scuffles at Manila Airport. On his return to London on 8 July, George told Tom Mangold on the BBC's *Today* news programme: 'We're going to have a couple of weeks to recuperate before we go and get beaten up by the Americans.'

During the break, John and Paul were interviewed for a programme scheduled for August Bank Holiday Monday (29 August 1966). There had previously been a discussion with Brian Epstein about his proposal for a radio 'Beatles Story'. The BBC concluded that, with insufficient archive interview material, they would have to 'start from scratch' on the project. Presumably, that scuppered the idea. But *The Lennon and McCartney Songbook*, a 'serious' examination of John and Paul's songwriting achievements, was accepted by Epstein. For the recording on 6 August, producer

Derek Chinnery and Keith Fordyce – a familiar figure from TV's *Ready Steady Go!* and radio shows *Pop Inn* and (from 1964) *Easy Beat* – visited Paul's house in Cavendish Avenue near Regent's Park, London.

The holiday show was scheduled to follow *The Billy Cotton Band Show* (featuring Mr Wakey-Wakey himself), *Swing Into Summer* and *Robinson Cleaver* at the theatre organ in the Granada, Tooting. Following such old-fashioned fare, it is perhaps not surprising that the 15 selections from *The Lennon-McCartney Songbook* were mostly by middle-of-the-road artists. It is doubtful that John and Paul had even heard half of the following records:

> The Band of the Irish Guards – 'She Loves You'
> Peggy Lee – 'A Hard Day's Night'
> Andy Williams – 'Michelle'
> Ella Fitzgerald – 'Can't Buy Me Love'
> Peter Sellers – 'Help'
> Nancy Sinatra – 'Day Tripper'
> Matt Monro – 'All My Loving'
> The Boston Pops Orchestra – 'I Want To Hold Your Hand'
> Lena Horne – 'And I Love Him'
> Frankie Vaughan – 'Wait'
> Keely Smith – 'If I Fell'
> The Mamas and the Papas – 'I Call Your Name'
> Brenda Lee – 'He Loves You'
> Pat Boone – 'Yesterday'
> The George Martin Orchestra – 'This Boy'

The interview might have been a bit more comfortable for Lennon and McCartney if 'I Wanna Be Your Man' by the Rolling Stones, Del Shannon's early pick-up on 'From Me To You', Motown's returned compliment of the Supremes' 'You Can't Do That' or Marianne Faithfull's delicate 'Yesterday' had been included. The funniest moment came when Keith Fordyce wondered aloud whether 'Wait' had been written specifically for the vaudeville song and dance man Frankie Vaughan. 'No! We weren't thinking of Frankie at the time,' said an incredulous John.

Paul was relaxed and co-operative, while John often seemed tired and uninterested. Before a retake of the show's farewells, John mutters 'Not a peep out of me' while Paul tries to encourage with, 'No, no, come on.' But the interview did offer some interesting insights into their approach to songwriting and their musical influences:

KEITH Have you got any thoughts on other composers – people whose work you particularly admire?

PAUL There's lots of them actually but they're not big as composers, mainly. I like, still I think, Goffin and King. They're the kind of writers we set out to be... what we wanted to be originally. They wrote all the big hits at the time...

JOHN And they were all nice as well.

PAUL ...always nice, commercial, great, easy to sing.

JOHN But not horrible.

PAUL Never sickly.

KEITH How far do you feel that your invididual talents are dependent upon each other? I mean, are you like Gilbert and Sullivan or Rodgers and Hammerstein? Do you need to work together as composers?

JOHN No, not really but it helps a lot... you get another point of view.

PAUL We can do them on our own but often one of us will just do a song and there'll be one verse in it that's very bad or very corny. If I've written it then I'll take it along and sing it to John and he'll say that verse is terrible and that verse is corny.

JOHN You still get so involved with something; you finish it and if you're on your own, you haven't got the energy to go over it and see if it really makes exactly what you want. So you [still] sing it over to one another, even if it's a finished song with almost the [complete] arrangement.

KEITH I don't know how many thousand times you've been asked which is your own favourite composition. I'm not going to ask you that, I'm

Studio Two at Abbey Road was the usual venue for EMI Beatles sessions but much of Revolver was recorded in Studio Three. Here, producer George Martin watches through the control-room window.

The Beatles had to complete their 1966 album before embarking on a tour and final day of studio work came only two days before the tour began in Germany on 24 June. The title Revolver *was decided upon in Japan but other suggestions were* Abracadabra, Magic Circles *and* Beatles on Safari..

going to tell you that one of mine is certainly 'Can't Buy Me Love'. It's got a zip and gaiety about it that is perhaps way ahead of the others. Were you in that sort of mood when you wrote this song?

PAUL Zipping away in Paris, we were, when we wrote that one.

JOHN I thought we just recorded it there.

PAUL I mean, you can draw your own conclusions from that, you know, Keith.

KEITH Do you both have to be in the right mood when you're working together, collaborating on a song? Does one have to wait for the other to start?

JOHN Very seldom, you know. If we both don't feel like it, we just have another ciggy.

PAUL The only time we've got to do that – to actually force ourselves to write it – is when we've got an LP coming up or a film. Then it's a bit of a drag for the first, say, two songs... In fact, the last LP [*Revolver*], wow! We took weeks just trying to get one written to get back into the swing of it. 'Cause we don't write in between LPs normally. Maybe just write one or two and then we have a great big batch [to do].

KEITH I would have thought it's quite impossible really to say, 'Right, we've got to write 12 songs for an LP. Let's settle down to it.'?

JOHN It is some days. This last time was very impossible. Holiday spirit.

KEITH Would you give me a personal reaction on 'Day Tripper' and 'We Can Work It Out'. Were these songs written under pressure or were they

inspired? To me, personally, they were less
inspired than all your other songs that I've heard.

JOHN 'Day Tripper' was under complete pressure,
based on an old folk song I wrote about the month
previous. It was very hard going, that, and it sounds
it. Glad you spotted that. Two house points!

PAUL *(Clears throat)* However…

JOHN 'We Can Work It Out' wasn't.

PAUL No. Bad marks for 'We Can Work It Out'. Lose
three Brownie points.

On the day of the interview, Brian Epstein had
hurriedly flown to New York to quell a storm of
controversy. America was in a frenzy over an
observation John had made a few months before in a
London newspaper interview: 'Christianity will go. It
will vanish and shrink. I needn't argue with that; I'm
right and I will be proved right. We're more popular
than Jesus now.' When printed in the US magazine
Datebook, his pronouncement had provoked the
banning and even burning of Beatles records. These
were less than ideal circumstances under which to
launch a tour. A week later, John was being pressed

for an apology at a Beatles press conference in
America. 'If I'd have said television is more popular
than Jesus, I might have got away with it… I'm not
saying that we're *better* or *greater* or comparing us
with Jesus Christ as a person, or God as a thing, or
whatever it is, you know. I just said what I said and it
was wrong or was taken wrong and now it's all
this…'

News reports on the BBC covered the shenanigans
occurring across the Atlantic and included the
'apology'. Here was another side of Beatlemania.
Mass adoration of the cute 'mop tops' had suddenly
turned to something much more sinister. The day *The
Lennon and McCartney Songbook* was heard in
Britain, the group knew they were playing their last
concert before a wailing wall of fans in San Francisco.

At the end of 1965, the BBC had expressed its
disappointment over the group's 'total absence' from
radio. Between August Bank Holiday 1966 and Easter
Monday 1967, the Beatles all but disappeared from
the BBC and public life. They rose again to great highs
– but now radio had to scrabble for a few words from
the enigmatic studio wizards.

CHAPTER THIRTEEN

'No More "She Loves You"s'

Radio silence was broken when three pre-recorded acceptance speeches by John and Paul were heard during *The Ivor Novello Awards For 1966*, broadcast on 27 March 1967. These were taped a week earlier at Abbey Road, where the Beatles were taking their time on a new album, *Sgt Pepper's Lonely Hearts Club Band*. On the same occasion Brian Matthew had his last encounter with John and Paul for BBC Transcription's *Top Of The Pops* programme.

The double-A-sided single 'Penny Lane'/'Strawberry Fields Forever' had just failed to top the British charts – the first Beatles single not to reach number one since their debut hit 'Love Me Do'. Their masterpiece had been eclipsed by the year's bestselling record, 'Release Me', by the king of smoochy ballads Engelbert Humperdinck:

BRIAN 'Penny Lane' failed to make number one… Did you feel at all put out by that?

PAUL No. The main thing is that it's fine if you're kept from being number one by a record like 'Release Me', 'cause you're not trying to do the same kind of thing… That's a completely different scene altogether.

BRIAN Can you, without giving away any trade secrets, tell us anything about this new album you're working on?

JOHN Oh, we've done about nine or ten… and there's a couple of strange ones, a couple of happy-go-lucky Northern Songs.

PAUL Mmm… couple of whimsical folk, folk-rock…

Between 1965 and 1968, George devoted daily hours of practice on the sitar. He is pictured with his teacher and friend, the virtuoso player Ravi Shankar at a concert at the Albert Hall, 20 October 1969.

BRIAN Have you augmented again, this time used any strange line-ups at all?

PAUL Well, we've used things that aren't us quite a bit.

JOHN We've used the Monkees on a few tracks!

PAUL and BRIAN *(Laughs)*

PAUL Yeah, right. But they wouldn't go along with the TV series that we had planned for them.

BRIAN Yeah, yeah. Has George written anything this time?

PAUL Oh yeah. He's done a great one. *(Laughs)* A great one.

JOHN A great Indian one. We came along one night and he had about 400 Indian fellas playing 'ere and it was a great swinging evening, as they say.

PAUL So there's a few things going on.

BRIAN Yeah. Is there going to be another Beatles film?

JOHN Yes.

PAUL Oh yeah.

JOHN As soon as we finish this LP we'll be starting on this mythical film that we've been on about for the last year.

PAUL We wanna do a TV show and a film, sort of next.

BRIAN And is touring now completely out? Everywhere?

JOHN I reckon so, yeah… says John.

PAUL Well, the thing is, we're working on an act where we run on in brightly coloured suits…

BRIAN *(Not fooled)* Yeah…

PAUL …and switch on five tapes…

BRIAN Ah! Yeah, yeah, that's a thought.

PAUL …and then we do a juggling act at the front of the stage while these tapes play Beatle melodies.

BRIAN Yeah. Why is it? I don't know why this microphone sends you barmy! Because when I was

Paul, John and George Martin during the recording of Sgt Pepper's Lonely Hearts Club Band. *In the foreground is the alarm clock heard ringing before Paul sings, 'Woke up, fell out of bed…' in 'A Day in the Life'. The refrain 'I'd love to turn you on' led to the BBC banning the song.*

talking to John earlier, he was quite serious and said, 'No, no more tours.'

PAUL No, that's the only possibility, you never know.

JOHN I said, 'No more tours, no more "She Loves You"s.' But going on with a million tape recorders and a brightly coloured suit… well, that's something else, you know.

Brian hopefully mentioned the rumoured stage musical that he had discussed with them previously, but his question was effectively evaded. His pay-off line on the *Top Of The Pops* programme was 'As unpredictable as ever, the Beatles!' How right he was.

Sgt Pepper's Lonely Hearts Club Band was released on 1 June 1967 and could not have been more of its time. That 'summer of love' saw the underground culture of hallucinogenic drugs, flamboyant clothes and trippy music starting to swirl about in the main-

stream and *Sgt Pepper* provided the era's soundtrack. But the album's qualities were also timeless and continued to reverberate, as strong as ever, through the decades that followed. The many innovations that went into the 700 hours of the album's recording could have been fruitfully examined in interviews. But that was not to be. Instead, three of the Beatles turned up very briefly in the Light Programme's preview of the LP on *Where It's At*.

Presented by former Radio Luxembourg and pirate Radio London DJ Chris Denning, *Where It's At* was launched in early 1967. Producer Johnny Beerling listened to and liked the pirates and wanted his show to sound just as 'groovy'. It even had jingles! 'On the station of the nation, this is *Where It's At*' intoned Duncan Johnson. Denning, his voice treated with echo and tape-reverb, speedily introduced the records, and *only* records. No versions of 'God Only Knows' or

'Paint It Black' by Joe Loss and his Orchestra! The running order between the two *Sgt Pepper* features is a good reflection of the music scene in May 1967.

Two Tamla Motown discs were played (Brenda Holloway's 'Just Look What You've Done' and the Marvelettes' 'When You're Young And In Love'); current Top 20 records by the Tremeloes ('Silence Is Golden'), the Who ('Pictures Of Lily'), the Kinks ('Waterloo Sunset'), the Beach Boys ('Then I Kissed Her'), the Bee Gees ('New York Mining Disaster 1941') and Arthur Conley ('Sweet Soul Music'); and future hits by the Young Rascals ('Groovin''), P.P. Arnold ('The First Cut Is The Deepest'), Petula Clark ('Don't Sleep In The Subway'), Dusty Springfield ('Give Me Time'), Procol Harum ('A Whiter Shade Of Pale') and Dave Dee, Dozy, Beaky, Mick and Tich ('Okay'). There were also a couple of early slices of British psychedelia by the Purple Gang ('Granny Takes A Trip') and the Mirage ('The Wedding Of Ramona Blair') and an update of 'Portrait Of My Love' by American vocal group the Tokens.

Where It's At opened and closed with the *Sgt Pepper* preview pieces put together with Liverpudlian DJ Kenny Everett. Encouraged to pursue a radio career by BBC producer Wilfred De'Ath, he had also worked on Luxembourg and Radio London. His playful tinkering with sound through tape-editing, echo and phasing was startlingly inventive in 1967; and his interview technique was on another planet to that of Brian Matthew. Kenny giggled and mumbled casually with the Beatles, keen to show he was locked onto their wave length.

John was heard delivering three amusing and rather stoned introductions. 'We're sitting in the hushed semi-circular theatre waiting for the *Sgt Pepper's Lonely Hearts Club Band* to come out and here they come now playing the first number, ah! let's go!... All right? I can't do it for them all, man, or I'll be dizzy.

'Now we'd like to play you one. It's a sad little song... Where's it gone?... Oh, this is it, yeah... "Picture yourself on an old-fashioned elephant". "Lucy In The Sky" for everyone... now.

'Phasing is great! Double-flanging, we call it... You name the one it isn't on. You spot it, you get a prize and you get a *Sgt Pepper* badge. Phasing is toooo much!'

Paul's musings were a little more informative:

KENNY How many takes did you usually do on this album before you got the perfect take?
PAUL We did quite a few on each one but it's just 'cause it's changed. Like in the old days of the LP *Please Please Me*, we went in and did it in a day 'cause we knew all the numbers; we'd rehearsed them and been playing them for about a year. But nowadays, we just take a song in and all we've got is the chords on a guitar and the words and the tune. So we've got to work out how to arrange it. So we do a lot of takes on each one.
KENNY Do you like to have a lot of people in the studio when you're recording or do you like to do it completely alone?
PAUL It doesn't matter. We had a lot of people on some of the tracks. Sometimes we use them – ask them to clap and that. Depends. If it's good people, who don't hassle anyone and don't try and mess a session up, then it's great, you know. 'Cause it's company, good company.
KENNY I hear you had the Rolling Stones in this session.
PAUL They came down 'cause we had a lot of people there. It was a big session and we wanted to make a 'happening' happen... and it happened!

It happened on 10 February 1967 when the orchestral cacophony was added to 'A Day In The Life'. Serious players wore a joke shop assortment of silly red noses and the like, while various friends – including some Stones and a Monkee – gathered in the studio. Images from the occasion were jumbled together into a film with the song as its soundtrack. It was never shown in the sixties – principally because 'A Day In The Life' was banned from both BBC radio and television.

The BBC's first warning regarding 'A Day In The Life' came from a front page news item in *Disc and Music Echo* (6 May 1967). Some Los Angeles radio stations with bafflingly early copies of four *Sgt Pepper* tracks had placed a ban on the song because of alleged drug references. An advance tape was acquired from Northern Songs and then Mark White, the Assistant Head of Gramophone Programmes, wrote a memo to the Assistant Head of Sound Broadcasting, Mr R.D. Marriott. 'Our Light Programme production *Where It's At* will be featuring the LP… and although they need not play this particular track, it is thought by the experts to be one of the best on the album, and other programmes may well want to play it later. Head of Gramophone Programmes [Anna Instone] and I have listened to the tape, and neither of us is sure about the content, nor about whether or not it should be broadcast. We would welcome a ruling from you at the earliest opportunity.'

There was also a worry that 'the word "Psychedelic" derives exclusively from the use of the drug LSD and it might be wise if we were to instruct all DJs not to use it'. The dubious word was heard on *Where It's At* (although further utterances were officially discouraged) but 'A Day In The Life' was not played. Roland Fox – Assistant Head of Publicity – wrote to his colleagues confirming that the BBC would not broadcast the song, as it could 'encourage a permissive attitude to drug-taking'.

On 23 May, Frank Gillard – the Director of Sound Broadcasting – wrote an explanatory letter to the Chairman of EMI, Sir Joseph Lockwood. 'I never thought the day would come when we would have to put a ban on an EMI record, but sadly, that is what has happened over this track. We have listened to it over and over again with great care, and we cannot avoid coming to the conclusion that the words "I'd love to turn you on", followed by the mounting montage of sound, could have a rather sinister meaning.

'"Turned on" is a phrase which can be used in many different circumstances, but it is currently much in vogue in the jargon of the drug-addicts. We do not feel that we can take the responsibility of appearing to favour or encourage those unfortunate habits…'

'A Day In The Life' was not heard on BBC radio until the early seventies and was one of only two 1960s tracks to be actively banned, as opposed to 'restricted'. The other song was, for obvious reasons, 'We Love The Pirate Stations'.

During the summer of 1967, watery wireless was outlawed by the Marine Offences Act and so, with the exception of plucky Radio Caroline, the radio dial was once again monopolized by the BBC. But the popularity of the pirates had signalled a need for a network that didn't schedule *Where It's At* within hours of *Those Were The Days* (with Old Time sequence dance music played by Sidney Davey and his Orchestra). BBC Radio was reorganized and a fourth channel was added to the mix: Radio One. It even had jingles promising that the station would 'turn you on'!

On the first day of broadcasting, 30 September 1967, an interview with George was heard in the pop magazine programme *Scene and Heard*. He talked to reporter Miranda Ward, who had joined the party filming *Magical Mystery Tour* at the Atlantic Hotel, Newquay. Listeners had not heard George talk on a pop show since June 1966 and it soon became clear that his fascination with Indian culture now went deeper than playing the sitar. 'I first noticed that I was interested in this with the music… first of all… and along with that I'd heard stories of people in caves – yogis as they're known – people levitating and dematerializing and doing all sorts of wondrous things! And then through the music, with meeting Ravi [Shankar], it was great – because he's a Brahmin, which is a high sect. Just all the groovy people are Brahmins – the scientists, religious people and musicians. And I learnt a lot from him and by going to India I realized there was more to all these rumours and mystic stories than you hear about in the West… They're actually there doing it and it's real and there are people like Jesus Christ, who are there all the time and they're always gonna be there.

'One thing led to another, just snowballed, got bigger and bigger. And then in the end, [I thought] I'd like to become this myself. I'd just like to have this

Replying, Sir Joseph wrote he 'appreciated why you have taken the action you have' but 'did not understand a good deal of the lyrics'.

23rd May 1967

Dear Sir Joseph,

"A Day in the Life"

I never thought the day would come when we would have to put a ban on an EMI record, but sadly, that is what has happened over this track. We have listened to it over and over again with great care, and we cannot avoid coming to the conclusion that the words "I'd love to turn you on", followed by that mounting montage of sound, could have a rather sinister meaning.

The recording may have been made in innocence and good faith, but we must take account of the interpretation that many young people would inevitably put upon it. "Turned on" is a phrase which can be used in many different circumstances, but it is currently much in vogue in the jargon of the drug-addicts. We do not feel that we can take the responsibility of appearing to favour or encourage those unfortunate habits, and that is why we shall not be playing the recording in any of our programmes, Radio or Television.

I expect we shall meet with some embarrassment over this decision, which has already been noted by the Press. We will do our best not to appear to be criticising your people, but as you will realise, we do find ourselves in a very difficult position. I thought you would like to know why we have, most reluctantly, taken this decision.

Warmest regards,

Yours ever,

FRANK GILLARD

(Frank Gillard)
Director of Sound Broadcasting

Sir Joseph Lockwood, Chairman,
E.M.I. House,
20 Manchester House,
London, W.1.

quality that these people have, which is a spiritual thing. And I think, with us having all the material wealth that we need, then… you know, the average person feels that if they had a car and a telly and a house then that's where it's at. But if you get a car and a telly and a house… and even a lot of money… your life's still empty because it's still all on this gross level. What we need isn't material, it's spiritual. We need some other form of peace and happiness.'

George gave a brief synopsis of *Magical Mystery Tour* – 'a typical coach tour but anything can happen… because it's magic' – and his view on TV shows like *Top Of The Pops* –'it was OK for whenever it was invented but it's still the same; the times change so fast, yet those TV shows go on and on and on being the same old thing'. When asked about the long-awaited third movie, George used an apt analogy. 'Over the last two years since *Help!*, we've had thousands of ideas [sent to us] but they've all been *Help!* and *A Hard Day's Night* revisited. It's no good… How we visualize the film, it's got to be at least the difference between the song 'Help' and *Sgt Pepper*. The movie's got to be that progression too.'

Presenter Johnny Moran promised the second part of the interview the following week, in which George would talk about the Maharishi and Transcendental Meditation. Unfortunately the tape has not survived. If the truth be told, the first part only did because Miranda Ward rescued the *Scene and Heard* programme tape from a waste bin!

Where It's At – the old Light Programme's hippest show – was given a slot on Radio One on Saturday afternoon. The edition of 25 November featured John chatting to Chris Denning and Kenny Everett. They seemed most interested in capturing some off-the-wall stream of consciousness thoughts for jingles:

KENNY 'Cause interviews are a bit old hat, as you'll have gathered… do a few Lennonisms that we can chuck in every now and then.

JOHN It's easier said than done, Ken. I mean, give us a clue as to what you want.

A 1967 photograph of Kenny Everett in front of a rather dated poster.

Subjects flitted in and out of the conversation, such as the equipment at Abbey Road ('EMI are just about to buy some eight-track machines and that's not enough!'), post-production work on *Magical Mystery Tour* ('we planned three weeks to edit it and put the sound on but it's taken eight weeks to edit and we're just getting into the sound now') and the songs in the TV film. The BBC had its knickers in a twist again about, well… knickers.

'I Am The Walrus', on the B-side of the Beatles' Christmas number one 'Hello, Goodbye', included the line 'Boy, you been a naughty girl, you let your knickers down'.

'Are you going to play 'Walrus'?' John asked. 'Somebody heard Joyce Grenfell singing about "Pull your knickers up!" yesterday. So listen Sir Henry Fielding, or whoever it is running the BBB…'

John and Kenny rambled together for Radio 1 on two occasions in 1968. The second took place on

6 June, during the sessions for *The Beatles* (the 'White Album'). The DJ was moving from his Sunday morning slot to a daily show and encouraged John, Paul and Ringo to improvise some 'goodbye jingles'. John strummed an unplugged electric guitar and was joined by Paul for an instantaneous song, 'Goodbye to Kenny Everett, he is our very pal'. Ringo also led a chorus of 'Goodbye Kenny, see you in the morning', which soon became 'Goodbye Kenny, we hear you got the sack!'.

As for 'the interview', even Kenny seemed to be aware of how bizarre it was:

KENNY Well, that's about 30 seconds worth.
JOHN Nah, there's an LP out of this, Ken... This is ad nauseam, straight from the mouth that bit me... I hope we're gonna hear this, listeners, because we have a lot of fun doing them. But never quite hear them, listeners, when you get home... So, Wonderful Radio One-ders!
KENNY Have you got anything to say that our listeners would understand?
JOHN How about 'Good Morning'?

John treated Kenny to a quick blast of the Leadbelly song 'Cottonfields' with a word change: 'When I was a little bitty baby, my mama used to *smash* me in the cradle!'. (In November 1968, the Beach Boys recorded it and reached the UK Top Ten in 1970.) Asked to choose a favourite new record, John picked Nilsson's 'River Deep Mountain High' or, as he called it, 'River Deep Mountain Dew'. It was on the singer's debut album *Pandemonium Shadow Show*, which also featured an ingenious version of 'You Can't Do That' incorporating snatches of other Beatles songs. Kenny Everett recorded a Nilsson composition from the same album, 'It's Been So Long'. In an unbroadcast version of the interview, all the Beatles are heard enthusing about the eccentric falsetto singer and ukelele plunker, Tiny Tim.

On the same day he looned around with Everett, John gave an extremely lucid and serious interview for the BBC 2 television show *Release*. Airing his increasingly radical political views, he and Victor Spinetti also discussed their stage adaptation of his two books called *In His Own Write*.

During the following year, it was this forthright side of John that was heard most on the radio as he campaigned vigorously for peace.

Paul, George and Ringo also pursued their own interests away from the group. So much so that speculation about the Beatles not remaining together became a regular interview topic...

CHAPTER FOURTEEN

'A Rebirth or a Death'

On 22 August 1968, Ringo walked out of the recording sessions for *The Beatles* (the 'White Album'), intending to leave the group for ever. But 12 days after quitting, he returned just in time to take part in a promotional film for 'Hey Jude' – the first Beatles record on the group's own Apple label. The month before, Apple Films had released the animated movie *Yellow Submarine* with a soundtrack of Beatles tracks including four new songs. It was a visual delight but the group had little to do with the project – even the voices for their cartoon characters were mimicked by actors. At the end of November 1968 the double 'White Album' was out, brimming with 30 new and extraordinarily varied tracks. Yet none of these projects were accompanied by any of the Beatles talking in detail about them on BBC radio.

Only an interview with George for *Scene and Heard*, broadcast two months before *The Beatles* was released, gave any clues. He told *New Musical Express* writer Alan Smith, 'This next album is much simpler than *Pepper* because it's more down to guitars, bass and drums, and maybe piano.' Although George's spiritual beliefs were as strong as ever, his songs would not be as mystical. 'It's all still 'Within You, Without You' but I don't want to go into that any more 'cause now I'm being a rock 'n' roll star! I now want to write songs that don't have any meaning, because I'm a bit fed up with people coming up and saying, "Hey, what's it all about? What does it mean"?'

After the 'White Album', their next project was intended to return the group to their origins as a live rock band. They rehearsed songs for a televised concert in the chilly atmosphere of a vast sound stage at Twickenham Film Studios where, as the cameras rolled, they documented the Beatles in the midst of a cold war. There were frequent skirmishes – but the most damaging erupted on 10 January 1969 when George quit the group. He was persuaded to rejoin five days later but only on condition that any plans for a live performance were abandoned.

When Ringo talked to *Daily Express* writer David Wigg for Radio 1's *Scene and Heard* programme on 21 January, he was asked about the reported tensions threatening the group's unity:

DAVID Last week was quite a controversial week for the Beatles – are you as close [as you used to be]?

RINGO Yes. There's that famous old saying 'You always hurt the one you love' and we all love each other and we all know that. But we still hurt each other occasionally, where we just misunderstand each other and we go off and it builds up to something bigger than it ever was. And then we have to come down to it and get it over with, sort it out. So we're still really very close people.

DAVID Do you see the Beatles going on like they are at the moment for a long time in the future? Or do you see a split very soon?

RINGO We'll never go... oh, I can't say never... but we won't go our separate ways after this album. We'll always be tied up with each other in some way, because we signed a lot of papers that say we stay together for 20 years or something!

They discussed the way the group was now perceived differently by the British public, who had once

John and Yoko during sessions for the album that was called for most its evolution Get Back, *until it received the sadly apt title* Let It Be.

cherished their fresh-faced cheekiness. 'It's because when we started we were the nice clean "mop-tops" and every mother's son and everyone loved us. Then suddenly there's a few things they don't understand; they don't like... and it turns them off us a bit.'

This was a topic that Paul also addressed in a *Scene and Heard* interview with David Wigg in September 1969. 'You see, you grow up. Everyone grows up. And it's always a great pity to see a baby turn into an adult, 'cause it's always nicer when they're a baby and they go "Goo! Goo!" and they do everything you want. It's lovely. In a certain period of our career, we were particularly nice. We had a very all-round appeal. It wasn't put on, we were more like that. But as you grow up, you become more individual... we're more true to ourselves these days.'

David Wigg seemed to have been cast in the role of father confessor during 1969 and early 1970. All four Beatles gave him several lengthy interviews for *Scene and Heard*, in which their individual concerns and the future of the Beatles as a unit were frequently discussed.In an interview with Wigg in March, George had spoken about his frustration with Britain's now less than positive attitude to the group – mainly expressed through the press. On 8 May 1969, John was asked whether he had noticed a change. 'Oh, we've experienced it before. We've always been treated the same; the Beatles are treated like Britain's children. And it's OK for the family to insult us but see what happens if abroad starts insulting us. The British will stick up for us and it's just like a family. And it's all right for them to slap our face, but if the neighbour does it, you watch out! And George was very depressed and it is depressing when the whole family's picking on you. We do get hurt because Britain appreciates us least.'

John and his new wife Yoko Ono were orchestrating an intense campaign for peace and were content to generate publicity for this cause, whatever ridicule might be heaped upon them. A month after their Amsterdam Bed-In, David Wigg's sympathetic questions elicited calm responses that always revolved around the central theme of peace:

DAVID John, you seem a lot more relaxed in yourself now. What has happened? What do you put it down to? Because before, you were always a little bit frightening.

JOHN I put it down to Yoko. She's brought out the real me. I get nervous and tense like anybody else, but I'm more relaxed than I ever was... since I was a child anyway.

DAVID But a lot of people are jeering, aren't they? And making fun, not taking you seriously.

JOHN But that is good. That's part of our policy not to be taken seriously because our opposition, whoever they may be in all their manifest forms, don't know how to handle humour. And we are humorists... Laurel and Hardy, that's John and Yoko. And we stand a better chance under that guise because all the serious people, like Martin Luther King and Kennedy and Gandhi, got shot. We're willing to be the world's clowns.

A week later Paul was interviewed for BBC Radio Merseyside by former school contemporary Roy Corlett and, in a relaxed mood, talked generously about his Beatle colleagues. Only a few days before, there had been acrimony when Paul had refused to add his name to papers appointing Allen Klein as Apple's business manager. But, with Roy Corlett, he was supportive both of the group and of John and Yoko. 'The truth about it all is that he loves Yoko. He said one thing to me which made me understand what they were up to. He said, "It's like holding hands on the back row of the pictures." And I suddenly realized they're not freaks. Because John says that, you know, "It's too bad if we look like this and people think we're funny. This is how we are and we're very straight." 'Cause they are, really. They're two great people and they're very much in love. You can't say anything more than that.

'As four people, we're all right. There's nothing seriously wrong. 'Cause we're each other's mates and we've come through all of this together so you can't help but be friends. Anyway, they're my three best friends. They're good lads, I'll tell you.'

'I don't see how we can retire. It's like Brigitte Bardot and Greta Garbo… you can't.' At the Beatles' headquarters, Apple Corps, Savile Row in 1969, Paul grants an audience to David Wigg reporting for the Radio 1 magazine programme Scene and Heard. The journalist talked frequently to all the group and extracts from these interviews were eventually released on an album entitled The Beatles Tapes.

In fairly harmonious sessions (compared to those for the now shelved project begun at Twickenham) the group worked on *Abbey Road* during the summer of 1969. To promote the album's release in September, three of the Beatles were featured on Radio One's *Scene and Heard* programme. David Wigg was again in attendance, ready to talk about the new record and the continuing rumours about the possible demise of the group. He talked to Paul on 19 September, when only six days earlier John had returned to the stage playing with a hastily convened Plastic Ono Band in Toronto.

Asked for his personal favourites on the new LP, Paul selected John's 'Come Together', George's 'Something', the 'Long One' (meaning the medley that concludes the album) and 'Because'. He explained the background to writing 'Golden Slumbers' and 'Her Majesty', boasted about his new baby Mary – 'the best-looking baby you've ever seen!' – and faced up to the inevitable question:

DAVID Paul, what about the future of the Beatles? I happen to know that the organizers of the Isle of Wight Pop Festival are going to ask you and the rest of the Beatles if you will top the bill next year at the Isle of Wight. What's your reaction to a thing like that? Are you likely to go back on stage and perhaps do a show like that?

PAUL I don't know. I've never known. I didn't know when we were playing the Cavern that we'd be on

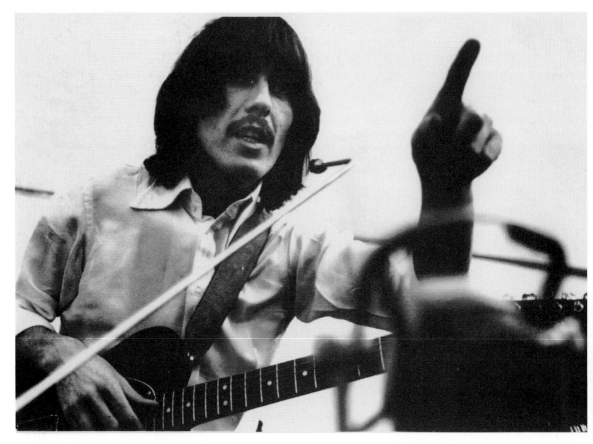

Let It Be *film director Michael Lindsay-Hogg recalls the day at Twickenham when 'we went up for lunch, George came up and said, "I'll see you round the clubs" and he left... they thought it was goodbye forever, and John said, "Let's call Eric Clapton and get him!"'*

the *Royal Variety Performance.* And after that all the papers said, 'Well, what's left for them?' So then we went to America. Then they said, 'What's left for them?' And then we got into making better albums and stuff. I mean, I just don't know what's going to happen. It'll be all right though... I don't see how we can retire. It's like Brigitte Bardot and Greta Garbo. Although they tried to retire, you can't, 'cause you're always there.

When it was George's turn to sit down with David Wigg in October 1969, he seemed equally sure that the group would survive. 'All I'm doing is acting out the part of Beatle George and we're all acting out our own parts. You know, the world is a stage and the people are the players. Shakespeare said that... and he's right... It's the same as any job. It's up and down.

Life is up and down all the time. Maybe for us it goes up higher but it comes down lower.'

He tried to explain what it was that bound the group together. 'I think it's a mental concept. To physically or spiritually split is impossible. Well, maybe not physically. Spiritually, you can't split because, if you're listening, I'm the walrus too!'

The same month, John and Yoko talked to David Wigg and the possibility of a Beatles concert was once again on the agenda. 'Performing as a Beatle is a harder problem than performing as John Lennon and Yoko, or the Plastic Ono Band, 'cause you don't have that big aura around you. You saw what happened to Dylan in the Isle of Wight. There was nothing wrong with his performance and the audience appreciated him but they were expecting Buddha or Jesus to appear! And if you imagine the four Beatles are going to come [together] on the Isle of Wight, whatever happens we're gonna get knocked. Whatever happens, we have such a thing to live up to. It's not out of the question. It's just a big responsibility. There's such a mystique about the Beatles that they'd be expecting God to perform and we're not.'

Having secretly asked for 'a divorce' from the group in September, John referred to the group in the third person when asked what he wanted for the Beatles in the future. 'For them to be happy. To do whatever they want to do. 'Cause whatever happens to the Beatles, so-called, we'll always be friends. So all I want for the Beatles is their individual happiness and whether that's in a collective form or not remains to be seen.'

As if the Beatles did not have enough to deal with, in October 1969 a preposterous rumour swept through America that Paul had died in 1966 and been replaced with a lookalike. The clues hidden on Beatles records that supposedly revealed this secret were first reported by Russ Gibbs – a DJ on Detroit station W-KNR. In the wake of this nonsense, Radio 4 newsman Chris Drake was granted an interview with Paul, who had retreated with his family to the Mull of Kintyre in Scotland. While he didn't actually persuade Paul to say, 'I'm alive!', Linda expressed the couple's annoyance – 'it ruins our life, that kind of thing'. Drake reported that Paul 'lives contentedly in isolation, walking in the day and watching television at night. He does have a telephone but it's nearly always left off the hook. He's in no hurry to return to civilization – there's no need to.' Paul explained, 'I've done all my work for this year, because the Beatles have... We've made a film and another album besides *Abbey Road*, which are unreleased yet. So I've finished my work till about March of next year, so I'm laughing! I may not be back in London at all this year.

While Paul remained out of the spotlight, Ringo recorded tracks for a solo album *Sentimental Journey* and George slipped into Delaney and Bonnie's band during their tour of Britain. John and Yoko also played on stage at the Lyceum Ballroom in London and pursued their many other activities in the cause of world peace. BBC reporter David Bellan caught up

with them just after 'Instant Karma!' had been written and recorded in one day for a Plastic Ono Band single:

BELLAN How much are you seeing, at the moment, of the other Beatles?
JOHN Well, George was on the session for 'Instant Karma!' and Ringo's away [in Los Angeles] and Paul's... I don't know what he's doing, you know. At the moment, I haven't got a clue.
BELLAN When did you last see him?
JOHN Before Toronto. When was it? I'll see him this week actually. If you're listening, I'm coming round!

John and Yoko had flown to Toronto on 16 December 1969 to discuss plans for a Peace Pop Festival in the city. While they were there they met the Canadian Prime Minister Pierre Trudeau. 'It's like he's running a business and he can't really know what the doormen and the caretakers are doing, but he cares about them. He was asking us – as, like, a shop steward of youth, maybe – what's going on out there? We were just giving our point of view, not necessarily as representatives of youth but just as people who have got something to do with youth... He gave us hope. That's the only one [world leader] I've really met. He was human, obviously, and he did care.'

When 'Instant Karma!' was released on 6 February 1970, David Wigg turned up at Apple to talk to John and Yoko:

DAVID Are you in fact going your own way with Yoko these days? Because that is the impression one has.
JOHN Well, each Beatle's doing his own thing at the moment and it's like... it could be a rebirth or a death, you know. We'll see what it is. It'll probably be a rebirth... for all of us.
DAVID When do you in fact plan to record with the Beatles again?
JOHN At the moment, there is no plan whatsoever. And maybe if one of us starts it off, the others will all come round and make an album. It's just like

that at the moment. To open the Beatles up, you know. And I've no idea if the Beatles will work together again or not... I never did have, it was always open.

DAVID It's the first time this situation has ever arisen, isn't it?

JOHN Well, let's say before *Sgt Pepper* there was nine months of nothing. So in between our albums now, there's a lot of other stuff going on, that's all. There might be nine months or a year before we decide that we're interested enough to produce that thing called the Beatles album. But there was nine months before *Sgt Pepper* and it's only been since September when we last worked together.

DAVID Do you care about making another one?

JOHN Yeah, I think [the] Beatles is a good communication medium and I wouldn't destroy it out of hand...

On 30 March 1970, the BBC broadcast that now rare treat – a Beatles Bank Holiday special – on Easter Monday. Called *The Beatles Today*, it featured George talking to Johnny Moran, the presenter of *Scene and Heard*. He talked about the Apple artists he had produced – Jackie Lomax, Billy Preston, Doris Troy and the Radha Krishna Temple – and the forthcomimg album and film *Let It Be*. He sounded very cheerful and his words conveyed a positive attitude to the Beatles. 'Ringo's completed a great album... it was gonna be called *Ringo Starrdust*... but it's called *Sentimental Journey*. It's all the songs Elsie and Harry – that's his mother and father – and his uncles and aunties used to sing at parties. Then John's doing a Plastic Ono album with Phil Spector. And I think Paul's doing an album, which is, I should imagine like... if you remember Eddie Cochran did a couple of tracks like 'C'Mon Everybody', where he played bass, drums, guitar and sang. So Paul's doing this sort of thing where he's gonna play all the instruments himself,

'There's that saying "You always hurt the one you love" and we all love each other... But we still hurt each other occasionally,... and it builds up to something bigger than it ever was.'

which is nice. Because he couldn't possibly do that in the Beatles. If it was a Beatle album, automatically Paul gets stuck on bass, Ringo gets on drums...

'In a way, it's a great relief for us all to work separately at the same time and so maybe, if I get a chance, I'd like to do an album as well, just to get rid of a lot of songs. So I'll try and get that together sometime during this summer. And I expect by that time we should be ready to do a new Beatle album. So I think really the next Beatle album should be a very good one because we would have had so much freedom that it will be a pleasure to get back and to do a compromise. Because [the] Beatles are compromising really, because you've got to allow that he's gonna do that and they're gonna do that... In a way you lose something by being the Beatles but what we gain is so much more than what we lose. It's definitely worth it.

'It's nice to go away from each other for a while, because then you can appreciate what it's like being together... I certainly don't want to see the end of the Beatles and I know I'll do anything... whatever Paul, John, Ringo would like to do, I'll do it.'

On 10 April 1970, 11 days after *The Beatles Today* was broadcast, advance copies of Paul's solo album *McCartney* were distributed with a long 'self-interview' press release. The only Beatle who had not wanted to split the group at one point, now seemed to be doing just that:

Q Are you planning a new album or single with the Beatles?

A No.

Q Is your break with the Beatles temporary or permanent, due to personal differences or musical ones?

A Personal differences, business differences, musical differences but most of all because I have a better time with my family. Temporary or permanent? I don't know.

As far as the news media knew, after months of speculation this was the end of the Beatles and the split was duly headlined around the world. On BBC

Radio News, a report by Chris Drake was introduced with the words 'now it seems the Beatles' story is *almost* over'. Drake lifted George's recent optimistic statements about the group's future and revisited his interview with Paul in Scotland, prefacing it with the thought that, 'the split will obviously suit Paul because he's done his best to keep away from the public for several months now.' Paul said, 'I haven't enjoyed doing interviews and getting a lot of publicity lately. I've preferred to sit more in the background and be more with the family [rather] than go to clubs and be seen everywhere. Like, I used to do an interview a week almost for a newspaper or something; just to keep my name in the headlines – because, I don't know, you go through a phase of wanting to be up there in the limelight. Well, I'm going through a phase now… where I *don't* want to be in the limelight.'

Listening again to the BBC's interviews from 1969 and early 1970, it seems that Paul's April announcement was unexpected, especially by the other Beatles. Even during the most tense times – particularly January and May 1969 – they had all been gracious and positive about their colleagues. There had been bitter disagreements concerning Allen Klein's management of Apple's affairs, yet the music had continued. Perhaps the divide between Paul and the others became unbridgeable when George, John and Klein gave Phil Spector the task of 're-producing' the album that became *Let It Be*. Paul was clearly not happy about the *auteur* producer being given free rein to salvage an album from the 16-month-old tapes. It might well have been the 'wall of sound' Spector built around 'The Long And Winding Road' that finally tipped the balance. Paul's press release was issued ten days after the producer's overdub of celestial orchestra and choir of angels.

As solo artists, the ex-Beatles continued to appear regularly and eloquently on BBC Radio but that's another story… As for the staying power of their work together, the rapid sale of seven million copies of *The Beatles Live At The BBC* at Christmas 1994 sent out a strong and clear signal. On that album, the world could hear the group just the way Britain had first fallen in love with them – affectionately sending up BBC announcers, laughing at their own crazy success, bringing a joyous rush of musical energy to shows creaking with dance bands and crooners! They even changed the BBC… By the end of the sixties, TV newsreaders were appearing with Beatle haircuts (albeit more like those of 1964 than 1969) and a less formal style of presentation was heard on the airwaves.

The BBC's legacy of Beatles recordings, including a wealth of unusual musical performances and revealing interviews, gives us an invaluable insight into the group's career and how they, as individuals, reacted to their success. We should be grateful for the enthusiasm and professionalism of the dedicated presenters, producers and studio managers who made these recordings and the prescience of those who preserved them.

The audition report comment made by producer Peter Pilbeam, who first opened the BBC's doors to the Beatles in 1962, now stands as a lovely understatement – 'A tendency to play music'. To that, borrowing a phrase used by *From Us To You* DJ Alan Freeman, we can only reply, 'Not 'alf!'.

The Beatles' BBC Radio Appearances

 For programmes with specially performed **music** the following information is given:

♪ **Programme Title**

BR: BROADCAST DATE

REC: RECORDING DATE

BBC Studio

Producer

Programme Presenter

Song title ✖ ● ✔(1)

Any other points of interest

❝❝ For programmes in which the Beatles made a **speech** contribution (individually or as a group) but did not perform any music, the following information is given:

❝ **Programme Title**

BR: BROADCAST DATE

REC: RECORDING DATE

A note on the nature of the contribution.

✖ Denotes that the song was not on any Beatles' records released on the Parlophone and Apple labels between October 1962 and April 1970.

● Denotes the BBC session songs released on *The Beatles Live At The BBC* (1994), the 'Baby It's You' single and *Anthology 1* (1995).

✔ Denotes that the song was included in the 1988 BBC Radio 1 series *The Beeb's Lost Beatles Tapes* (in the above example – Part 1).

ALL INFORMATION RELATES TO UK BROADCASTS ONLY

PROGRAMMES BROADCAST ON THE BBC LIGHT PROGRAMME UNLESS OTHERWISE INDICATED

1♪ Teenagers Turn – Here We Go

BR: 8 MARCH 1962

REC: 7 MARCH 1962

Playhouse Theatre, Manchester

Producer: Peter Pilbeam

Presenter: Ray Peters

Dream Baby ✖ ✔(1)

Memphis Tennessee ✖

Please Mister Postman

Recorded in front of an audience.

Pete Best – Drummer

2♪ Here We Go

BR: 15 JUNE 1962

REC: 11 JUNE 1962

Playhouse Theatre, Manchester

Producer: Peter Pilbeam

Presenter: Ray Peters

Ask Me Why

Besame Mucho ✖

A Picture Of You ✖

Recorded in front of an audience.

Pete Best – Drummer

March 1, 1962 · RADIO TIMES · 49

Third Programme

SOUND 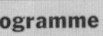 MARCH 8

Light Programme

THURSDAY evening

VHF and Wavelengths: page 6

8.0
BERLIOZ
La Damnation de Faust
Régine Crespin (soprano)
André Turp (tenor)
Michel Roux (baritone)
L.S.O. Chorus
London Symphony Orchestra
Leader, Hugh Maguire
Conductor,
Pierre Monteux
Part 1
From the Royal Festival Hall,
London
See below and page 42

9.0 app.
IN ANOTHER COUNTRY
Story by
ERNEST HEMINGWAY
read by William Sylvester
'The tall boy with a very pale face
who was to be a lawyer had been a
lieutenant of Arditi and had three
medals of the sort we each had only
one of. He had lived a very long time
with death and was a little detached.
We were all a little detached, and there
was nothing that held us together except that we met every afternoon at
the hospital...'
BBC recording: second broadcast

9.15 app.
BERLIOZ
La Damnation de Faust
Part 2

10.15
E. E. CUMMINGS
reads
a selection
from his poetry
introduced by D. G. Bridson
BBC recording

10.45-11.5
R. W. WOOD
String Quartet No. 3
played by the
Quartet Pro Musica
Patrick Halling (violin)
Ernest Scott (violin)
Gwynne Edwards (viola)
Peter Halling (cello)
BBC recording: second broadcast
The tenth of a series of contemporary
British music
*Richard Arwyn's String Trio (first broad-
cast performance) and Beethoven's Trio
in E flat major, Op. 3, played by the
Oromonte String Trio: March 13*

Andy Cole — Doreen Hume — William Davies

are featured in tonight's edition of

TORCHLIGHT PARADE at 9.31

4.31
RACING RESULTS

4.34 app.
PLAYTIME
Records for the Young
Introduced by John Webster

5.0
TEENAGERS TURN
Here We Go
with the N.D.O.
Directed by Bernard Herrmann
with The Trad Lads
Brad Newman
The Beatles
Introduced by Ray Peters
Produced by Peter Pilbeam
BBC recording

5.31
ROUNDABOUT
A daily round of music
news, views, and information
on all manner of topics
Introduced by John Anthony
Today's record stars include:
Anne Shelton and
Luis Alberto Del Parana'
BBC Revue Orchestra
Leader, Julien Gaillard
Conducted by Malcolm Lockyer
Producer, Frank Hooper
Editor, Peter Duncan

6.33
SPORTS REVIEW
including news, comment
interviews, and racing results

6.45
THE ARCHERS
Written by
David Turner and Geoffrey Webb
Edited by Godfrey Baseley
Produced by Tony Shryane
BBC recording

7.0
NEWS and
RADIO NEWSREEL

7.31
WHAT DO YOU KNOW?
Franklin Engelmann
is the chairman of this general
knowledge contest, in which
listeners from all over the
United Kingdom compete for
the title 'Brain of Britain 1962'
11: Wales (II)
The second panel of contestants
representing Wales is
Lilian Turton
Caernarvonshire
University Lecturer
Mrs. Ann James
Montgomeryshire
William Strang, Monmouthshire
Civil Servant
John Kelly, Swansea
Schoolmaster
The programme also includes
'Hear! Hear!'
A test of memory for listeners
at home and in the audience
The programme devised and written
by John P. Wynn
Produced by Joan Clark
BBC recording
Repeated on Saturday at 12 noon

8.0
WHACK-O!
Professor Jimmy Edwards
endures a further outbreak
of pandemonium
at Chiselbury School
with
June Whitfield as Matron
Roddy Maude-Roxby
as Aubrey Potter
Frederick Treves as Sir Wilfred
John Caxall as Phipps
Roger Shepherd as Lumley
and Graham Ann and David Lott
Script adapted by David Climie
from an original by
Frank Muir and Denis Norden
Produced by Edward Taylor
BBC recording

8.31
ALL TOGETHER
Community singing from
Barnstaple, Devon, with
Sheila Harris (soprano)
Arthur Parkman at the piano
and local choirs
and their friends
Conducted by Lawrence Adam
Master of Ceremonies,
Bernard Fishwick
Produced by Brian Patten
BBC recording

9.0
ANY ANSWERS?
A radio correspondence column
in which listeners add their
comments to some of the views
expressed in last Friday's 'Any
Questions?' from the Village
Hall, Axbridge, Somerset
Introduced by
Freddy Grisewood
Produced by Michael Bowen
Repeated on Friday at 12.15 (Home
Service, not Scottish)

9.31
TORCHLIGHT PARADE
Sidney Torch
conducts music
from the theatres of the world
featuring
Doreen Hume, Andy Cole
William Davies
with the
New Metropolitan Orchestra
Leader, Reginald Leopold
and including
TORCHLIGHT ON A STAR
Al Jolson
with records
Introduced by Peter King
Produced by Edward Nash
BBC recording

10.30
NEWS
followed by
SPORT and TONIGHT'S TOPIC

10.41
JAZZ CLUB
A farewell party for pianist
Eddie Thompson
on the eve of his
departure for America
To bid him bon voyage are
The Eddie Thompson Trio
Sandy Brown, Keith Christie
Kathleen Stobart, Kenny Baker
Introduced by Alan Dell
Produced by Terry Henebery
See page 42

11.31
MOOD INDIGO
Music in cool style
with Yolande Bavan
Produced by Joanna Hollas
BBC recording

11.55
LATE NEWS
Close Down at 12 midnight

IN THE THIRD PROGRAMME

Pierre Monteux

CONDUCTS

La Damnation de Faust

BY BERLIOZ

Part 1 at 8.0 • Part 2 at 9.15
FROM THE ROYAL FESTIVAL
HALL, LONDON

From the Radio Times, the diverse delights of the Light Programme during the evening of the Beatles' radio debut – 8 March 1962. The Archers and Any Answers? can still be heard on BBC Radio 4. If you missed Teenagers Turn, perhaps you were watching Crackerjack on BBC television.

3.♪ Here We Go

BR: 26 OCTOBER 1962

REC: 25 OCTOBER 1962

Playhouse Theatre, Manchester

Producer: Peter Pilbeam

Presenter: Ray Peters

Love Me Do

A Taste Of Honey

P.S. I Love You

Recorded in front of an audience.

Performed but not broadcast:

Sheila ✖

Ringo Starr – Drummer from this session onwards

4.♪ The Talent Spot

BR: 4 DECEMBER 1962

REC: 27 NOVEMBER 1962

BBC Paris Theatre, London

Producer: Brian Willey

Presenter: Gary Marshal

Love Me Do

P.S. I Love You

Twist And Shout

First session in London.

1.❝ Pop Inn

BR: 22 JANUARY 1963

LIVE

Interview with Keith Fordyce and the record of 'Please Please Me' was featured.

5.♪ Here We Go

BR: 25 JANUARY 1963

REC: 16 JANUARY 1963

Playhouse Theatre, Manchester

Producer: Peter Pilbeam

Presenter: Ray Peters

Chains

Please Please Me

Ask Me Why

Recorded in front of an audience.

Performed but not broadcast:

Three Cool Cats ✖

6.♪ Saturday Club

BR: 26 JANUARY 1963

REC: 22 JANUARY 1963

Playhouse Theatre, London

Producer: Jimmy Grant

Presenter: Brian Matthew

Some Other Guy ✖

Love Me Do

Please Please Me

Keep Your Hands Off My Baby ✖ ●

Beautiful Dreamer ✖

7.♪ The Talent Spot

BR: 29 JANUARY 1963

REC: 22 JANUARY 1963

BBC Paris Theatre, London

Producer: Brian Willey

Presenter: Gary Marshal

Please Please Me

Ask Me Why

Some Other Guy ✖

8.♪ Parade of the Pops

BR: 20 FEBRUARY 1963

LIVE

Playhouse Theatre, London

Producer: John Kingdon

Presenter: Denny Piercy

Love Me Do

Please Please Me

9.♪ Here We Go

BR: 12 MARCH 1963

REC: 6 MARCH 1963

Playhouse Theatre, Manchester

Producer: Peter Pilbeam

Presenter: Ray Peters

Misery

Do You Want To Know A Secret

Please Please Me

Recorded in front of an audience.

Performed but not broadcast:

I Saw Her Standing There

10♪ Saturday Club

BR: 16 MARCH 1963

LIVE

Studio 3A, Broadcasting House, London

Producers: Jimmy Grant and Bernie Andrews

Presenter: Brian Matthew

I Saw Her Standing There

Misery

Too Much Monkey Business ✖

I'm Talking About You ✖

Please Please Me

The Hippy Hippy Shake ✖

11♪ On the Scene

BR: 28 MARCH 1963

REC: 21 MARCH 1963

Number 1 Studio, BBC Piccadilly Theatre, London

Producer: Brian Willey

Presenter: Craig Douglas

Misery

Do You Want To Know A Secret

Please Please Me

12♪ Easy Beat

BR: 7 APRIL 1963

REC: 3 APRIL 1963

Playhouse Theatre, London

Producer: Ron Belchier

Presenter: Brian Matthew

Please Please Me

Misery

From Me To You

Recorded in front of an audience.

2✇ Pop Inn

BR: 9 APRIL 1963

LIVE

An interview with Keith Fordyce and the record of 'From Me To You' was played.

13♪ Swinging Sound '63

BR: 18 APRIL 1963

LIVE

The Royal Albert Hall, London

Producers: Terry Henebery and Ron Belchier

Presenters: George Melly and Rolf Harris

Twist And Shout

From Me To You

Performed in front of an audience.

14♪ Side By Side

BR: 22 APRIL 1963

REC: 1 APRIL 1963

Number 1 Studio, BBC Piccadilly Theatre, London

Producer: Bryant Marriott

Presenter: John Dunn

Side By Side (with the Karl Denver Trio) ✖

I Saw Her Standing There

Do You Want To Know A Secret

Baby It's You

Please Please Me

From Me To You

Misery

15♪ Side By Side

BR: 13 MAY 1963

REC: 1 APRIL 1963

Number 1 Studio, BBC Piccadilly Theatre, London

Producer: Bryant Marriott

Presenter: John Dunn

Side By Side (with the Karl Denver Trio) ✖

From Me To You

Long Tall Sally

A Taste Of Honey

Chains

Thank You Girl

Boys

Thursday

POPS for everyone

The final concert in the Light Programme series— from the Royal Albert Hall

Now these I could scream for . . .

LIGHT 9.10 TONIGHT the Royal Albert Hall will be filled to capacity for the third and final Light Programme pop concert. And when the last echo of an electric guitar has died away twenty-seven soloists, six vocal and instrumental groups, seven bands, and two BBC orchestras will have performed in the series. **Frankie Vaughan** is the compère for this show and he will be introducing, among others, the bands of **Bilk and Ball**, and **Susan Maughan** who have all appeared in previous concerts. **Joe Brown and the Bruvvers, Christine Campbell**, and **Bert Weedon** are a few of the new faces.

As a result of my reactions to the first pop concert I was accused of being—horror of horrors!—square and not with it. Just to prove that my heart is in the right place I invited a girl—who is anything but square—to accompany me to the second concert—for *her* impressions of the show.

Jane Asher, a favourite *Juke Box Jury* panelist (David Frost, I am told, has to be dragged away from the set when she is on), has very definite views on pop music and speaks her mind with disarming frankness. As we sat in the stalls (a football-pitch length from the stage) I took down her comments—those I could hear above the roar.

After a few minutes Jane turned to me: 'It's weird how the sound fills the entire hall, seeing the singers at such a distance. It gives you a funny feeling.' Or as The Vernons Girls put it vocally, 'Funny All Over.' Jane studied the faces around her: 'It seems only the girls are enjoying themselves. It really is a girl's show.'

The Beatles bounded on stage and the noise of their reception reached the threshold of pain. 'Now these I could scream for,' said Jane—with a little prompting from our photographer she did, and felt better for it. (Listen tonight for the response to Gerry and the Pacemakers.) 'Isn't that fantastic (Rolf Harris's wobble board) —it sounds like bath water running out.' And as the bath water ran out, the Sun Arose.

Of the show in general, Jane said: 'It ran very smoothly. It's fabulous to see all these singers together.' And in a word? 'Noisy.' Which all goes to prove that the sentiments of a square equal the sum of the sentiments of the non-square on my left.   TONY ASPLER

In the Radio Times *edition that billed a third live pop concert from the Royal Albert Hall, Tony Aspler reported on the previous event featuring the Beatles. 'Now these I could scream for,' says Jane Asher, who met her future fiancé Paul McCartney for the first time that evening, 18 April 1963. Only the second half of the concert was broadcast and so the audience in the hall heard two extra items – 'Please Please Me' and 'Misery'.*

16♪ Saturday Club

BR: 25 MAY 1963

REC: 21 MAY 1963

Playhouse Theatre, London

Producers: Jimmy Grant and Bernie Andrews

Presenter: Brian Matthew

I Saw Her Standing There

Do You Want To Know A Secret

Boys ✔(2)

Long Tall Sally ✔(2)

From Me To You

Money (That's What I Want)

17♪ Steppin' Out

BR: 3 JUNE 1963

Whit Monday Bank Holiday

REC: 21 MAY 1963

Playhouse Theatre, London

Producer: Terry Henebery

Presenter: Diz Disley

Please Please Me

I Saw Her Standing There

Roll Over Beethoven

Thank You Girl

From Me To You

Recorded in front of an audience.

Performed but not broadcast:

Twist And Shout

Beatles Meet Bachelors

LIGHT
5.0

Two days after the first broadcast in the *Pop Go The Beatles* series, the producer Terry Henebery received over one hundred cards from listeners all over the country expressing their delight that this remarkable group now have their own programme, and that their fans could at last have a hearty helping of the Merseyside sound.

Each week The Beatles play host to another vocal group and this evening it is **The Bachelors**. The close harmony of these three young men, spiced with Country and Western flavouring, should provide a neat contrast to the free-wheeling, casual style of the four lads from Liverpool. There is no need to remind chart-enthusiasts that the Bachelors' most recent hit was 'Charmaine' and that The Beatles are still riding high with 'From Me to You.'

The compère is the actor-disc-jockey **Lee Peters** whom listeners may recognise as David Owen of *The Dales*.

The fourth Pop Go The Beatles *featured the sugary country style of Irish group the Bachelors, whose first hit had come earlier in the year with 'Charmaine'. Declan Cluskey explained on the show that Bobby Darin had sent a telegram congratulating the group on their version of his song 'Jailer, Bring Some Water'. Without missing a beat, presenter Lee Peters dived in with, 'He liked your treatment?… Well, treat us to it!'*

18.♪ Pop Go The Beatles (1)

BR: 4 JUNE 1963

REC: 24 MAY 1963

Number 2 Studio, Aeolian Hall, London

Producer: Terry Henebery

Presenter: Lee Peters

Pop Go The Beatles ✖

From Me To You

Everybody's Trying To Be My Baby

Do You Want To Know A Secret

You Really Got A Hold On Me

Misery

The Hippy Hippy Shake ✖

Pop Go The Beatles ✖

Guest group: the Lorne Gibson Trio

19.♪ Pop Go The Beatles (2)

BR: 11 JUNE 1963

REC: 1 JUNE 1963

BBC Paris Theatre, London

Producer: Terry Henebery

Presenter: Lee Peters

Pop Go The Beatles ✖

Too Much Monkey Business ✖

I Got To Find My Baby ✖ ✔(3) ●

Young Blood ✖ ✔(3) ●

Baby It's You ✔(3) ●

Till There Was You

Love Me Do

Pop Go The Beatles ✖

Guest group: the Countrymen

20♪ Pop Go The Beatles (3)

BR: 18 JUNE 1963

REC: 1 JUNE 1963

BBC Paris Theatre, London

Producer: Terry Henebery

Presenter: Lee Peters

Pop Go The Beatles ✖

A Shot Of Rhythm And Blues ✖ ✔(3)

Memphis, Tennessee ✖

A Taste Of Honey

Sure To Fall (In Love With You) ✖ ✔(3) ●

Money (That's What I Want) ✔(3)

From Me To You

Pop Go The Beatles ✖

Guest group: Carter-Lewis and the Southerners

A rowdy version of 'Happy Birthday To You' was also featured before 'A Taste Of Honey' to celebrate Paul's twenty-first birthday.

21♪ Easy Beat

BR: 23 JUNE 1963

REC: 19 JUNE 1963

Playhouse Theatre, London

Producer: Ron Belchier

Presenter: Brian Matthew

Some Other Guy ✖ ✔(2) ●

A Taste Of Honey ✔(2)

Thank You Girl ●

From Me To You

Recorded in front of an audience.

22♪ Side By Side

BR: 24 JUNE 1963

REC: 4 APRIL 1963

BBC Paris Theatre, London

Producer: Bryant Marriott

Presenter: John Dunn

Side By Side (with the Karl Denver Trio) ✖ ✔(1)

Too Much Monkey Business ✖ ✔(1)

Love Me Do

Boys ✔(1)

I'll Be On My Way ✖ ✔(1) ●

From Me To You ✔(1)

23♪ Pop Go The Beatles (4)

BR: 25 JUNE 1963

REC: 17 JUNE 1963

Studio Number 5, BBC Maida Vale, London

Producer: Terry Henebery

Presenter: Lee Peters

Pop Go The Beatles ✖

Anna (Go To Him) ✔(3)

I Saw Her Standing There

Boys ●

Chains

P.S. I Love You

Twist And Shout ✔(3)

Pop Go The Beatles ✖

Recorded but not broadcast:

A Taste Of Honey

Guest group: the Bachelors

24♪ Saturday Club

BR: 29 JUNE 1963

REC: 24 JUNE 1963

Playhouse Theatre, London

Producers: Jimmy Grant and Bernie Andrews

Presenter: Brian Matthew

I Got To Find My Baby ✖

Memphis, Tennessee ✖

Money (That's What I Want)

Till There Was You

From Me To You

Roll Over Beethoven

25♪ The Beat Show

BR: 4 JULY 1963

REC: 3 JULY 1963

Playhouse Theatre, Manchester

Producer: Geoff Lawrence

Presenter: Gay Byrne

From Me To You

A Taste Of Honey

Twist And Shout

26♪ Pop Go The Beatles (5)

BR: 16 JULY 1963

REC: 2 JULY 1963

Number 5 Studio, BBC Maida Vale, London

Producer: Terry Henebery

Presenter: Rodney Burke

Pop Go The Beatles ✖

That's All Right Mama ✖ ✔(4) ●

There's A Place

Carol ✖ ✔(4) ●

Soldier Of Love ✖ ✔(4) ●

Lend Me Your Comb ✖ ✔(4) ●

Clarabella ✖ ✔(4) ●

Pop Go The Beatles ✖

Guest group: Duffy Power and the Graham Bond
  Quartet

Recorded but not broadcast:

Three Cool Cats ✖

Sweet Little Sixteen ✖

Ask Me Why

27♪ Easy Beat

BR: 21 JULY 1963

REC: 17 JULY 1963

Playhouse Theatre, London

Producer: Ron Belchier

Presenter: Brian Matthew

I Saw Her Standing There

A Shot Of Rhythm And Blues ✖

There's A Place

Twist And Shout

Recorded in front of an audience.

28♪ Pop Go The Beatles (6)

BR: 23 JULY 1963

REC: 10 JULY 1963

Number 2 Studio, Aeolian Hall, London

Producer: Terry Henebery

Presenter: Rodney Burke

Pop Go The Beatles ✖

Sweet Little Sixteen ✖ ✔(4) ●

A Taste Of Honey ●

Nothin' Shakin' ✖ ✔(4) ●

Love Me Do ●

Lonesome Tears In My Eyes ✖ ✔(4) ●

So How Come (No One Loves Me) ✖ ✔(4) ●

Pop Go The Beatles ✖

Guest group: Carter-Lewis and the Southerners

29♪ Pop Go The Beatles (7)

BR: 30 JULY 1963

REC: 10 JULY 1963

Number 2 Studio, Aeolian Hall, London

Producer: Terry Henebery

Presenter: Rodney Burke

Pop Go The Beatles ✖

Memphis, Tennessee ✖ ●

Do You Want To Know A Secret ✔(5)

Till There Was You

Matchbox ✔(5) ●

Please Mister Postman ✔(5)

The Hippy Hippy Shake ✖ ●

Pop Go The Beatles ✖

Guest group: the Searchers

30♪ Pop Go The Beatles (8)

BR: 6 AUGUST 1963

REC: 16 JULY 1963

BBC Paris Theatre, London

Producer: Terry Henebery

Presenter: Rodney Burke

Pop Go The Beatles ✖

I'm Gonna Sit Right Down And Cry (Over You) ✖
  ✔(5) ●

Crying, Waiting, Hoping ✖ ✔(5) ●

Kansas City/Hey!-Hey!-Hey!-Hey! ●

To Know Her Is To Love Her ✖ ✔(5) ●

The Honeymoon Song ✖ ✔(5) ●

Twist And Shout

Pop Go The Beatles ✖

Guest group: The Swinging Blue Jeans
          [produced by Ian Grant]

31♪ Pop Go The Beatles (9)

BR: 13 AUGUST 1963

REC: 16 JULY 1963

BBC Paris Theatre, London
Producers: Terry Henebery and Ian Grant
Presenter: Rodney Burke
Pop Go The Beatles ✖
Long Tall Sally ●
Please Please Me
She Loves You
You Really Got A Hold On Me
I'll Get You
I Got A Woman ✖ ●
Pop Go The Beatles ✖
Guest group: the Hollies

32♪ Pop Go The Beatles (10)

BR: 20 AUGUST 1963
REC: 16 JULY 1963
BBC Paris Theatre, London
Producer: Terry Henebery
Presenter: Rodney Burke
Pop Go The Beatles ✖
She Loves You [also broadcast in PGTB(9)]
Words Of Love
Glad All Over ✖ ✔(6) ●
I Just Don't Understand ✖ ✔(6) ●
Devil In Her Heart ●
Slow Down ●
Pop Go The Beatles ✖
Guest group: Russ Sainty and the Nu-Notes

33♪ Saturday Club

BR: 24 AUGUST 1963
REC: 30 JULY 1963
Playhouse Theatre, London
Producers: Jimmy Grant and Bernie Andrews
Presenter: Brian Matthew
Long Tall Sally
She Loves You
Glad All Over ✖
Twist And Shout
You Really Got A Hold On Me ●
I'll Get You

34♪ Pop Go The Beatles (11)

BR: 27 AUGUST 1963
REC: 1 AUGUST 1963
Playhouse Theatre, Manchester
Producer: Ian Grant
Presenter: Rodney Burke
Pop Go The Beatles ✖
Ooh! My Soul ✖ ●
Don't Ever Change ✖ ✔(6) ●
Twist And Shout
She Loves You
Anna (Go To Him)
A Shot Of Rhythm And Blues ✖ ●
Pop Go The Beatles ✖
Guest group: the Cyril Davies Rhythm and Blues All Stars with Long John Baldry

3⁶⁶ Non Stop Pop

BR: 30 AUGUST 1963
REC: 30 JULY 1963
Bandleader Phil Tate talked to the group for the 'Pop Chat' section of the show. The interview was recorded at the beginning of a *Saturday Club* session.

35♪ Pop Go The Beatles (12)

BR: 3 SEPTEMBER 1963
REC: 1 AUGUST 1963
Playhouse Theatre, Manchester
Producer: Ian Grant
Presenter: Rodney Burke
Pop Go The Beatles ✖
From Me To You
I'll Get You
Money (That's What I Want)
There's A Place
Honey Don't (John on lead vocal) ✔(6) ●
Roll Over Beethoven
Pop Go The Beatles ✖
Recorded but not broadcast:
Lucille ✖
Baby It's You
She Loves You
Guest group: Brian Poole and the Tremeloes

36♪ Pop Go The Beatles (13)

BR: 10 SEPTEMBER 1963

REC: 3 SEPTEMBER 1963

Number 2 Studio, Aeolian Hall, London

Producer: Ian Grant

Presenter: Rodney Burke

Pop Go The Beatles ✘

Too Much Monkey Business ✘ ●

Till There Was You

Love Me Do

She Loves You

I'll Get You

A Taste Of Honey

The Hippy Hippy Shake ✘

Pop Go The Beatles ✘

Guest group: Johnny Kidd and the Pirates

37♪ Pop Go The Beatles (14)

BR: 17 SEPTEMBER 1963

REC: 3 SEPTEMBER 1963

Number 2 Studio, Aeolian Hall, London

Producer: Ian Grant

Presenter: Rodney Burke

Pop Go The Beatles ✘

Chains ✔(6)

You Really Got A Hold On Me ✔(6)

Misery

Lucille ✘ ✔(6)

From Me To You

Boys

Pop Go The Beatles ✘

Recorded but not broadcast:

A Taste Of Honey

Guest group: the Marauders

38♪ Pop Go The Beatles (15)

BR: 24 SEPTEMBER 1963

REC: 3 SEPTEMBER 1963

Number 2 Studio, Aeolian Hall, London

Producer: Ian Grant

Presenter: Rodney Burke

Pop Go The Beatles ✘

She Loves You

Ask Me Why

Devil In Her Heart

I Saw Her Standing There

Sure To Fall (In Love With You) ✘

Twist And Shout ✔(6)

Pop Go The Beatles ✘

Plus a short chant of 'Goodbye George, Goodbye John, Ringo, Paul, Ringo, Paul, Rodney Burke!'.

Guest group: Tony Rivers and the Castaways

39♪ Saturday Club

BR: 5 OCTOBER 1963

REC: 7 SEPTEMBER 1963

Playhouse Theatre, London

Producers: Jimmy Grant and Bernie Andrews

Presenter: Brian Matthew

I Saw Her Standing There ✔(2)

Memphis, Tennessee ✘ ✔(2)

Happy Birthday Dear Saturday Club ✘ ✔(2)

I'll Get You ✔(2)

She Loves You ✔(2)

Lucille ✘ ✔(2) ●

40♪ Easy Beat

BR: 20 OCTOBER 1963

REC: 16 OCTOBER 1963

Playhouse Theatre, London

Producer: Ron Belchier

Presenter: Brian Matthew

I Saw Her Standing There ✔(7) ●

Love Me Do ✔(7)

Please Please Me

From Me To You

She Loves You ✔(7)

Recorded in front of an audience.

4⁴⁴ The Public Ear

BR: NOVEMBER 1963

REC: 3 OCTOBER 1963

The magazine programme included a 12-minute feature presented by Tony Hall on the Beatles and the Liverpool scene, in which he interviewed the group and other Mersey figures.

41♪ The Ken Dodd Show

BR: 3 NOVEMBER 1963

REC: 9 OCTOBER 1963

BBC Paris Theatre, London

Producer: Bill Worsley

She Loves You

42♪ The Royal Variety Performance

BR: 10 NOVEMBER 1963

REC: 4 NOVEMBER 1963

Prince of Wales Theatre, London

Producer: Arthur Phillips

Compère: Dickie Henderson

Linked by Brian Johnston

From Me To You

Till There Was You ●

Twist And Shout ●

5" Voice of the North

BR: 20 NOVEMBER 1963

REC: 20 NOVEMBER 1963

Michael Barton recorded a two-minute interview backstage at the ABC Cinema, Ardwick, Manchester, for this programme broadcast on the BBC North Home Service.

6" A World of Sound

BR: 21 NOVEMBER 1963

REC: 7 SEPTEMBER 1963

An edition subtitled 'Liverpool: A Swinging City' included an interview with Paul conducted by the programme's producer Rosemary Hart.

7" Wacker, Mach Schau

BR: 27 NOVEMBER 1963

REC: 20 NOVEMBER 1963

Michael Barton talked to George for a North Home Service programme which discussed the Liverpool and Hamburg music scenes.

43♪ Saturday Club

BR: 21 DECEMBER 1963

Christmas Edition

REC: 17 DECEMBER 1963

Playhouse Theatre, London

Producers: Jimmy Grant and Bernie Andrews

Presenter: Brian Matthew

All My Loving

This Boy ✔(13)

I Want To Hold Your Hand

Till There Was You

Roll Over Beethoven ✔(13)

She Loves You

Beatles Chrimble Muddley ✔(13)

8" Top Pops Of 1963

BR: 25 DECEMBER 1963

Christmas Day

REC: 7 DECEMBER 1963

A two-minute interview was included in Alan Freeman's Christmas Day 'survey of the year's pop scene'.

44♪ The Beatles Say From Us To You

BR: 26 DECEMBER 1963

Boxing Day Bank Holiday

REC: 18 DECEMBER 1963

BBC Paris Theatre, London

Producer: Bryant Marriott

Presenter: Rolf Harris

From Us To You ✖ ✔(13)

She Loves You ✔(13)

All My Loving

Roll Over Beethoven

Till There Was You

Boys

Money (That's What I Want)

I Saw Her Standing There

Tie Me Kangaroo Down, Sport (with Rolf Harris!) ✖ ✔(13)

I Want To Hold Your Hand ✔(13)

From Us To You ✖ ✔(13)

9⁶⁶ The Public Ear

BR: 12 JANUARY 1964

REC: 5 JANUARY 1964

George and Ringo were heard reading their letter for the programme's 'Air Mail' slot.

10⁶⁶ Saturday Club

BR: 8 FEBRUARY 1964

REC: 7 FEBRUARY 1964

On the day of the Beatles' arrival in the USA they answered questions put to them over the phone by Brian Matthew. The interview – in which George advised Bernie Andrews 'to get his hair cut!' – was broadcast the following day, together with a description by BBC correspondent Malcolm Davis of the Beatles' ecstatic New York welcome. 'Well, they have arrived and such a reception has never been given a head of state. New Yorkers are now without doubt besieged with Beatlemania.'

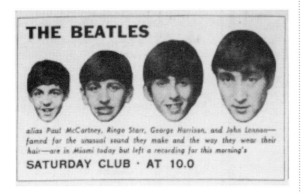

THE BEATLES

alias Paul McCartney, Ringo Starr, George Harrison, and John Lennon— famed for the unusual sound they make and the way they wear their hair—are in Miami today but left a recording for this morning's

SATURDAY CLUB · AT 10.0

45♪ Saturday Club

BR: 15 FEBRUARY 1964

REC: 7 JANUARY 1964

Playhouse Theatre, London

Producers: Jimmy Grant and Bernie Andrews

Presenter: Brian Matthew

All My Loving

Money (That's What I Want)

The Hippy Hippy Shake ✘

I Want To Hold Your Hand ✔(7)

Roll Over Beethoven

Johnny B. Goode ✘ ✔(7) ●

I Wanna Be Your Man

11⁶⁶ Saturday Club

BR: 22 FEBRUARY 1996

REC: 22 FEBRUARY 1996

The Beatles talked to Brian Matthew on the phone from London Airport just after their return flight from America had touched down.

12⁶⁶ Today

BR: 18 MARCH 1964

REC: 17 MARCH 1964

On location for the movie *A Hard Day's Night* at the London club Les Ambassadeurs, John was interviewed by presenter Jack de Manio about his forthcoming book *In His Own Write*.

13⁶⁶ The Public Ear

BR: 22 MARCH 1964

REC: 18 AND 19 MARCH 1964

While on the set at Twickenham Film Studios for *A Hard Day's Night*, the Beatles recorded various speech items for *The Public Ear*. George interviewed Ringo about *In His Own Write* and also talked to John who read 'Alec Speaking'. The next day, George interviewed Paul about the movie while in a car heading to the Variety Club Awards at the Dorchester Hotel. George and Ringo read out the programme's production credits... including themselves in the list!

46♪ From Us To You Say The Beatles

BR: 30 MARCH 1964

Easter Monday

REC: 28 FEBRUARY 1964

Number 1 Studio, Piccadilly Theatre, London

Producer: Bryant Marriott

Presenter: Alan Freeman

From Us To You ✘ ✔(8) ●

You Can't Do That

Roll Over Beethoven ✔(8) ●

Till There Was You ✔(8) ●

I Wanna Be Your Man ✔(8) ●

Please Mister Postman

All My Loving ✔(8) ●

This Boy

Can't Buy Me Love ✔(8) ●

From Us To You ✖

This is the only Beatles session from which five songs were actually kept in the main BBC Sound Archive on a one-sided LP disc.

47♪ Saturday Club

BR: 4 APRIL 1964

REC: 31 MARCH 1964

Playhouse Theatre, London

Producers: Jimmy Grant and Bernie Andrews

Presenter: Brian Matthew

Everybody's Trying To Be My Baby

I Call Your Name

I Got A Woman ✖ ✔(9)

You Can't Do That ✔(8)

Can't Buy Me Love

Sure To Fall (In Love With You) ✖ ✔(9)

Long Tall Sally

14❝ Movie-Go-Round

BR: 12 APRIL 1964

REC: 19 AND 20 MARCH 1964

Interviews conducted by film columnist Peter Noble at Twickenham Film Studios.

15❝ Scottish News

BR: 29 APRIL 1964

REC: 29 APRIL 1964

The Scottish Home Service broadcast an interview recorded with Bill Aitkenhead in the Beatles' dressing room in the ABC Cinema, Edinburgh.

16❝ A Slice of Life

BR: 2 MAY 1964

REC: 31 MARCH 1964

This edition of the Home Service programme focussed on hobbies and John was interviewed by Brian Matthew about his pastime of writing the unusual poems and prose published in his first book.

48♪ From Us To You Say The Beatles

BR: 18 MAY 1964

Whit Monday

REC: 1 MAY 1964

BBC Paris Theatre, London

Producer: Bryant Marriott

Presenter: Alan Freeman

From Us To You ✖

I Saw Her Standing There

Kansas City/Hey!-Hey!-Hey!-Hey!

I Forgot To Remember To Forget ✖ ✔(8) ●

You Can't Do That

Sure To Fall (In Love With You) ✖ ✔(8)

Can't Buy Me Love

Matchbox

Honey Don't (John on lead vocal) ✔(8)

From Us To You ✖

Plus two versions of 'Whit Monday To You' – an adaptation of 'Happy Birthday To You'.

17❝ Roundabout

BR: 27 JUNE 1964

REC: 20 JUNE 1964

The Beatles were recorded talking on the telephone from Sydney on the third day of their concerts at the local Stadium for a programme billed as 'an easy-going mixture of news, views and music'.

18❝ The Teen Scene

BR: 9 JULY 1964

REC: 7 JULY 1964

New Musical Express editor Chris Hutchins talked to John about the movie *A Hard Day's Night*, which had received its world première that week.

49♪ Top Gear

BR: 16 JULY 1964

REC: 14 JULY 1964

Studio S2, Broadcasting House, London

Producer: Bernie Andrews

Presenter: Brian Matthew

Long Tall Sally ✔(9)

Things We Said Today ✔(9) ●

A Hard Day's Night ✔(9) ●
And I Love Her ✔(9)
If I Fell
You Can't Do That
Played from a disc: *I Should Have Known Better*

50♪ The Beatles Say From Us To You

BR: 3 AUGUST 1964
August Bank Holiday Monday
REC: 17 JULY 1964
BBC Paris Theatre, London
Producer: Bryant Marriott
Presenter: Don Wardell
From Us To You ✖
Long Tall Sally
If I Fell
I'm Happy Just To Dance With You
Things We Said Today
I Should Have Known Better
Boys
Kansas City/Hey!-Hey!-Hey!-Hey!
A Hard Day's Night
From Us To You ✖

19" The Teen Scene

BR: 13 AUGUST 1964
REC: 12 AUGUST 1964
Chris Hutchins interviewed Ringo, who talked about the North American concert tour beginning the following week.

51♪ Top Gear

BR: 26 NOVEMBER 1964
REC: 17 NOVEMBER 1964
Playhouse Theatre, London
Producer: Bernie Andrews
Presenter: Brian Matthew
I'm A Loser ✔(10) ●
Honey Don't ✔(10)
She's A Woman ✔(10) ●
Everybody's Trying To Be My Baby ●
I'll Follow The Sun ✔(10) ●
I Feel Fine ✔(9) ●

In 1988, a tape – marked 'Reel 2 of 2' – was uncovered in a BBC Archive, with false starts, several takes (complete and incompete) of 'I Feel Fine' and 'She's A Woman'. This reel is the original tape that a BBC Transcription recording engineer will have been running during the session. Sadly, Reel 1 remains lost.

20" The Teen Scene

BR: 29 NOVEMBER 1964
REC: 28 NOVEMBER 1964
Chris Hutchins interviewed John about his new house 'Kenwood' in Weybridge, Surrey.

52♪ Saturday Club

BR: 26 DECEMBER 1964
Boxing Day Bank Holiday
REC: 25 NOVEMBER 1964
Number 2 Studio, Aeolian Hall
Producers: Jimmy Grant and Brian Willey
Presenter: Brian Matthew
Rock And Roll Music ✔(11) ●
I'm A Loser ●
Everybody's Trying To Be My Baby ✔(11) ●
I Feel Fine ●
Kansas City/Hey!-Hey!-Hey!-Hey! ✔(11)
She's A Woman ●
'I'm A Loser', 'Everybody's Trying To Be My Baby', 'I Feel Fine' and 'She's A Woman' were actually repeats of the versions recorded in the November *Top Gear* session.

21" Saturday Club

BR: 20 MARCH 1965
REC: 19 MARCH 1965
The group talked to Brian Matthew over the phone from a hotel room in Obertauen, Austria, where they were on location for their second movie *Help!*

22" Pop Inn

BR: 13 APRIL 1965
100th edition
LIVE
Sitting in a BBC radio car, the Beatles' voices were beamed from Twickenham Film Studios onto the air.

The BBC's Radio Times pushed the boat out for 'Bernie's new vessel' Top Gear when they featured the programme on the front cover. No mean exposure as the magazine has long been one of the biggest sellers in Europe. The Beatles were first featured on its cover to celebrate a fab Saturday evening of TV when all four were panel members for Juke Box Jury and It's the Beatles showed them in concert.

53♪ The Beatles Invite You To Take A Ticket To Ride

BR: 7 JUNE 1965

Whit Monday Bank Holiday

REC: 26 MAY 1965

Number 1 Studio, Piccadilly Theatre, London

Producer: Keith Bateson

Presenter: Denny Piercy

Ticket To Ride (short version)

Everybody's Trying To Be My Baby

I'm A Loser

The Night Before

Honey Don't

Dizzy Miss Lizzy ✔(11) ●

She's A Woman

Ticket To Ride ✔(11) ●

23" Late Night Extra

BR: 11 JUNE 1965

REC: 11 JUNE 1965

Paul was interviewed over the telephone when news broke of the Beatles receiving MBEs in the Queen's Birthday Honours List.

24" Today

BR: 21 JUNE 1965

REC: 16 JUNE 1965

The Home Service news programme included John talking to reporter Tim Matthews and reading two verses of 'The National Health Cow' from his new book *A Spaniard in the Works*.

25" The World of Books

BR: 3 JULY 1965

REC: 16 JUNE 1965

John was interviewed about *A Spaniard in the Works* by BBC producer Wilfred De'Ath for the Home Service programme *The World of Books*.

26" Lance A' GoGo

BR: 31 JULY 1965

REC: 30 JULY 1965

The group were interviewed by singer and actor Lance Percival for his show, billed as 'half an hour of quiet pandemonium'.

27" The Beatles Abroad

BR: 30 AUGUST 1965

August Bank Holiday Monday

REC: 15-20 AUGUST 1965

Brian Matthew presented a 45-minute behind-the-scenes feature about the Beatles tour of North America and particularly the Shea Stadium concert. The Beatles were heard talking – and George strumming – in hotel rooms.

28" Saturday Club

BR: 25 DECEMBER 1965

Christmas Day

REC: 29 NOVEMBER 1965

Brian Matthew engaged the group in merry banter, including a 'Beatle Box Jury' verdict on his performance of Stanley Holloway's monologue 'Brahn Boots' and a sung version of the show's instrumental theme 'Saturday Jump'.

29" Saturday Club

BR: 4 JUNE 1966

REC: 2 MAY 1966

400th edition

The Beatles were featured several times in conversation with Brian Matthew but it was Cliff Richard and the Shadows who topped the musical bill for this special show.

30" Today

BR: 8 JULY 1966

REC: 8 JULY 1966

George and Ringo were interviewed by reporter Tom Mangold on their arrival from India (after concerts in Tokyo and the Philippines).

31⁶⁶ David Frost at the Phonograph

BR: 6 AUGUST 1966

REC: 1 AUGUST 1966

Paul was interviewed for this programme of gramophone records and chat.

32⁶⁶ The Lennon and McCartney Songbook

BR: 29 AUGUST 1966

August Bank Holiday Monday

REC: 6 AUGUST 1966

Keith Fordyce sought comments on a collection of cover versions by mostly conservative artists. Paul was diplomatic and tried hard; John remained subdued and did not pay attention.

33⁶⁶ The Lively Arts

BR: 11 DECEMBER 1966

REC: 20 SEPTEMBER 1966

The Home Service programme featured George, who was interviewed in Bombay by the BBC's correspondent Donald Milner about his burgeoning interest in India in an item entitled 'A Beatle Goes East'.

34⁶⁶ The Ivor Novello Awards for 1966

BR: 27 MARCH 1967

Easter Monday

REC: 20 MARCH 1967

John and Paul won three awards, for 'Yellow Submarine', 'Michelle' and 'Yesterday', but did not attend the ceremony. Their acceptance speeches were taped a week before during recording sessions for *Sgt Pepper* at Abbey Road.

35⁶⁶ Where It's At

BR: 20 MAY 1967

REC: MAY 1967

Kenny Everett put together features with John, Paul and Ringo that introduced all but two of the tracks on *Sgt Pepper's Lonely Hearts Club Band*. The Light Programme's 'hippest' show was presented by Chris Denning.

36⁶⁶ Where It's At

BR: 1 JULY 1967

REC: JUNE 1967

Paul talked to Kenny Everett about the forthcoming single 'All You Need Is Love' which was first heard on the global TV broadcast *Our World*.

37⁶⁶ Scene and Heard

BR: 30 SEPTEMBER 1967

REC: 13 SEPTEMBER 1967

Radio 1

George was interviewed by Miranda Ward for the first edition of a pop magazine programme broadcast on the launch day of Radio 1. Recorded at the Atlantic Hotel in Newquay, he talked about the filming of *Magical Mystery Tour* and his enthusiasm for Indian spirituality.

38⁶⁶ Scene and Heard

BR: 7 OCTOBER 1967

REC: 13 SEPTEMBER 1967

Radio 1

Part 2 of Miranda Ward's interview with George.

39⁶⁶ Scene and Heard

BR: 14 OCTOBER 1967

REC: 14 SEPTEMBER 1967

Radio 1

During filming of the Cornish scenes for *Magical Mystery Tour*, Miranda Ward also caught up with Ringo at the Atlantic Hotel, Newquay.

40⁶⁶ Where It's At

BR: 25 NOVEMBER 1967

REC: NOVEMBER 1967

Radio 1

Kenny Everett and Chris Denning interviewed John and during their casual ramblings some details emerged about the making of *Magical Mystery Tour*. Paul also recorded a musical jingle with the repeated line 'Kenny Everett and Chris Denning all together on the wireless machine'.

41 Late Night Extra

BR: 5 DECEMBER 1967

REC: 5 DECEMBER 1967

Radio 1/Radio 2

John and Cilla Black talked to Brian Cullingford at the launch party of the Apple shop in Baker Street.

42 Kenny Everett

BR: 4 FEBRUARY 1968

REC: 27 JANUARY 1968

Radio 1

John was interviewed for Kenny Everett's Sunday morning show at his house in Weybridge, Surrey.

43 Kenny Everett

BR: 9 JUNE 1968

REC: 6 JUNE 1968

Radio 1

An interview primarily with John, who toyed with an unplugged electric guitar and burst into song occasionally. Paul and Ringo joined in for some 'goodbye jingles' to mark Kenny's transfer from his Sunday slot to a weekday evening show called *Foreverett*. The interview was recorded at Abbey Road during the first phase of recording of *The Beatles* ('White Album').

44 Late Night Extra

BR: 6 AUGUST 1968

REC: 6 AUGUST 1968

Radio 1/Radio 2

BBC reporter Matthew Robinson interviewed John – and Pattie Harrison and fashion editor Suzy Menkes – at a fashion show in the Revolution Club.

45 Scene and Heard

BR: 28 SEPTEMBER 1968

REC: 18 SEPTEMBER 1968

Radio 1

George was interviewed by *New Musical Express* writer Alan Smith for the pop magazine programme presented by Johnny Moran.

46 Night Ride

BR: 11 DECEMBER 1968

LIVE

Radio 1/Radio 2

John and Yoko took part in the filming of *The Rolling Stones' Rock and Roll Circus* in Wembley and then visited John Peel during his eclectic hour of the Wednesday *Night Ride* programme. They discussed *Unfinished Music No. 1: Two Virgins*, which was released the previous week. One reverend gentleman complained about the programme – describing the silences as obscene!

47 Scene and Heard

BR: 25 JANUARY 1969

REC: 21 JANUARY 1969

Radio 1

During a car journey to London, *Daily Express* writer David Wigg interviewed Ringo about the rumours of a Beatles split and the group's financial state.

48 Scene and Heard

BR: 8 MARCH 1969

REC: 4 MARCH 1969

Radio 1

George was interviewed at the Apple office in Savile Row, London, by David Wigg.

49 Scene and Heard

BR: 12 APRIL 1969

REC: 4 MARCH 1969

Radio 1

More from the David Wigg interview with George.

50 Night Ride

BR: 1 APRIL 1969

REC: 1 APRIL 1969

Radio 1/Radio 2

On his return from Amsterdam, John discussed with Ian Ross the events of the Bed-In he and Yoko had staged for peace.

51 " The World at One

BR: 3 APRIL 1969

REC: 3 APRIL 1969

Radio 4

George talked to Sue MacGregor about his friend and sitar teacher, the virtuoso player Ravi Shankar.

52 " Scene and Heard

BR: 11 MAY 1969

REC: 8 MAY 1969

Radio 1

John and Yoko talked to David Wigg about their campaign for peace, including their recent Amsterdam Bed-In.

53 " Scene and Heard

BR: 18 MAY 1969

REC: 8 MAY 1969

Radio 1

More from David Wigg's John and Yoko interview.

54 " Light and Local

BR: 16 MAY 1969

REC: 15 MAY 1969

BBC Radio Merseyside

Paul gave a very relaxed and candid interview to Ray Corlett, one of his former school friends, at the Liverpool Institute.

55 " Everett Is Here

BR: 20 SEPTEMBER 1969

REC: 14 AUGUST 1969

Radio 1

A Kenny Everett interview with John, which had been delayed until the release of the *Abbey Road* album at the end of September.

56 " Scene and Heard

BR: 21 SEPTEMBER 1969

REC: 19 SEPTEMBER 1969

Radio 1

Paul talked to David Wigg about tracks from the new album *Abbey Road*.

57 " Everett Is Here

BR: 27 SEPTEMBER 1969

REC: 14 AUGUST 1969

Radio 1

More from the interview with John recorded at Abbey Road studios for Kenny's Saturday morning show.

58 " Scene and Heard

BR: 28 SEPTEMBER 1969

REC: 19 SEPTEMBER 1969

Radio 1

A continuation of David Wigg's conversation with Paul.

59 " Scene and Heard

BR: 12 OCTOBER 1969

REC: 8 OCTOBER 1969

Radio 1

George discussed financial matters, songwriting, his spiritual beliefs and his recent production of the Radha Krishna Temple's UK hit 'Hare Krishna Mantra'. David Wigg was in attendance, of course.

60 " Scene and Heard

BR: 19 OCTOBER 1969

REC: 8 OCTOBER 1969

Radio 1

More from the interview with George.

61 " The World This Weekend

BR: 26 OCTOBER 1969

REC: 24 OCTOBER 1969

Radio 4

When the 'Paul is dead' myth was concocted and disseminated by an American DJ, BBC reporter Chris Drake journeyed to the McCartneys' remote Scottish farmhouse. On the windswept moorland he talked to the harassed couple who had wanted to retreat from the world for a while.

Above: Radio Times gets groovy for the launch of Radio 1 on 30 September 1967. Next page: Visiting the group in the studio in 1963. From left, former singer Dick James — who formed the music publishing company Northern Songs for Lennon-McCartney compositions — and their manager Brian Epstein.

62 " Scene and Heard

BR: 26 OCTOBER 1969

REC: 21 OCTOBER 1969

Radio 1

Beatle domination of this weekly show continued with David Wigg's interview with John.

63 " Today

BR: 26 NOVEMBER 1969

REC: 25 NOVEMBER 1969

Radio 4

John returned his MBE medal as an act of protest 'against Britain's involvement in the Nigeria-Biafra thing, against our support of America in Vietnam and against 'Cold Turkey' slipping down the charts'. Naturally, this generated more publicity for his peace campaign and John's interview with David Bellan was included in this breakfast news programme.

64 " Late Night Extra

BR: 15 DECEMBER 1969

REC: 3 DECEMBER 1969

Radio 2

During the first week of December 1969, John and Yoko were filmed for the BBC TV documentary series *24 Hours*. The night the programme was shown, this Radio 2 programme broadcast an extract – the Lennons' fiery encounter with American writer Gloria Emerson. She had no patience for John and Yoko's antics for peace – 'You've made yourself look ridiculous' – but the couple were unbowed. (The footage was later included in the 1988 film documentary *Imagine John Lennon*)

65 " Kenny Everett's Christmas Show

BR: 25 DECEMBER 1969

Christmas Day

REC: 15 DECEMBER 1969

Radio 1

During this show, Ringo made an appeal on behalf of The British Wireless for the Blind Fund.

66 " Scene and Heard

BR: 15 FEBRUARY 1970

REC: 6 FEBRUARY 1970

Radio 1

On the day 'Instant Karma' was released, David Wigg talked to John and Yoko about the uncertain future of the Beatles – 'it could be a rebirth or a death'.

67 " Scene and Heard

BR: 15 MARCH 1970

REC: 11 MARCH 1970

Radio 1

Short extracts were included from an interview with George conducted by the programme's presenter Johnny Moran. Their conversation was featured in a 44-minute special two weeks later.

68 " Scene and Heard

BR: 29 MARCH 1970

REC: 25 MARCH 1970

Radio 1

Ringo was interviewed by David Wigg (natch!).

69 " Scene and Heard

BR: 5 APRIL 1970

REC: 25 MARCH 1970

Radio 1

Another extract from the Ringo interview.

70 " The Beatles Today

BR: 30 MARCH 1970

Easter Monday

REC: 11 MARCH 1970

Radio 1

George talked about his songwriting, his production of Apple artists and the *Let It Be* film and album.

71 " Open House

BR: 31 MARCH 1970

LIVE

Radio 1/Radio 2

Pete Murray talked to Ringo about his just released album *Sentimental Journey*.

Complete Radio Songs Listing

....

For each song the following information is given:

Song Title   Lead vocal
   [Composer]
BBC programme
   DATE OF BROADCAST
Any other points of interest

✖ Denotes that the song was not on any Beatles records released on the Parlophone and Apple labels between October 1962 and April 1970.

● Denotes the BBC performances featured on the album *The Beatles Live at the BBC* (November 1994) and two other releases:
In March 1995, 'Baby It's You' (*Pop Go The Beatles* 11 June 1963) was made the lead track of a single. Three BBC recordings not included on *Live at the BBC* were also featured on this release – 'I'll Follow The Sun' (*Top Gear* 26 November 1964), 'Devil In Her Heart' (*Pop Go The Beatles* 20 August 1963) and 'Boys' (*Pop Go The Beatles* 25 June 1963).

Among the tracks excavated for *Anthology I* in November 1995, were 'Lend Me Your Comb' (*Pop Go The Beatles* 16 July 1963) and 'Till There Was You' and 'Twist And Shout' from the *Royal Variety Performance* broadcast on BBC Radio on 10 November 1963.

◆ Denotes which of the BBC performances of the song was released.

(PB) Denotes that Pete Best is playing drums, not Ringo Starr.

....

All My Loving ●   Paul   30 MARCH 1964 ◆
   [Lennon-McCartney]   One of the strongest tracks from the second album
Saturday Club   *With The Beatles* released in November 1963, this
   21 DECEMBER 1963   became the title track of their fourth EP in February
From Us To You   1964. It was also the opening song of their live debut
   26 DECEMBER 1963   on American television's top-rated *The Ed Sullivan*
Saturday Club   *Show*, a performance available on *Anthology 1*. The
   15 FEBRUARY 1964   song's melodic strengths reached out to older listeners,
From Us To You   mainly through jazz and easy listening versions. In the

August 1966 BBC radio show *The Lennon and McCartney Songbook*, John commented that English balladeer Matt Monro 'did it how people imagined it should be done' and Paul agreed: '...it changed a few people's minds about us... everyone said, "Oh, that's a nice song isn't it?", whereas beforehand they thought it was just a gay little ditty!'.

And I Love Her   Paul

[Lennon-McCartney]

Top Gear

16 JULY 1964

Featured in the film and released on the soundtrack album of *A Hard Day's Night* in July 1964, this song quickly acquired standard status with smooth versions by Lena Horne, Sarah Vaughan and Jack Jones. During this BBC performance, George played his solo on electric guitar rather than the nylon acoustic used on the record, placing the BBC arrangement midway between the early EMI takes (as on *Anthology 1*) and the finished master.

Anna (Go To Him)   John

[Alexander]

Pop Go The Beatles

25 JUNE 1963

Pop Go The Beatles

27 AUGUST 1963

Originally a Top Ten hit in the US R & B chart for Southern soul singer Arthur Alexander, the Beatles' version was released on their debut album *Please Please Me*.

Ask Me Why   John

[Lennon-McCartney]

Here We Go

15 JUNE 1962 **(PB)**

Here We Go

25 JANUARY 1963

The Talent Spot

29 JANUARY 1963

Pop Go The Beatles

24 SEPTEMBER 1963

First issued as the B-side of 'Please Please Me' in January 1963 but also captured in December 1962 on an amateur recording in the Star-Club, Hamburg. That decidedly lo-fi recording eventually escaped in May 1977 and has made further breakouts since then.

Baby It's You ●   John

[David-Bacharach-Williams]

Side By Side

22 APRIL 1963

Pop Go The Beatles

11 JUNE 1963 ◆

Great admirers of the American girl-groups of the early sixties, the Beatles covered this Top Ten hit for the Shirelles on their first album *Please Please Me*. The BBC interpretations feature a cute ending rather than the familiar fade-out on the record.

Beautiful Dreamer ✗   Paul

[Foster]

Saturday Club

26 JANUARY 1963

The song was written in the late nineteenth century by American writer Stephen Foster and subsequent recordings by crooners Bing Crosby and Al Jolson ensured its endurance as a popular standard. In the late fifties, there was a fashion for reviving 'oldies' by adding a faster rock beat – British singer Jackie Lynton specialized in this with 'Over the Rainbow', 'Teddy Bears' Picnic' and 'All of Me'. As Paul recalled in 1988, 'I looked at the recording scene and realized that a few people were taking offbeat songs, putting them in their acts and modernizing them a bit.' Later in 1963, other Liverpool acts – Rory Storm and the Hurricanes, the Searchers and Billy J. Kramer – had their versions of the song released.

Besame Mucho ✗   Paul

[Velazquez-Skylar]

Here We Go

15 JUNE 1962 **(PB)**

A standard that was popularized during the Second World War by the likes of 'Hutch', Vera Lynn, Carroll

Gibbons' Savoy Hotel Orpheans and Joe Loss. The Beatles' version, however, was inspired by a quirky rendition by one of their favourite American R & B groups, the Coasters, whose take on the song was spread over two sides of a single in 1960. With Pete Best still their drummer, they taped it at their first EMI session in June 1962 but the track remained unreleased until its inclusion on *Anthology 1*.

Boys ●   Ringo
    [Dixon-Farrell]
Side By Side
    13 MAY 1963
Saturday Club
    25 MAY 1963
Side By Side
    24 JUNE 1963
Pop Go The Beatles
    25 JUNE 1963 ◆
Pop Go The Beatles
    17 SEPTEMBER 1963
From Us To You
    26 DECEMBER 1963
From Us To You
    3 AUGUST 1964
The Shirelles' original was on the flip-side of their biggest British hit 'Will You Love Me Tomorrow'. The Beatles' first album includes 'Boy's and the many performances at the BBC reflect the song's position as Ringo's featured vocal on stage.

Can't Buy Me Love ●   Paul
    [Lennon-McCartney]
From Us To You
    30 MARCH 1964 ◆
Saturday Club
    4 APRIL 1964
From Us To You
    18 MAY 1964
Released as a single in March 1964 and then featured both in the film and on the album *A Hard Day's Night*. There is also a live version recorded on 30 August 1965 at the Hollywood Bowl and an early

EMI take on *Anthology 1*. When jazz diva Ella Fitzgerald selected the song, the group were accorded recognition as something other than a mere teen phenomenon. 'I love it,' said Paul of her swinging seal of approval. 'She was *the* first [to do a Beatles song] of the sort of great, big, all-time, who do you like? Oh, Ella! singers!' In the same interview, featured in *The Lennon and McCartney Songbook*, John reflected: 'That was a little click of time: we thought, "Oh, one of those has done one, have they?"'

Carol ✗ ●   John
    [Berry]
Pop Go The Beatles
    16 JULY 1963 ◆
A US Top Twenty hit for Chuck Berry in 1958, which the Rolling Stones included on their first album in June 1964. 'If you tried to give rock 'n' roll another name, you might call it "Chuck Berry",' John later suggested!

Chains   George
    [Goffin-King]
Here We Go
    25 JANUARY 1963
Side By Side
    13 MAY 1963
Pop Go The Beatles
    25 JUNE 1963
Pop Go The Beatles
    17 SEPTEMBER 1963
The original by the Cookies – female backing singers on many other Goffin and King hits on the Dimension label – was climbing the US charts when the Beatles first tried this song out in a studio. Their version was released on *Please Please Me* in March 1963 and also the EP *The Beatles (No.1)* six months later.

Chrimble Muddley ✗   John
    [Lennon-McCartney; Marks; Eddy-Hazlewood]
Saturday Club
    21 DECEMBER 1963
A half-minute of Christmas fun, in which John –

double-tracked! – sings the titles or snatches of lyrics from the five Beatles hit singles to date ('Love Me Do', 'Please Please Me', 'From Me To You', 'She Loves You' and 'I Want To Hold Your Hand')… and Rudolph The Red-Nosed Reindeer. Presenter Brian Matthew describes it as a 'muddley… I'm sorry… medley'. The linking riff played on guitar and bass was borrowed from Duane Eddy's 'Shazam!'.

Clarabella ✘ ●   Paul

[Pingatore]

Pop Go The Beatles

16 JULY 1963 ◆

In the Beatles' set list since 1960, this obscure favourite of Paul's was originally recorded in 1956 by the Jodimars – *JO*ey Di'Ambrosia, *DI*ck Richards and *MAR*rshall Lytle – who were refugees from Bill Haley's Comets.

Crying, Waiting, Hoping ✘ ●   George

[Holly]

Pop Go The Beatles

6 AUGUST 1963 ◆

First recorded by Buddy Holly in his New York apartment just weeks before he died in a plane crash in February 1959. His rudimentary demo was overdubbed by two different groups of musicians for release in the year he died and later in 1963. The Beatles played it at their audition for Decca Records on 1 January 1962.

Devil In Her Heart ●   George

[Drapkin]

Pop Go The Beatles

20 AUGUST 1963 ◆

Pop Go The Beatles

24 SEPTEMBER 1963

The first BBC performance of this obscure song by girl-group the Donays was released on the 'Baby It's You' single in 1995. It was one of 18 songs recorded at a marathon session on 16 July 1963. Two days later the EMI version was taped for the second album *With The Beatles*, by which time George had a firmer grasp of the words!

Dizzy Miss Lizzy ●   John

[Williams]

The Beatles Invite You To Take A Ticket To Ride

7 JUNE 1965 ◆

A minor American hit on Specialty Records – the label that issued Little Richard's classics – and one of three Larry Williams rockers the Beatles covered on record. The other two were 'Slow Down' (featured on the *Long Tall Sally* EP) and 'Bad Boy' (released in the UK on *A Collection of Beatles Oldies* 18 months after its inclusion on the American album *Beatles VI*).

Don't Ever Change ✘ ●   George

[Goffin-King]

Pop Go The Beatles

27 AUGUST 1963 ◆

A UK Top Five hit in the summer of 1962 for the Crickets, the group who had backed Buddy Holly on most of his hits before his tragic death in February 1959.

Do You Want To Know A Secret   George

[Lennon-McCartney]

Here We Go

12 MARCH 1963

On The Scene

28 MARCH 1963

Side By Side

22 APRIL 1963

Saturday Club

25 MAY 1963

Pop Go The Beatles

4 JUNE 1963

Pop Go The Beatles

30 JULY 1963

The first BBC performance of this song was heard 10 days before its release on the *Please Please Me* album. The Beatles' Parlophone producer George Martin recorded it again with Billy J. Kramer and the Dakotas, who were also managed by Brian Epstein. Released as a single in April 1963, it peaked at number two – stuck behind the Beatles second chart topper 'From Me To You'.

During The Ken Dodd Show, *the BBC Variety Orchestra watch the Beatles perform 'She Loves You' while squeezed onto the stage of the Paris Theatre. Originally a cinema, the venue in Lower Regent Street, London was used for many acclaimed BBC comedy shows, including* The Goon Show, *and also for the Radio 1* In Concert *series.*

Dream Baby ✖   Paul

[Walker]

Teenagers Turn – Here We Go

8 MARCH 1962 **(PB)**

The Roy Orbison original had just entered the UK
Top 30 when the group recorded this song for their
radio debut. A little over a year later, the Beatles and
'The Big O' appeared together on a 21-date tour of
Britain. Much much later, Orbison – as Lefty – played
with George/Nelson in the Traveling Wilburys.

Everybody's Trying To Be My Baby ●   George

[Perkins]

Pop Go The Beatles

4 JUNE 1963

Saturday Club

4 APRIL 1964

Top Gear

26 NOVEMBER 1964 ◆

Saturday Club

26 DECEMBER 1964 ◆

The Beatles Invite You to Take A Ticket To Ride

7 JUNE 1965

Featured on the 1959 UK London-American album *Carl Perkins*, the group had been performing this song for over three years before its release on their LP *Beatles For Sale*. They had taped the first BBC performance 17 months before knocking it off for record in one take at Abbey Road. *Anthology 2* features the song played live at their first ground-breaking – and ear-shattering – 1965 concert at Shea Stadium, New York.

From Me To You   John and Paul

[Lennon-McCartney]

Easy Beat

   7 APRIL 1963

Swinging Sound '63

   18 APRIL 1963

Side By Side

   22 APRIL 1963

Side By Side

   13 MAY 1963

Saturday Club

   25 MAY 1963

Steppin' Out

   3 JUNE 1963

Pop Go The Beatles

   4 JUNE 1963

Pop Go The Beatles

   18 JUNE 1963

Easy Beat

   23 JUNE 1963

Side By Side

   24 JUNE 1963

Saturday Club

   29 JUNE 1963

The Beat Show

   4 JULY 1963

Pop Go The Beatles

   3 SEPTEMBER 1963

Pop Go The Beatles

   17 SEPTEMBER 1963

Easy Beat

   20 OCTOBER 1963

Royal Variety Performance

   10 NOVEMBER 1963

With 16 broadcasts, their third single was the group's most frequently performed song at the BBC. Number one in the UK throughout May and June 1963, 'From Me To You' was the first Lennon-McCartney song to crack the US charts when Del Shannon's cover entered in July. *Cashbox* described it as 'an infectious thump-a-twist version' but Shannon's record only dented the lower end of the magazine's Top 100. The American singer topped the bill of the live radio concert *Swinging Sound '63* and, following the group onto the stage of the Royal Albert Hall, he witnessed the developing Beatles phenomenon at first hand.

From Us To You ✗ ●   John and Paul

(Two versions: Opening and Closing with extended instrumental)

[Lennon-McCartney]

From Us To You

   26 DECEMBER 1963

From Us To You

   30 MARCH 1964 ◆

From Us To You

   18 MAY 1964 ◆

From Us To You

   3 AUGUST 1964 ◆

The signature tune and title of four programmes broadcast on public holidays. This adaptation of *From Me To You* was heard on Boxing Day 1963 and the three 1964 shows broadcast on the Easter, Whitsun and August Bank Holidays. In this variation, the lyrics more closely mirrored the song's inspiration – the title of the *New Musical Express* letters page 'From You To Us'.

Glad All Over ✗ ●   George

[Bennett-Tepper-Schroeder]

Pop Go The Beatles

   20 AUGUST 1963 ◆

Saturday Club

   24 AUGUST 1963

The third British single release for Carl Perkins in December 1958 and a Beatles' live number since 1960. George played the song with a 'dream team' band assembled to pay tribute to Carl in a TV concert in

1985. It was the first time Ringo and George had appeared on a British stage together since 1966, as they bopped the blues with Eric Clapton, Dave Edmunds and their rockabilly hero.

Happy Birthday Dear Saturday Club ✖ John

[Hill-Hill)

Saturday Club

5 OCTOBER 1963

On the fifth birthday edition of the Light Programme's most successful live music show, the Beatles performed this in an arrangement inspired by a current Top Ten hit by Heinz – 'Just Like Eddie' (Cochran, that is). Brian Matthew's response was: 'Isn't that nice? And thank you, Dear Beatles!'.

A Hard Day's Night ● John and Paul

[Lennon-McCartney]

Top Gear

16 JULY 1964 ◆

From Us To You

3 AUGUST 1964

The first Beatles' movie was about to open and the title song was on its way to number one when they taped the first BBC performance. The instrumental section, of 12-string guitar doubled with a piano, was rather obviously dubbed from the record and cut into the session tape. Producer Bernie Andrews remembers that they were expecting George Martin to come to the studio to play the piano part, but he never made it. The solo on the *From Us To You* version, made three days later, was picked out on an electric 12-string with generous echo. A live Beatles performance recorded in August 1965 appeared on the *Hollywood Bowl* album in 1977. Peter Sellers' hilarious oration of 'A Hard Day's Night', as if he were Laurence Olivier portraying Richard III, was produced by George Martin and released for Christmas 1965.

The Hippy Hippy Shake ✖ ● Paul

[Romero]

Saturday Club

16 MARCH 1963

Pop Go The Beatles

4 JUNE 1963

Pop Go The Beatles

30 JULY 1963 ◆

Pop Go The Beatles

10 SEPTEMBER 1963

Saturday Club

15 FEBRUARY 1964

Originally recorded by Chan Romero in 1959, this song became a Liverpool anthem which gave the Swinging Blue Jeans a British hit in early 1964. Cheekily, the Beatles' taped their last BBC performance of the song when their Merseybeat *compadrés* were in the Top Three with it. The 1962 Star-Club tape also features a live Beatles' rendition.

Honey Don't ● Ringo

[Perkins]

Pop Go The Beatles

3 SEPTEMBER 1963 (JOHN) ◆

From Us To You

18 MAY 1964 (JOHN)

Top Gear

26 NOVEMBER 1964 (RINGO)

The Beatles Invite You To Take A Ticket To Ride

7 JUNE 1965 (RINGO)

The B-side of Carl Perkins' Top Ten UK hit 'Blue Suede Shoes' and a Beatles stage favourite for several years before it appeared on their fourth album. The BBC recordings show how brilliantly John swaggered through the song before generously surrendering it to Ringo for his number on *Beatles For Sale*. The first released Lennon vocal performance of a Perkins song was, therefore, delayed until December 1969 when the Plastic Ono Band's *Live Peace In Toronto* featured 'Blue Suede Shoes'.

The Honeymoon Song ✗ ●   Paul

[Theodorakis-Sansom]

Pop Go The Beatles

6 AUGUST 1963 ◆

The theme tune from the film *Honeymoon*, written by Greek composer Theodorakis. A vocal version was released in June 1959 by Marino Marini and his Quartet – an Italian pop combo who made a big impression when they played in Liverpool. Local group, the Remo Four, were even inspired to assume an Italian-sounding name! Paul was still fond of the song in 1969, as he selected it for the *Postcard* album he produced for Mary Hopkin.

I Call Your Name   John

[Lennon-McCartney]

Saturday Club

4 APRIL 1964

John and Paul gave this song to Billy J. Kramer and the Dakotas, who released it in July 1963 on the flip-side of their second single. The top side – another Lennon-McCartney gift, 'Bad To Me' – was number one for three weeks before 'She Loves You' arrived. The writers also provided exclusive hit songs for Tommy Quickly, the Fourmost and Cilla Black in 1963. As John later commented in the radio programe *The Lennon and McCartney Songbook*, 'We thought we had some to spare!'. The Beatles version was released almost a year afterwards on the *Long Tall Sally* EP. Check out the lustrous cover by the Mamas And The Papas too!

I Feel Fine ●   John

[Lennon-McCartney]

Top Gear

26 NOVEMBER 1964 ◆

Saturday Club

26 DECEMBER 1964 ◆

The rare survival of an unedited *Top Gear* session tape of 'I Feel Fine' reveals that the distinctive feedback opening took quite a few attempts to get right – and that riff was pretty tricky too! Their eighth single topped both the UK and US charts during Christmas 1964, bringing their tally of American number ones that year to six.

If I Fell   John and Paul

[Lennon-McCartney]

Top Gear

16 JULY 1964

From Us To You

3 AUGUST 1964

John's innocent lyric is set over a wrist-twisting bar-chord sequence. A high point of *A Hard Day's Night*, it was coupled with Paul's ballad 'And I Love Her' on an American single and also featured on the British EP *Extracts From The Film A Hard Day's Night*.

I Forgot To Remember To Forget You ✗ ●

[Kesler-Feathers]   George

Easter Monday

From Us To You

18 MAY 1964 ◆

During the second *From Us To You* that Alan Freeman presented, the Beatles slipped in this Elvis cover. It was on the flip-side of Presley's fifth and last single for Sun Records, 'Mystery Train', but first released in the UK on the album *Elvis' Golden Records, Vol 1.* in October 1958. There are also versions by its composer, Charlie Feathers, and two other Sun luminaries, Johnny Cash and Jerry Lee Lewis.

I Got A Woman ✗ ●   John

[Charles-Richards]

Pop Go The Beatles

13 AUGUST 1963 ◆

Saturday Club

4 APRIL 1964

This song was an American R & B hit for Ray Charles in 1954, but the Beatles probably learnt it from the first Elvis Presley UK album called *Rock 'n' Roll No.1*. Both BBC takes are assured performances. The later version – with a double-tracked vocal from John – is a touch more studio-polished than the *Live At The BBC* track.

I Got To Find My Baby ✘ ●   John

[Berry]

Pop Go The Beatles

11 JUNE 1963 ◆

Saturday Club

29 JUNE 1963

A Chuck Berry rocker that developed out of a 1954 recording by his Chess label-mate and ace harmonica man, Little Walter. Berry's record was released in 1960 and the song was hammered out by many British R & B groups during the early sixties.

I Just Don't Understand ✘ ●   John

[Wilkin-Westberry]

Pop Go The Beatles

20 AUGUST 1963 ◆

Swedish-born movie starlet Ann-Margret (Olson) had an American Top Twenty hit with this in August 1961. Freddie and the Dreamers later covered the song and may have discovered it through the Beatles. Paul is convinced the Manchester group's first hit – 'If You Gotta Make A Fool Of Somebody' – went into their set list once the Beatles had played it at their local club, the Oasis. Both songs are 'rock 'n' roll waltzes', a musical hybrid the group experimented with for 'Baby's In Black' and an early take of 'I'll Be Back' heard on *Anthology 1*.

I'll Be On My Way ✘ ●   John and Paul

[Lennon-McCartney]

Side By Side

24 JUNE 1963 ◆

The only recording by the Beatles of this early Lennon-McCartney original. The song, dating from 1961, had been given to another Epstein-managed group – Billy J. Kramer and the Dakotas – and put on the B-side of their hit version of 'Do You Want To Know A Secret' in April 1963.

I'll Follow The Sun ●   Paul

[Lennon-McCartney]

Top Gear

26 NOVEMBER 1964 ◆

An early song of Paul's that was at least four years old by the time it was revisited for *Beatles For Sale*. Glyn Johns recorded a version in 1965 but enjoyed less success as a singer than as a recording engineer and producer. He worked closely with the Beatles amid the tense conditions of the *Get Back/Let It Be* sessions.

I'll Get You   John and Paul

[Lennon-McCartney]

Pop Go The Beatles

13 AUGUST 1963

Saturday Club

24 AUGUST 1963

Pop Go The Beatles

3 SEPTEMBER 1963

Pop Go The Beatles

10 SEPTEMBER 1963

Saturday Club

5 OCTOBER 1963

The other side of the 'She Loves You' single and also abounding in the group's trademark nasal 'yeahs', this is a Beatles B-side gem. *Anthology 1* presents their live TV performance of the song on *Sunday Night At The London Palladium* on 13 October 1963. The British press described the screaming enthusiasm of fans outside the theatre that night as 'Beatlemania' and the hysteria was set to increase from then on.

I'm A Loser ●   John

[Lennon-McCartney]

Top Gear

26 NOVEMBER 1964 ◆

Saturday Club

26 DECEMBER 1964 ◆

The Beatles Invite You To Take A Ticket To Ride

7 JUNE 1963

This song's first broadcast was 10 days before its release on *Beatles For Sale* in December 1964. Unusually, the recording made for *Top Gear* was used again in *Saturday Club*. The song was taped once more during the group's last BBC music session when John cheekily changed 'Beneath this smile, I am wearing a frown' to the rather less dramatic 'Beneath this wig, I am wearing a tie'!

I'm Gonna Sit Right Down And Cry (Over You) ✕ ●   John

[Thomas-Biggs]
Pop Go The Beatles
6 AUGUST 1963 ◆

Like two other Elvis covers performed for the BBC, this song was released in the UK on Presley's 1956 debut album *Rock 'n' Roll No. 1.*

I'm Happy Just To Dance With You   George

[Lennon-McCartney]
From Us To You
3 AUGUST 1964

This was one of only two tracks written by John and Paul on which George took the lead vocal (the other was 'Do You Want to Know a Secret'). It came from *A Hard Day's Night* – the first and last Beatles' album entirely consisting of Lennon-McCartney songs. Brian Epstein managed an American folk-rock group, the Cyrkle (spelling courtesy of John), who covered this song in 1967.

I'm Talking About You ✕   John

[Berry]
Saturday Club
16 MARCH 1963

Chess Records released Chuck Berry's disc in February 1961. The Beatles performed the song the following year and the Star-Club tape preserves their fiery New Year's Eve interpretation. The BBC version was live from the *Saturday Club* on-air studio, as they had been forced to cancel the pre-recording session because of John's heavy cold.

I Saw Her Standing There ●   Paul

[Lennon-McCartney]
Saturday Club
16 MARCH 1963
Side By Side
22 APRIL 1963
Saturday Club
25 MAY 1963
Steppin' Out
3 JUNE 1963
Pop Go The Beatles
25 JUNE 1963
Easy Beat
21 JULY 1963
Pop Go The Beatles
24 SEPTEMBER 1963
Saturday Club
5 OCTOBER 1963
Easy Beat
20 OCTOBER 1963 ◆
From Us To You
26 DECEMBER 1963
From Us To You
18 MAY 1964

Written in late 1962, this song was captured on tape at the Beatles' final Star-Club performance on the last night of that year. Six weeks later they recorded it at Abbey Road during the EMI one-day session that yielded all 10 new tracks needed for the debut album *Please Please Me*. The first BBC performance was as live as it gets – straight onto the air – from *Saturday Club*'s small compilation studio. The two *Easy Beat* recordings were made in front of an audience. On the second occasion, the show's presenter Brian Matthew pleaded for the screaming to cease and commented, 'Alfred Hitchcock's *Birds* have got nothing on you lot!'.

I Should Have Known Better   John

[Lennon-McCartney]
From Us To You
3 AUGUST 1964

The Beatles appeared in session for *Top Gear* on 16 July 1964 and the extant BBC running order listed

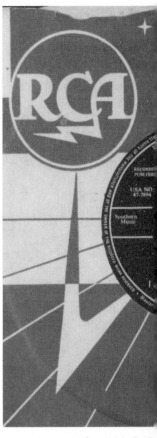

45rpm singles that the Beatles covered at the BBC. These labels specialized in releasing American artists and anyone with a passion for rock 'n' roll will turn misty-eyed at the sight of RCA – home of Elvis's hits at the time – and London-American, which released most of the finest records of the era!

this song as recorded with five others from the current album *A Hard Day's Night*. The recent emergence of a tape of the programme reveals that the disc was played instead. However three days later the song was taped in a BBC session for the final *From Us To You*.

I Wanna Be Your Man ●   Ringo

[Lennon-McCartney]

Saturday Club

   15 FEBRUARY 1964

From Us To You

   30 MARCH 1964 ◆

This song gave the Rolling Stones their first Top Twenty hit. Their manager Andrew Oldham, a former Epstein employee, had received the song from John and Paul after bemoaning his new group's lack of single success to them in a chance meeting.

I Want To Hold Your Hand   John and Paul

[Lennon-McCartney]

Saturday Club

   21 DECEMBER 1963

From Us To You

   26 DECEMBER 1963

Saturday Club

   15 FEBRUARY 1964

With advance orders of one million, the group's fifth single quickly replaced their previous disc – 'She Loves You' – at the top of the UK charts. Just two months later, it was number one in America – only the third occasion a British record had achieved this. It began their musical domination of the world and remains their biggest seller, with global sales of 15 million copies. In January 1964 they recorded the German translation 'Komm, Gib Mir Deine Hand'. Howard

Morrison and the Hu Hus spoke for some worried parents when they sang 'I Wanna Cut Your Hair'.

Johnny B. Goode ✗ ●   John

[Berry]

Saturday Club

15 FEBRUARY 1964 ◆

Not a British hit for Chuck Berry in 1958, but the UK London single, with 'Around And Around' on the other side, must have been owned by every British beat group of the sixties. It was one of the most frequently performed tunes on *Saturday Club*.

Kansas City/Hey!-Hey!-Hey!-Hey! ●   Paul

[Leiber-Stoller]/[Penniman]

Pop Go The Beatles

6 AUGUST 1963 ◆

From Us To You

18 MAY 1964

From Us To You

3 AUGUST 1964

Saturday Club

26 DECEMBER 1964

'Kansas City' was an American number one for Wilbert Harrison in May 1959. It was a very early 1952 composition by Leiber and Stoller – the production and writing wizards behind the Coasters' records that the Beatles loved so much. Little Richard's 1959 medley of 'Kansas City' with his previously released 'Hey!-Hey!-Hey!-Hey! (Goin' Back To Birmingham)' was the inspiration for the group's version. The first BBC broadcast was well over a year before it was recorded for *Beatles For Sale*.

Keep Your Hands Off My Baby ✗ ●   John

[Goffin-King]

Saturday Club

26 JANUARY 1963 ◆

Looking for a singer for their novelty dance tune 'The Loco-motion', the married songwriting team of Gerry

Goffin and Carole King chose their babysitter, Little Eva. This was the follow-up hit (her baby-sitting days were obviously over!) and the Beatles played it on their *Saturday Club* debut, the week Little Eva's record dropped out of the Top Forty. They also performed the song during their tour with Helen Shapiro which opened in glamorous Bradford in February 1963.

Lend Me Your Comb ✗ ●   John and Paul

[Twomey-Wise-Weisman]

Pop Go The Beatles

16 JULY 1963 ◆

Released in the UK in 1958 on the flip-side of the fourth Carl Perkins single 'That's Right', this song was a staple of the Beatles' act for several years before they made this BBC recording. When the infamous *Live! At The Star-Club* album became available in 1977, it was just possible to discern the song through the audience bustle and muffled recording quality of the tape.

Lonesome Tears In My Eyes ✗ ●   John

[J. and D. Burnette-Burlison-Mortimer]

Pop Go The Beatles

23 JULY 1963 ◆

A cover of a record by Johnny Burnette and his Rock 'n' Roll Trio (including his brother Dorsey), who made several influential rockabilly discs in the late fifties. The shuffling mood of the Beatles' 1969 single 'The Ballad Of John And Yoko' echoes the feel of this performance.

Long Tall Sally ●   Paul

[Johnson-Penniman-Blackwell]

Side By Side

13 MAY 1963

Saturday Club

25 MAY 1963

Pop Go The Beatles

13 AUGUST 1963 ◆

Saturday Club

24 AUGUST 1963

Saturday Club

4 APRIL 1964

Top Gear

16 JULY 1964

From Us To You

3 AUGUST 1964

Four of the seven BBC takes were broadcast well ahead of the song's release in June 1964 on the *Long Tall Sally* EP. It had been in the Beatles' repertoire since its appearance on a Little Richard single with the equally thunderous 'Tutti Frutti' in 1957. It endured as a stage number to the very end when it was the final song at the last official Beatles' concert in San Francisco (29 August 1966). Other versions can be found on the Star-Club tape, the *Hollywood Bowl* album and *Anthology 1*.

Love Me Do ●   John and Paul

[Lennon-McCartney]

Here We Go

26 OCTOBER 1962

The Talent Spot

4 DECEMBER 1962

Saturday Club

26 JANUARY 1963

Parade Of The Pops

20 FEBRUARY 1963

Pop Go The Beatles

11 JUNE 1963

Side By Side

24 JUNE 1963

Pop Go The Beatles

23 JULY 1963 ◆

Pop Go The Beatles

10 SEPTEMBER 1963

Easy Beat

20 OCTOBER 1963

The group's first Top Twenty hit in the UK and eventually a US Number one in June 1964. EMI's American outlet Capitol had decided not to issue 'Love Me Do' in 1962, allowing Tollie to license the track. The small independent label rode the wave of Beatlemania (engendered by Capitol's campaign for 'I Want To Hold Your Hand') all the way to the top. There are three EMI recordings of the song available, each with a different drummer: the British single take with Ringo, the *Please Please Me* album track with session player Andy White, and the earliest recording with Pete Best included on *Anthology 1*.

Lucille ✗ ●   Paul
[Collins-Penniman]
Pop Go The Beatles
    17 SEPTEMBER 1963
Saturday Club
    5 OCTOBER 1963 ◆

Little Richard's rocker went Top Ten in the UK during the summer of 1957. The Beatles' second BBC performance was for the fifth birthday edition of *Saturday Club*. Brian Matthew gave a nod to the Everlys in his voice-over because the brothers were fellow guests that day and had also scored a big hit with 'Lucille'. The *Pop Go The Beatles* version is equally good, with a wild tremolo guitar solo by George. Paul returned to the song at the 1979 Concert for Kampuchea and for his 1988 album, initially available only in the USSR – *CHOBA B CCCP*.

Matchbox ●   Ringo
[Perkins]
Pop Go The Beatles
    30 JULY 1963 ◆
From Us To You
    18 MAY 1964

Rooted in a blues recorded in 1927 by Blind Lemon Jefferson, 'Matchbox' by Carl Perkins was the unsuccessful follow-up single to 'Blue Suede Shoes'. Pete Best first sang it with the Beatles and, after his departure, John took it over. As with 'Honey Don't', he passed it over to Ringo for these BBC performances, and the later version included on the EP *Long Tall Sally*. Carl Perkins attended the Abbey Road session and witnessed the first Beatles' EMI recording of one of his songs.

Memphis, Tennessee ✗ ●   John
[Berry]
Teenagers Turn – Here We Go
    8 MARCH 1962 **(PB)**
Pop Go The Beatles
    18 JUNE 1963
Saturday Club
    29 JUNE 1963
Pop Go The Beatles
    30 JULY 1963 ◆
Saturday Club
    5 OCTOBER 1963

First released on the flip-side of Chuck Berry's 'Back In The USA' in the summer of 1959, 'Memphis, Tennessee' made the British charts four years later when Dave Berry and the Cruisers were also in the Top Twenty with the song. Paul remembers learning it in John's bedroom in 1959 and the two lads thinking it was 'the greatest riff ever, it killed us!'.

Misery   John and Paul
[Lennon-McCartney]
Here We Go
    12 MARCH 1963
Saturday Club
    16 MARCH 1963
On The Scene
    28 MARCH 1963
Easy Beat
    7 APRIL 1963
Side By Side
    22 APRIL 1963
Pop Go The Beatles
    4 JUNE 1963
Pop Go The Beatles
    17 SEPTEMBER 1963

Offered to precocious teenage *chanteuse* Helen Shapiro while the group were touring with her, this song was instead picked up by Liverpool actor Kenny Lynch who was also on the bill. The BBC performances lack the descending piano runs that George Martin overdubbed onto the EMI master made at Abbey Road on 11 February 1963.

Money (That's What I Want)   John

[Bradford-Gordy]

Saturday Club

25 MAY 1963

Pop Go The Beatles

18 JUNE 1963

Saturday Club

29 JUNE 1963

Pop Go The Beatles

3 SEPTEMBER 1963

From Us To You

26 DECEMBER 1963

Saturday Club

15 FEBRUARY 1964

Motown founder Berry Gordy notched up his first hit as a label owner in 1960 with this co-composition recorded by Barrett Strong. The last song on *With The Beatles*, it was the climax of the group's second album (in the same way as 'Twist And Shout' had been on the first). In 1969, John's live version, with Eric Clapton, Klaus Voormann and Ringo Starr, was featured on *Live Peace In Toronto*.

The Night Before   Paul

[Lennon-McCartney]

The Beatles Invite You To Take A Ticket To Ride

7 JUNE 1965

The last radio show featuring specially recorded Beatles' tracks gave this song its 'first airing', as host Denny Piercy rather quaintly put it.

Nothing Shakin' ✗ ●   George

[Fontaine-Colacrai-Lampert-Gluck]

Pop Go The Beatles

23 JULY 1963 ◆

George's affection for rockabilly led him to *Nothin' Shakin'* by Eddie Fontaine, who the Beatles would have spotted singing 'Cool It Baby' in the best ever rock movie *The Girl Can't Help It*. The 1958 British cover of 'Nothin' Shakin'' by Craig Douglas was – as with most 1950s British attempts at rock 'n' roll – light years away from the sound and spirit of the American original. Comparing Craig's dreary version

with the Beatles' rollicking BBC performance clearly demonstrates why British pop has to be characterized as pre- or post- 'Love Me Do'!

Ooh! My Soul ✗ ●   Paul

[Penniman]

Pop Go The Beatles

27 AUGUST 1963 ◆

Little Richard's last Top Forty US hit on Specialty came in the summer of 1958 with this song. The one-off Beeb performance was one of four rockers by 'The Georgia Peach' that the Beatles selected for a radio show.

A Picture Of You ✗   George

[Beveridge-Oakman]

Here We Go

15 JUNE 1962 **(PB)**

At the time of this broadcast, the song was a Top Ten hit for Joe Brown and the Bruvvers. With his slick playing on an impressive-looking Grimshaw guitar, Joe's was the more credible face – cheeky grin, spiky hair and all – of pre-Beatles British pop. George also used to sing songs from Brown's early repertoire: 'Darktown Strutters Ball', 'What A Crazy World We're Living In', 'I'm Henry The Eighth, I Am' and 'The Sheik Of Araby' (recorded at the fruitless audition for Decca Records).

Please Mister Postman   John

[Holland-Bateman-Garrett-Dobbins-Gorman]

Teenagers Turn – Here We Go

8 MARCH 1962 **(PB)**

Pop Go The Beatles

30 JULY 1963

From Us To You

30 MARCH 1964

After a tortuous 15-week climb up the charts, the Marvelettes' record became the first American number one for Motown in December 1961. Nothing doing in Britain, of course, where it was released on the Fontana label. Motown's records had been shamefully neglected by the BBC in the early sixties, and when the Beatles became successful they were tireless champions of the label. Significantly, even their humble Light Programme debut gave a Motown song some rare radio exposure.

Please Please Me   John and Paul

[Lennon-McCartney]

Here We Go

25 JANUARY 1963

Saturday Club

26 JANUARY 1963

The Talent Spot

29 JANUARY 1963

Parade Of The Pops

20 FEBRUARY 1963

Here We Go

12 MARCH 1963

Saturday Club

16 MARCH 1963

On The Scene

28 MARCH 1963

Easy Beat

7 APRIL 1963

Side By Side

22 APRIL 1963

Steppin' Out

3 JUNE 1963

Pop Go The Beatles

13 AUGUST 1963

Easy Beat

20 OCTOBER 1963

George Martin was convinced the group had a potential number one when the recording was completed at Abbey Road. Following the single's release on 11 January 1963, there was a flurry of media activity. After their *Thank Your Lucky Stars* TV appearance on 19 January, the group were heard plugging their new single on *Pop Inn* three days later. Three live performances followed in quick succession. The next week *Please Please Me* entered the Top Twenty and quickly rose to number one on most charts, including that used by the BBC's *Pick Of The Pops* programme.

Pop Go The Beatles ✗   Instrumental

Opening and closing signature tunes

[Arrangement of the nursery rhyme 'Pop Goes The Weasel']

Pop Go The Beatles

ALL 15 PROGRAMMES

The short 20-second version always opened the show and the other variation of over a minute was fadeable play-out music to close the programme on time. With the usual mid-1963 Beatles' trademarks of wailing harmonica and falsetto whooping, this tune was recorded on 24 May 1963 in a session for the first show. Guesting on the show were radio veterans the Lorne Gibson Trio and their leader remembers his group lending a hand on this recording.

P.S. I Love You   Paul

[Lennon-McCartney]

Here We Go

26 OCTOBER 1962

The Talent Spot

4 DECEMBER 1962

Pop Go The Beatles

25 JUNE 1963

This was the B-side of the Beatles' first single 'Love Me Do' released in October 1962. The Cavern DJ Bob Wooler remembers that one of the reasons for not making it the lead track was to avoid confusion with the current revival of a different song with the same title. Gordon Jenkins and Johnny Mercer wrote their 'P.S. I Love You' in 1934, Frank Sinatra popularized it in 1956 but it was Ketty Lester's version that was around in late 1962 – soon after her big hit 'Love Letters'.

Rock And Roll Music ●   John

[Berry]

Saturday Club

26 DECEMBER 1964 ◆

Chuck Berry's record went to number eight in the Billboard Top 100 at the end of 1957 but saw no chart action in the UK. That did not stop the Beatles seeking out the song and performing it live from 1959 to 1966. When they were digging into their extensive repertoire to complete *Beatles For Sale* quickly, they pulled this out. One take later, it was in the can.

Roll Over Beethoven ● George

[Berry]

Steppin' Out

　3 JUNE 1963

Saturday Club

　29 JUNE 1963

Pop Go The Beatles

　3 SEPTEMBER 1963

Saturday Club

　21 DECEMBER 1963

From Us To You

　26 DECEMBER 1963

Saturday Club

　15 FEBRUARY 1964

From Us To You

　30 MARCH 1964 ◆

A year after its American Top Thirty success, Chuck Berry's 1956 original was released in the UK but made no headway in the charts. John sang it until 1961; after that it was George who invited Beethoven to roll over. Following the three BBC broadcasts in summer 1963, the song became available in November as the side two opener of *With The Beatles*. There are three released live versions, recorded in Germany (*Star-Club*), the USA (*Hollywood Bowl*) and Sweden (*Anthology 1*).

She Loves You John and Paul

[Lennon-McCartney]

Pop Go The Beatles

　13 AUGUST 1963

Pop Go The Beatles

　20 AUGUST 1963

Saturday Club

　24 AUGUST 1963

Pop Go The Beatles

　27 AUGUST 1963

Pop Go The Beatles

　10 SEPTEMBER 1963

Pop Go The Beatles

　24 SEPTEMBER 1963

Saturday Club

　5 OCTOBER 1963

Easy Beat

　20 OCTOBER 1963

The Ken Dodd Show

　3 NOVEMBER 1963

(Repeated 6 November 1963 and 1 February 1964)

Saturday Club

　21 DECEMBER 1963

From Us To You

　26 DECEMBER 1963

The Beatles' fourth single became their biggest seller in Britain, spending a staggering 12 weeks in the Top Three, with two stints at number one. Capitol in the States declined to release it and Philadelphian Independent Swan Records picked it up. On 3 January 1964, *The Jack Paar Show* on NBC featured footage of the Beatles taken from BBC TV's *The Mersey Sound*. The clip of 'She Loves You' was America's first glimpse of the Beatles – already causing considerable excitement with the rush-released '*I Want To Hold Your Hand*'. A month later, that single was number one and after seven weeks at the top it was replaced by 'She Loves You' (in turn, followed by 'Can't Buy Me Love!'). Other versions available are the German translation 'Sie Liebt Dich' and live performances at the 1963 *Royal Variety Show* (included on *Anthology 1*) and the *Hollywood Bowl* in August 1964.

She's A Woman ● Paul

[Lennon-McCartney]

Top Gear

　26 NOVEMBER 1964 ◆

Saturday Club

　26 DECEMBER 1964 ◆

The Beatles Invite You To Take A Ticket To Ride

　7 JUNE 1965

The flip-side of the group's Christmas 1964 single 'I Feel Fine'. During *Top Gear*, John and Paul described how they completed writing 'She's A Woman' on the morning of the EMI session. John explained they had 'about one verse and we had to finish it off rather quickly, and that's why they're such rubbishy lyrics!'. An American group (affecting an English sounding name), the Sir Douglas Quintet, picked up on the track's infectious groove with their 1965 hit 'She's About A Mover'.

A Shot Of Rhythm And Blues ✗ ●   John

[Thompson]

Pop Go The Beatles

18 JUNE 1963

Easy Beat

21 JULY 1963

Pop Go The Beatles

27 AUGUST 1963 ◆

Rhythm and Blues singer Arthur Alexander, who was a particular favourite of John's, first released this in March 1962 on the B-side of another British beat boom staple 'You Better Move On'. (The Rolling Stones released a version of that song on their first EP in January 1964.) In a letter from the Star-Club, Hamburg – dated April 1962 – John asked his future wife Cynthia to 'send me the words of "A Shot Of Rhythm + Blues" please? There's not many'.

Side By Side ✗   Karl Denver and John and Paul

With the Karl Denver Trio

[Woods]

Side By Side

22 APRIL 1963

Side By Side

13 MAY 1963

Side By Side

24 JUNE 1963

The Karl Denver Trio hosted a radio series in which they traded numbers with a guest group. Named after the old standard, the programme required the visiting group to sing 'Side By Side' with yodelling Karl (whose biggest hit was 'Wimoweh').

Slow Down ✗   John

[Williams]

Pop Go The Beatles

20 AUGUST 1963 ◆

A Larry Williams song that was broadcast almost a year before its inclusion on the Beatles' EP *Long Tall Sally*. It was the B-side of Larry's 'Dizzy Miss Lizzy' and a Merseybeat favourite that Gerry and the Pacemakers also released on their album *How Do You Like It?* Another Williams classic – 'Bony Moronie' – was later covered by John on his 1975 album *Rock 'N' Roll*.

So How Come (No One Loves Me) ✗ ●

George

[Bryant]

Pop Go The Beatles

23 JULY 1963

The song was included on *A Date With The Everly Brothers*, a Top Three album in 1961. The Beatles are known to have played three other tracks by the duo – 'I Wonder If I Care As Much', 'Love Of My Life' and 'Cathy's Clown'.

Soldier Of Love ✗ ●   John

[Cason-Moon]

Pop Go The Beatles

16 JULY 1963 ◆

The group performed four songs cut by the Alabama-born singer Arthur Alexander. '*Anna*' was recorded for the first album and 'A Shot Of Rhythm And Blue's taped at the BBC, but they also covered both sides of a single released in June 1962. 'Where Have You Been All My Life?' can just about be identified on the Star-Club tape but the BBC recording of 'Soldier Of Love' takes no prisoners! A Lennon *tour de force*, it could have enhanced any of the Beatles' early discs.

George, Paul and John during the live broadcast of Swinging Sound '63 *on 18 April 1963. 'Fantastic… people here twisting all over the Albert Hall!' observed wobble board specialist Rolf Harris. After a set by top of the bill act Del Shannon, all the artists – including the Beatles – returned to the stage for the finale number 'Mack the Knife'.*

Some Other Guy ✗ ●

[Leiber-Stoller-Barrett]

Saturday Club

26 JANUARY 1963

The Talent Spot

29 JANUARY 1963

Easy Beat

23 JUNE 1963 ◆

'Some Other Guy' was first recorded in 1962 by

John

Ritchie Barrett as a direct imitation of the gospel call-and-response style of Ray Charles. Though not much of a hit anywhere, it became a Liverpool anthem as almost every Mersey group tackled it. On 22 August 1962, Granada Television filmed the Beatles at the Cavern Club playing this song. The footage remained unseen until November 1963, when it gave a historic glimpse of the group on their old stomping ground before they had scored a hit.

Sure To Fall (In Love With You) ✕ ●   Paul

[Perkins-Claunch-Cantrell]

Pop Go The Beatles

18 JUNE 1963 ◆

Pop Go The Beatles

24 SEPTEMBER 1963

Saturday Club

4 APRIL 1964

From Us To You

18 MAY 1964

A Carl Perkins favourite included on his first album recorded in 1956, this song was absorbed into the Beatles' act the next year. Paul, who took the lead on these BBC performances, produced Ringo singing it on the 1981 album *Stop And Smell The Roses*. Paul also invited Carl to sing 'Get It' with him on the 1982 album *Tug Of War*.

Sweet Little Sixteen ✕ ●   John

[Berry]

Pop Go The Beatles ◆

23 JULY 1963

This was Chuck Berry's first British Top Twenty hit in June 1958. The Beatles were recorded romping through it at the Star-Club at the close of play in 1962, and 11 years later John revived the song during the unruly, Phil Spector-produced sessions for his album *Rock 'N' Roll*.

A Taste Of Honey ●   Paul

[Marlow-Scott]

Here We Go

26 OCTOBER 1962

Side By Side

13 MAY 1963

Pop Go The Beatles

18 JUNE 1963

Easy Beat

23 JUNE 1963

The Beat Show

4 JULY 1963

Pop Go The Beatles

23 JULY 1963 ◆

Pop Go The Beatles

10 SEPTEMBER 1963

The interpretation by Lenny Welch had inspired the Beatles' version of this song recorded first for the BBC and then the *Please Please Me* LP. The song's middle-of-the-road credentials were confirmed with other covers by Mr Acker Bilk, Herb Alpert, Peggy Lee, Barbra Streisand, Andy Williams and Tom Jones.

Thank You Girl ●   John and Paul

[Lennon-McCartney]

Side By Side

13 MAY 1963

Steppin' Out

3 JUNE 1963

Easy Beat

23 JUNE 1963 ◆

'Thank You Girl' was the B-side of the Beatles' third single 'From Me To You' and also included on the second EP *The Beatles' Hits*.

That's All Right (Mama) ✕ ●   Paul

[Crudup]

Pop Go The Beatles

16 JULY 1963 ◆

Written by Arthur 'Big Boy' Crudup, this was Elvis Presley's first American single on the Sun label. Its inclusion on his first British album in October 1956 led to Paul singing it as early as the skiffle days of the Quarry Men. It was also recorded by Paul in 1987 for *CHOBA B CCCP* – his rock 'n' roll album made exclusively for the Soviet Union.

There's A Place   John and Paul

[Lennon-McCartney]

Pop Go The Beatles

16 JULY 1963

Easy Beat

21 JULY 1963

Pop Go The Beatles

3 SEPTEMBER 1963

John's mature lyric displays a hint of the myriad mind games to come and explores a theme still evident in

In the foreground are Jane Asher and Ringo watching Paul and Lee Peters at the (4038) microphone during a Pop Go The Beatles *session in BBC Maida Vale Studio Five. To commemorate Beatles' sessions there, a plaque was unveiled at the* Live at the BBC *launch party in 1994.*

one of his last songs 'Watching The Wheels'. It was the penultimate track on *Please Please Me* and the B-side of 'Twist And Shout' in the USA.

Things We Said Today   Paul

[Lennon-McCartney]

Top Gear

16 JULY 1964 ◆

From Us To You

3 AUGUST 1964

This was issued in July 1964 as the B-side of the film title song 'A Hard Day's Night' and on side two of the British soundtrack album. In the States, the song was first included on the LP *Something New*.

This Boy   John, Paul and George

[Lennon-McCartney]

Saturday Club

21 DECEMBER 1963

From Us To You

30 MARCH 1964

Released on the flip-side of 'I Want To Hold Your Hand' in November 1963, this tune was orchestrated by George Martin for the movie *A Hard Day's Night*. As 'Ringo's Theme', it accompanies a sequence where the errant drummer goes parading through the streets of Twickenham and along the banks of the Thames. The 1995 'Free As A Bird' single also featured two giggly EMI out-takes of 'This Boy'.

Ticket To Ride ●   John

[Lennon-McCartney]

The Beatles Invite You To Take A Ticket To Ride

7 JUNE 1965 ◆

Featured on the soundtrack album for the group's second movie *Help!*, 'Ticket To Ride' provided the unwieldy title of the last Bank Holiday programme with specially recorded Beatles' music. *Anthology 2* has a live television performance of the song broadcast from the ABC Theatre in Blackpool on 1 August 1965. The *Live At The Hollywood Bowl* album includes a scream-drenched version from the same month.

Tie Me Kangaroo Down, Sport ✖   Rolf Harris

With Rolf Harris

[Harris]

From Us To You

26 DECEMBER 1963

The first Beatles Bank Holiday special was presented by Rolf Harris, who at the time of this broadcast was appearing in The Beatles' Christmas Show at the Astoria in Finsbury Park. 'Fellas, do you feel like singing a chorus with me?' Rolf inquired and off he went, with his wobble board quivering and the Beatles as his backing group. In the British Top Ten back in 1960, his record (produced by George Martin) had recently hopped to number three in the States. Rolf customized the lyric, building verses around the group's Christian names and their look – 'Cut your hair once a year, boys' – and extracted some 'She Loves You'-ish falsetto 'Woo!'s too!

Till There Was You ●   Paul

[Willson]

Pop Go The Beatles

11 JUNE 1963

Saturday Club

29 JUNE 1963

Pop Go The Beatles

30 JULY 1963

Pop Go The Beatles

10 SEPTEMBER 1963

Royal Variety Performance

10 NOVEMBER 1963

Saturday Club

21 DECEMBER 1963

From Us To You

26 DECEMBER 1963

From Us To You

30 MARCH 1964 ◆

This song was a highlight of Meredith Willson's Broadway musical success *The Music Man*, which also included a Light Programme jolly perennial 'Seventy-Six Trombones'. Paul was inspired by the silky Peggy Lee version, which made the Top 30 in April 1961. In the group's stage act for two years, the song was released on *With The Beatles* in November 1963. It was one of their selections for the 1963 *Royal Variety Performance*, released eventually on *Anthology 1* with Paul's introductory quip that it had also been recorded by 'our favourite American group… Sophie Tucker!'.

To Know Her Is To Love Her ✖ ●   John

[Spector]

Pop Go The Beatles

6 AUGUST 1963 ◆

The Teddy Bears' American number one was written by Phil Spector, who had been inspired by the inscription on his father's gravestone 'To know him was to love him'. In the UK, the record climbed to number two during the first months of 1959. John, Paul and George made their first attempt at three-part harmony – later so effectively employed on 'This Boy' and 'Yes It Is' – when learning this song.

Too Much Monkey Business ✖ ●   John

[Berry]

Saturday Club

16 MARCH 1963

Pop Go The Beatles

11 JUNE 1963

Side By Side

24 JUNE 1963

Pop Go The Beatles

10 SEPTEMBER 1963 ◆

On 16 April 1956, Chuck Berry rocked Chess Studios with a session that included three Top Ten American R & B hits: 'Roll Over Beethoven', 'Brown-Eyed Handsome Man' and this song. It became a British beat group favourite, covered on record by the Kinks, the Hollies, Wayne Fontana and the Mindbenders, the Applejacks and the Yardbirds.

Twist And Shout   John

[Medley-Russell (Burns)]

The Talent Spot

  4 DECEMBER 1962

Swinging Sound '63

  18 APRIL 1963

Pop Go The Beatles

  25 JUNE 1963

The Beat Show

  4 JULY 1963

Easy Beat

  21 JULY 1963

Pop Go The Beatles

  6 AUGUST 1963

Saturday Club

  24 AUGUST 1963

Pop Go The Beatles

  27 AUGUST 1963

Pop Go The Beatles

  24 SEPTEMBER 1963

Royal Variety Performance

  10 NOVEMBER 1963 ◆

The Beatles latched on to 'Twist And Shout' when it was an American hit for the Isley Brothers in the summer of 1962 and it became the rousing closer of their debut album and countless live shows. The song was written by Phil Medley and Bert Berns (using one of his pseudonyms, Bert Russell) and first recorded at an hysterical pace by the Top Notes on Atlantic Records. Brian Poole and the Tremeloes – the group signed by Decca in preference to the Beatles – took it to number four in the singles chart of July 1963. However, their record was outsold by the Beatles' first EP, with 'Twist And Shout' as the title track.

Words Of Love   John and Paul

[Holly]

Pop Go The Beatles

  20 AUGUST 1963

First recorded in 1957 by Buddy Holly and the Crickets, a version by the Beatles was broadcast 15 months before the song's inclusion on the album *Beatles For Sale*. John and Paul take the harmony parts which, through primitive but effective overdubbing, Holly had sung himself.

You Can't Do That   John

[Lennon-McCartney]

From Us To You

  30 MARCH 1964

Saturday Club

  4 APRIL 1964

From Us To You

  18 MAY 1964

Top Gear

  16 JULY 1964

Released on the other side of 'Can't Buy Me Love' though, by March 1964, it was clear that B-side status could not devalue any Beatles' song. 'You Can't Do That' is a cocksure R & B workout that was also included on the non-film-songs side of the A *Hard Day's Night* album. A vibrant alternate take was released on *Anthology 1*.

Young Blood ✖ ●   George

[Leiber-Stoller-Pomus]

Pop Go The Beatles

  11 JUNE 1963 ◆

The Coasters made the US Top Ten in 1957 with both titles on their third Atco single – 'Searchin'' and 'Young Blood'. The record even scraped into the British Top 30 for one week and Paul recalls cycling across Liverpool trying to track down someone rumoured to own a copy. Both sides were performed by the Beatles. 'Searchin'' – sung by Paul – was one of the 15 songs recorded at their Decca audition. As George usually took the lead on the quirkier novelty numbers in their early repertoire, he was upfront for

'Young Blood' (as he was on another of the Coasters'
musical cartoons, 'Three Cool Cats').

You Really Got A Hold On Me ●   John

[Robinson]

Pop Go The Beatles

  4 JUNE 1963

Pop Go The Beatles

  13 AUGUST 1963

Saturday Club

  24 AUGUST 1963 ◆

Pop Go The Beatles

  17 SEPTEMBER 1963

All four BBC performances were broadcast before
the EMI version was released on *With The Beatles* in
November 1963. Smokey Robinson wrote the song
for his group, the Miracles, and it climbed into the
Billboard Top Ten at the beginning of 1963. At this
time, the humble Oriole label was the British conduit
for Motown, whose American hits had not yet
penetrated the UK charts. (The breakthrough came
in May 1964 with 'My Guy', written by Smokey
Robinson and sung by Mary Wells. Always keen to
beat the drum for Motown, the Beatles ensured she
closed the first half of their 1964 British tour.)

Compact Discography

I THE BEATLES:

Sixty-two of the Beatles' performances for BBC Radio are available on the following CDs:

The Beatles Live At The BBC

(Apple 7243 8 31796 2 6)

(NOVEMBER 1994)

Fifty-six songs and thirteen speech tracks featuring the Beatles in conversation with presenters Rodney Burke, Alan Freeman, Brian Matthew and Lee Peters.

'Baby It's You' (4-track CD Single)

(Apple 7243 8 82073 2 4)

(MARCH 1995)

Three more previously unreleased BBC recordings augmenting the already available 'Baby It's You'.

Anthology I

(Apple 7243 8 34445 2 6)

(NOVEMBER 1995)

The *Pop Go The Beatles* track 'Lend Me Your Comb' was finally allowed out and joined 'Till There Was You' and 'Twist And Shout' from the *Royal Variety Performance* broadcast 10 November 1963 on BBC Radio (in addition to ITV).

Every home should have the complete Beatles catalogue and the following CDs include every track released between 1962 and 1970:

Please Please Me

(Parlophone CDP 7 46435 2)

UK LP released: 22 MARCH 1963

1: I Saw Her Standing There; Misery; Anna; (Go To Him); Chains; Boys; Ask Me Why; Please Please Me;

2: Love Me Do; P.S. I Love You; Baby It's You; Do You Want To Know A Secret; A Taste Of Honey; There's A Place; Twist And Shout.

With The Beatles

(Parlophone CDP 7 46436 2)

UK LP released: 22 NOVEMBER 1963

1: It Won't Be Long; All I've Got To Do; All My Loving; Don't Bother Me; Little Child; Till There Was You; Please Mister Postman;

2: Roll Over Beethoven; Hold Me Tight; You Really Got A Hold On Me; I Wanna Be Your Man; Devil In Her Heart; Not A Second Time; Money.

A Hard Day's Night

(Parlophone CDP 7 46437 2)

UK LP released: 10 JULY 1964

1: A Hard Day's Night; I Should Have Known Better; If I Fell; I'm Happy Just To Dance With You; And I Love Her; Tell Me Why; Can't Buy Me Love;

2: Any Time At All; I'll Cry Instead; Things We Said Today; When I Get Home; You Can't Do That; I'll Be Back.

Beatles For Sale

(Parlophone CDP 7 46438 2)

UK LP released: 4 DECEMBER 1964

1: No Reply; I'm A Loser; Baby's In Black; Rock And Roll Music; I'll Follow The Sun; Mr Moonlight; Kansas City/Hey!-Hey!-Hey!-Hey!;

2: Eight Days A Week; Words Of Love; Honey Don't; Every Little Thing; I Don't Want To Spoil The Party; What You're Doing; Everybody's Trying To Be My Baby.

Help!

(Parlophone CDP 7 46439 2)

UK LP released: 6 AUGUST 1965

1: Help!; The Night Before; You've Got To Hide Your Love Away; I Need You; Another Girl; You're Going To Lose That Girl ;Ticket To Ride;

2: Act Naturally; It's Only Love; You Like Me Too Much; Tell Me What You See; I've Just Seen A Face; Yesterday; Dizzy Miss Lizzy.

Rubber Soul

(Parlophone CDP 7 46440 2)

UK LP released: 3 DECEMBER 1965

1: Drive My Car; Norwegian Wood (This Bird Has Flown); You Won't See Me; Nowhere Man; Think For Yourself; The Word; Michelle;

2: What Goes On; Girl; I'm Looking Through You; In My Life; Wait; If I Needed Someone; Run For Your Life.

Revolver

(Parlophone CDP 7 46441 2)

UK LP released: 5 AUGUST 1966

1: Taxman; Eleanor Rigby; I'm Only Sleeping; Love You To; Here, There And Everywhere; Yellow Submarine; She Said She Said;

2: Good Day Sunshine; And Your Bird Can Sing; For No One; Doctor Robert; I Want To Tell You; Got To Get You Into My Life; Tomorrow Never Knows.

Sgt Pepper's Lonely Hearts Club Band

(Parlophone CDP 7 46442 2)

UK LP released: 1 JUNE 1967

1: Sgt. Pepper's Lonely Hearts Club Band; With A Little Help From My Friends; Lucy In The Sky With Diamonds; Getting Better; Fixing A Hole; She's Leaving Home; Being For The Benefit Of Mr Kite!;

2: Within You Without You; When I'm Sixty-Four; Lovely Rita; Good Morning Good Morning; Sgt Pepper's Lonely Hearts Club Band (Reprise); A Day In The Life.

The Beatles [the 'White Album']

(Parlophone CDP 7 46443 2)

UK Double LP released: 22 NOVEMBER 1968

1: Back In The U.S.S.R; Dear Prudence; Glass Onion; Ob-La-Di, Ob-La-Da; Wild Honey Pie; The Continuing Story Of Bungalow Bill; While My Guitar Gently Weeps; Happiness Is A Warm Gun;

2: Martha My Dear; I'm So Tired; Blackbird; Piggies; Rocky Raccoon; Don't Pass Me By; Why Don't We Do It In The Road; I Will; Julia;

3: Birthday; Yer Blues; Mother Nature's Son; Everbody's Got Something To Hide Except Me And My Monkey; Sexy Sadie; Helter Skelter; Long, Long, Long;

4: Revolution 1; Honey Pie; Savoy Truffle; Cry Baby Cry; Revolution 9; Good Night.

Yellow Submarine

(Parlophone CDP 7 46445 2)

UK LP released: 17 JANUARY 1969

1: Yellow Submarine; Only A Northern Song; All Together Now; Hey Bulldog; It's All Too Much; All You Need Is Love.

2: Instrumentals by the George Martin Orchestra.

Abbey Road

(Parlophone CDP 7 46446 2)

UK LP released: 26 SEPTEMBER 1969

1: Come Together; Something; Maxwell's Silver Hammer; Oh! Darling; Octopus's Garden; I Want You (She's So Heavy);

Before introducing the Beatles, Cavern DJ Bob Wooler built up the excitement by spinning 'Piltdown Rides Again', a rocked-up version of Wagner's 'William Tell Overture'. They played the Liverpudlian cellar for the last time on 3 August 1963 after nearly 300 performances in two-and-a-half years.

2: Here Comes The Sun; Because; You Never Give Me Your Money; Sun King; Mean Mr Mustard; Polythene Pam; She Came In Through The Bathroom Window; Golden Slumbers; Carry That Weight; The End; Her Majesty.

Let It Be

(Parlophone CDP 7 46447 2)

UK LP released: 8 MAY 1970

1: Two Of Us; Dig A Pony; Across The Universe; I Me Mine; Dig It; Let It Be; Maggie Mae;

2: I've Got A Feeling; One After 909; The Long And Winding Road; For You Blue; Get Back.

Magical Mystery Tour

(Parlophone CDP 7 48062 2)

An LP not originally released in the UK.

First US release: 27 NOVEMBER 1967

[These six tracks appeared in a double EP package in the UK:] Magical Mystery Tour; The Fool On The Hill; Flying; Blue Jay Way; Your Mother Should Know; I Am The Walrus; [The remainder were released on 1967 singles] Hello, Goodbye; Strawberry Fields Forever; Penny Lane; Baby, You're A Rich Man; All You Need Is Love.

Past Masters Volume One

(Parlophone CDP 7 90043 2)

Special 1988 compilation of non-album tracks from 1962–1965 ('Bad Boy' first surfaced a year late in the UK on *A Collection Of Beatles Oldies* released 9 December 1966).

Love Me Do (single version); From Me To You; Thank You Girl; She Loves You; I'll Get You; I Want To Hold Your Hand; This Boy; Komm, Gib Mir Deine Hand; Sie Liebt Dich; Long Tall Sally; I Call Your Name; Slow Down; Matchbox; I Feel Fine; She's A Woman; Bad Boy; Yes It Is; I'm Down.

Past Masters Volume Two

(Parlophone CDP 7 90044 2)

More non-album tracks from 1965–1970

Day Tripper; We Can Work It Out; Paperback Writer; Rain; Lady Madonna; The Inner Light; Hey Jude; Revolution; Get Back (single version); Don't Let Me Down; The Ballad Of John And Yoko; Old Brown Shoe; Across The Universe (alternative version); Let It Be (single version); You Know My Name (Look Up The Number).

When those twelve albums were transferred to Compact Disc in 1987 and 1988, three others were also made available to collect together any tracks not included on a UK Beatles LP.

Original British single couplings and EPs were later transferred to individual CDs and issued in box sets.

The Beatles CD Singles Collection

Parlophone CD BSCP 1

The Beatles Compact Disc EP Collection
Parlophone CD BEP 14

In 1993, the original 1973 'Red' and 'Blue' compilation albums were pressed onto CD:

The Beatles/1962-1966 [Red]
(Apple CDS 7 97036 2)

The Beatles/1967-1970 [Blue]
(Apple CDS 7 97039 2)

In addition to the aforementioned *Anthology 1*, there is more previously unreleased material on the following:

'Free As A Bird' (4-track CD Single)
(Apple 7243 8 82587 2 2)
(NOVEMBER 1995)

'Real Love' (4-track CD Single)
(Apple 7243 8 82646 2 4)
(MARCH 1996)

Anthology 2
(Apple 7243 8 34448 2 3)
(MARCH 1996)

Anthology 3 is waiting in the wings...

The Beatles Tapes
(Polydor 847 185-2)
(1994)
This collection was originally a double LP released in 1976 and features *Scene And Heard* interviews with all of the group by David Wigg, plus instrumental versions of Beatles' songs. The interview recording dates are unreliable but can be corrected as follows:

DISC ONE:
John And Yoko: Tracks 1 and 3–8 May 1969; Track 5–21 October 1969 and 6 February 1970; Track 7–October 1971.
Paul: Tracks 8 and 10–19 September 1969;

DISC TWO:
Paul: Tracks 1–19 September 1969
George: Tracks 3 and 5–8 October 1969
Ringo: Tracks 7–21 January 1969; Tracks 8–25 March 1970; Tracks 9 and 11–3 January 1973.

Rockin' At The Star Club, 1962
(Columbia COL 468950 2)
Sixteen songs extracted from the infamous tape recorded on 31 December 1962 at the Star-Club in Hamburg.

2 UNDER THE INFLUENCE:

The choice of songs performed for the BBC clearly reveals the seminal influences on the group. The following CDs provide a primer for anyone wishing to hear the Beatles' heroes and the original versions of the BBC tracks.

A – VARIOUS ARTISTS COMPILATIONS:

Under The Influence – The Original Versions of the songs the BEATLES Covered
(Sequel Records NEX CD 226)
Contains the original versions of all 24 covers released on their discs in the sixties.

**Love 'Em Do!
(24 Hits That Inspired The Beatles)**
(Instant CD INS 5063)
A less focussed collection including originals of songs heard on solo Beatle records and the *Live! At The Star-Club* album. Flawed by the inclusion of Little Richard's re-recordings of his Specialty hits.

Motown Sings The Beatles
(Connoisseur Collection NSP CD 500)
...featuring three Motown songs the Beatles sang.

The Colpix-Dimension Story
(Sequel Records NED CD 271)
Lots of Goffin-King magic including 'Chains' and
'Keep Your Hands Off My Baby'.

**British Beat Before The Beatles 1955–1962/
Volumes One to Seven**
(EMI 0777 7 89220 2 to 0777 7 89226 2)
The dark ages but yet a few bright sparks – Cliff
Richard, Johnny Kidd, Joe Brown, Billy Fury, Marty
Wilde – were breaking through.

The Girl Can't Help It
(EMI CDP 7 99093 2)
The influential 1956 rock film did not receive a
'soundtrack album' until the release of this CD in 1992.

B – SINGLE ARTIST ALBUMS

Arthur Alexander **The Greatest**
(Ace CDCHD 922)

Chuck Berry **The Chess Box**
(MCA CHD3-80,001) [Box Set]

Johnny Burnette **Rock 'N' Roll Trio/Tear It Up**
(Beat Goes On Records BGOCD177)

The Coasters **The Very Best Of**
(Rhino 9548-32656-2)

Eddie Cochran **The Eddie Cochran Box Set**
(EMI ECB 1) [Box Set]

Fats Domino **The Best Of**
(EMI CDP 7902942)

Duane Eddy **Because They're Young**
(BR Music BR 149-2)

The Everly Brothers **Heartaches & Harmonies**
(Rhino R2-71779) [Box Set]

Marvin Gaye **That Stubborn Kinda Fellow/How
Sweet It Is**
(Tamla Motown ZD72562)

Buddy Holly **From Original Master Tapes**
(MCA MCAD-5540)

The Isley Brothers **Shout And Twist With
Rudolph, Ronald And O'Kelly**
(Ace CDCH 928)

Jerry Lee Lewis **The EP Collection**
(See For Miles SEECD 307)

Little Richard **His Greatest Recordings**
(Ace CDCH 109)

Roy Orbison **The Legendary Roy Orbison**
(Telstar TDC 2330)

Carl Perkins **The Best Of The Sun Sessions**
(Music Club MCCD 191)

Elvis Presley **The King Of Rock 'N' Roll – The
Complete 50s Masters**
(BMG/RCA PD90689(5)-1 to PD90689(5)-5
[Box Set]

Smokey Robinson & The Miracles **Anthology**
(Tamla Motown ZD72531(2))

The Shirelles **The Best Of**
(Ace CDCHD 356)

Gene Vincent And His Blue Caps **The Best Of**
(EMI CDP 7903282)

Mary Wells **22 Greatest Hits**
(Motown ZD72448)

Larry Williams **The Best Of**
(Ace CDCHD 917)

Selective Bibliography

BEATLES REFERENCE/ INFORMATION/ IN THEIR OWN WORDS:

The following books give the 'what, when and how' guide to the Beatles' career. Mark Lewisohn's work is exhaustively researched, reliable and readable; his *Chronicle* is the essential reference work.

The Beatles: An Illustrated Record
Carr, Roy and Tyler, Tony
(LONDON: NEW ENGLISH LIBRARY, 1975)

All Together Now
Castleman, Harry and Podrazik, Wally
(ANN ARBOR: PIERIAN PRESS, 1975)

The Art Of The Beatles
Evans, Mike
(LONDON: ANTHONY BLOND, 1984)

The Beatles: 25 Years In The Life
Lewisohn, Mark
(LONDON: SIDGWICK & JACKSON, 1987)

The Beatles Live!
Lewisohn, Mark
(LONDON: PAVILION, 1986)

The Complete Beatles Chronicle
Lewisohn, Mark
(LONDON: PYRAMID BOOKS, 1992)

The Complete Beatles Recording Sessions
Lewisohn, Mark
(LONDON: HAMLYN, 1988)

Revolution In The Head
MacDonald, Ian
(LONDON: FOURTH ESTATE, 1994)

The Beatles In Their Own Words
Miles, ed.
(LONDON: OMNIBUS PRESS, 1978)

The Art & Music Of John Lennon
Robertson, John
(LONDON: OMNIBUS PRESS, 1990)

The Beatles London
Schreuders, Piet; Lewisohn, Mark; Smith, Adam
(LONDON: HAMLYN, 1994)

The Beatles: The Long And Winding Road – A History Of The Beatles On Record
Stannard, Neville
(LONDON: VIRGIN, 1982)

Lennon Remembers – The Rolling Stone Interviews
Wenner, Jann, ed
(LONDON: PENGUIN, 1973)

BEATLES BIOGRAPHIES

There are hundreds out there but these are essential. The Braun and Davies books were written while the story was unfolding and so are refreshingly free of any revisionism.

Love Me Do: The Beatles Progress
Braun, Michael
(LONDON: PENGUIN, 1964 – reprinted, at last, in 1995)

John Winston Lennon, Volume One 1940–1966
Coleman, Ray
(LONDON: SIDGWICK & JACKSON, 1984

John Ono Lennon, Volume Two 1967–1980
Coleman, Ray
(LONDON: SIDGWICK & JACKSON, 1984)

The Beatles
Davies, Hunter
(LONDON: HEINEMANN, 1968)

Apple To The Core: The Unmaking Of The Beatles
McCabe, Peter and Schonfield, Robert D
(LONDON: MARTIN BRIAN & O'KEEFE, 1972)

Shout! The True Story Of The Beatles
Norman, Philip
(LONDON: ELM TREE, 1981)

WRITTEN BY THE BEATLES:

John's two books of poetry, prose and drawings are essential. George's compendium of notes on his songs includes illustrations of his first sketches of lyrics.

I Me Mine
Harrison, George
(LONDON: WH ALLEN, 1982)

In His Own Write
Lennon, John
(LONDON: JONATHAN CAPE, 1964)

A Spaniard In The Works
Lennon, John
(LONDON: JONATHAN CAPE, 1965)

'FIFTH BEATLE' BOOKS:

Pete Best and Stuart Sutcliffe played in the group before Ringo's arrival. Brian Epstein, George Martin and Derek Taylor were three trusted members of the inner creative circle.

Beatle! The Pete Best Story
Best, Pete and Doncaster, Patrick
(LONDON: PLEXUS, 1985)

Brian Epstein: The Man Who Made The Beatles
Coleman, Ray
(LONDON: VIKING, 1989)

A Cellarful Of Noise
Epstein, Brian
(LONDON: SOUVENIR PRESS, 1964)

All You Need Is Ears
Martin, George with Hornsby, Jeremy
(LONDON: MACMILLAN, 1979)

Summer Of Love: The Making Of Sgt Pepper
Martin, George with Pearson, William
(LONDON: MACMILLAN, 1994)

Backbeat – Stuart Sutcliffe: The Lost Beatle

Clayson, Alan and Sutcliffe, Pauline

(LONDON: PAN BOOKS, 1994)

As Time Goes By

Taylor, Derek

(LONDON: DAVIS-POYNTER, 1973)

Fifty Years Adrift

Taylor, Derek

(GUILDFORD: GENESIS PUBLICATIONS, 1984)

BROADCASTING:

Two pioneering works by authors who have studiously researched this neglected genre of popular broadcasting.

Selling The Sixties – The Pirates And Pop Music Radio

Chapman, Rob

(LONDON: ROUTLEDGE, 1992)

In Session Tonight – The Complete Radio 1 Recordings

Garner, Ken

(LONDON: BBC BOOKS, 1993)

MAGAZINES:

The monthly **Record Collector** has featured excellent articles both on the Beatles and the artists they admired; many are still available through its back issues service.

Mojo magazine often focusses on the sixties and its Beatles edition (NO:24 – NOVEMBER 1995) was fab.

Index

....

Picture Acknowledgements

....

BBC Books would like to thank Apple Corps Ltd for use of the following photographs:
© Apple Corps Ltd (Dezo Hoffman) page 2, 15, 16, 20, 30, 34, 48, 62, 65, 84, 128, 144,
(Robert Freeman) page 81, 82; (Peter Kaye) page 150, (Dick Matthews) page 8,
(Ethan Russell) page 92, 96, 98, (photographer unknown) page 86.

Camera Press (Philip Gotlop) page 122/123; Press Association page 39;
Courtesy David Wigg page 95;

All other photographs © BBC.